Donald L. Hamilton

HOMILETICAL HANDBOOK

BROADMAN PRESS
NASHVILLE, TENNESSEE

© 1992 • Broadman & Holman Publishers
Nashville, Tennessee
All rights reserved

4216-26
IBSN: 0-8054-1626-9

Dewey Decimal Classification: 251
Subject Heading: PREACHING
Library of Congress Catalog Number: 91-28607
Printed in the United States of America

Library of Congress Cataloging-in-Publication Data
Hamilton, Donald L.
    Homiletical handbook /Donald L. Hamilton
        p   cm.
    Includes bibliographical references.
    ISBN 0-8054-1626-9 (pbk)
    1. Preaching. 2. Bible—Homiletical use. I. Title.
BV4211.2.H27   1992
251—dc20   91-28607
                                                                CIP

99 00 01 8 7 6 5

ACKNOWLEDGMENTS

As the preparation of this manuscript nears completion, I am reminded of several people who have been partners in the effort, sometimes unknowingly. They deserve special thanks for their advice and encouragement.

First, I am grateful to my wife, Joyce. She has been both my sweetheart and best friend for almost three decades of marriage. She has encouraged me faithfully through both good and bad times and has been especially patient through the many months when writing and editing lessened our time together.

I am appreciative to the administration of Columbia Bible College and Seminary (Columbia, South Carolina) for the opportunity of devoting a sabbatical to the writing of this book. Likewise, my colleagues on the seminary faculty have been an encouragement. I am especially thankful for a teaching faculty that holds the ministry of preaching in high regard. Their classes, though often in other disciplines, enhance the ability of our students to preach the Word with biblical authority, clarity, and power.

Rev. Greg Holladay, a long-time friend and former copastor, carefully proofread the manuscript and interacted with many of the ideas contained in it. I am grateful for his generosity in the use of his time to help in this way.

Finally, I must acknowledge the many people in my past who have contributed to my growth, first as a Christian, then as a preacher. These include former pastors, classroom teachers, colaborers in the ministry, and church members. Some of these, not surprisingly, have had a greater effect than others. As I reflect on my own development as a preacher, and then as one who teaches preaching, it is not difficult to isolate the one person whose influence has had the greatest impact on my understanding of the preaching task. That person is Lloyd M. Perry, former professor of preaching at Trinity Evangelical Divinity School in Deerfield, Illinois.

Much of what is found on the following pages can be attributed to my understanding of Dr. Perry's philosophy of preaching, as well as his homiletical methods. Some of his methods are borrowed almost verbatim. Others only distantly reflect his methodology. In either case, his philosophy of the preaching task was seldom far from my thoughts as I worked my way, hesitantly at times, through old and new ideas in sermon methodology.

I am truly grateful for the positive influence of Dr. Perry on my life and ministry.

INTRODUCTION

When wise Solomon complained that "of making many books there is no end" (Eccl. *12:12*, NIV), he could easily have been writing prophetically about modern publication of books on preaching.

Why, then, yet another such attempt? Are there not already enough publications about the preacher, the nature of the preaching task, sermon construction, sermon delivery, and other related themes? Is another book on preaching simply an unnecessary redundancy?

Perhaps. Yet, as I have read and pondered many books on preaching, I have concluded that relatively few are thoroughly helpful. Some are based on highly questionable views of Scripture. Weak bibliology, faulty hermeneutics, and unrestrained higher criticism hinder the truthful proclamation of the Word of God. Some books offer helpful insights into the theoretical aspects of the preacher and the message but offer little help in actual sermon construction. Some fail to apply homiletical methods to sample texts or to recognize that various kinds of biblical literature exist. Some teach only one method of sermon structure with the result that variety in the pulpit seldom occurs. Some books on preaching try to cover too many facets of the task and end up generalizing rather than dealing with specific issues.

This handbook does not discuss everything related to the preaching task. It does not, for example, address the subject of the preacher's personal life, although the reader must understand that personal and spiritual qualifications are foundational. Neither does the handbook speak to the matter of sermon delivery, for that subject is too large to cover adequately in a few pages.

Rather, this volume is meant to dwell on homiletics, the "science" of sermon construction. The book is divided into three sections: the first part is introductory and definitional; the second presents methodological ideas for specific homiletical arrangements; and the third makes some applications of these homiletical methods to the various kinds of literature found in Scripture.

This book is primarily intended to be an introductory treatment of homiletics. It is anticipated that beginning preaching students will benefit most from reading this book. Yet, much of this material has been used productively with experienced preachers who have desired to broaden their understanding and practice of the task.

No higher calling occurs among the people of God than to declare His Word to others. The task deserves to be done well. Hopefully, these pages will instruct and encourage others in that direction.

CONTENTS

PART 1

UNDERSTANDING OUR HOMILETICAL TASK

1

THE IMPORTANCE
OF PREACHING

Preachers invest much of their lives in thinking about sermons. If they preach regularly, they are all too aware that their praying, Bible reading, planning, studying, outlining, writing, practicing, and delivery involve a major time expenditure.

The typical evangelical pastor preaches two sermons weekly. He may also be responsible for other presentations, such as a Sunday School lesson or a brief devotional message for a midweek service. Even if he possesses the keenest of minds, the pastor will find that the major part of his work week is spent in study and sermon/lesson preparation. The preacher will most certainly ask himself on occasion, "Is it really worth all the effort?"

Apparently, most preachers believe it is. The extensive Gallup Poll conducted for *Christianity Today* in 1979 indicated that a large majority of American pastors (56 percent) felt that preaching was one of the most important things they did. (The second closest item was the administration of the sacraments or ordinances, marked by only 15 percent of the respondents.) However, in the same poll, only 10 percent of those surveyed mentioned preaching as being especially successful.[1] Evidently, pastors want to preach well but feel they are not very effective at it.

What Is Preaching?

In his book *A Primer for Preachers*, Ian Pitt-Watson titles his first chapter "What comes first."[2] He explains that he is using these words as a statement, not as a question. Just as he argues that "what?" must necessarily precede the "how?" issue, so it should be understood that "what?" must also precede the "why?" question. If we correctly understand what preaching is, then we can better understand why it should be done and how.

The biblical concept of preaching is centered in one word from the Old Testament and four from the New Testament. Other words come into play, but these predominate. The Old Testament word is *naba*, which translated into English means "prophesy"; it is used over 110 times. In the New Testament we find *kerusso* ("to proclaim," about 60 times), *euaggelizo* ("to declare good news," 50 times), *kataggello* ("to tell thoroughly," 17 times), and *didasko* ("to teach," 97 times). In addition, the New Testament word *parakaleo* ("to beseech, comfort, exhort," 103 times) is sometimes used in the sense of preaching, although this is not its usual meaning.

Much of the preaching in the Old Testament appears to involve direct revelation from God. During or after the exile, preaching began to take the shape of textual exposition as a part of synagogue worship. In the New Testament, the terms seem to be used somewhat interchangeably, although *kerusso* and *kataggello* emphasize the activity of preaching, while *euaggelizo* and *parakaleo* emphasize the nature and purpose of the message being preached.

The inclusion of *didasko* with the more traditional terms raises the issue concerning the difference, if any, between preaching and teaching. The issue needs to be addressed on two levels: biblical and theological, practical and cultural.

In regard to the former, the distinction between preaching and teaching has been advocated most effectively by C. H. Dodd.[3] He argued in favor of a clear difference between the two, saying that preaching *(kerusso)* had to do with the *kerygma* (that is, the basic gospel, as found in 1 Corinthians 15:3-4), while the concept of teaching *(didasko)* had to do with *didache* (that is, the body of doctrine and ethics meant for believers). Thus, in Dodd's view, New Testament preaching was always evangelistic, while teaching involved the doctrinal and ethical matters of Christianity. Preaching was carried on outside the church, while teaching was carried on inside.

Some recent scholarship has disputed Dodd's thesis,[4] pointing out that the two categories Dodd suggested are not, in reality, all that unique. It has also shown that a careful study of New Testament word usage indicates that *kerusso* and *euaggelizo* are sometimes used interchangeably with *didasko*. (Compare Matt. 4:23, "teaching in their synagogues," with Mark 1:39, "preached in their synagogues." The concepts also appear to overlap in texts like Acts 5:42; 28:31; Col. 1:28.)

As far as the practical and/or cultural distinction between preaching and teaching is concerned, several things enter the picture. (1) In some circles, a topical treatment of the text has been called preaching, while an "expository" treatment of a passage is said to be teaching. (2) In some circles, the word *preach* and its cognates have been thought to communicate too much dogmatism or authority, and the usage of *teacher* (rather than *preacher*) has become popular. (The expression "don't preach at me" clearly has a negative connotation.) (3) Some who prefer the term *teacher* do so because Ephesians 4:11 uses the phrase "pastors and teachers" v to refer to one leadership position in the church. Likewise, 1 Timothy 3:2 says that the bishop must be "able to teach" (NIV). (4) In some cultures (Japan, for example), a teacher is traditionally looked upon with great respect, and this results in the use of that title in those cultural situations.

Still, is there a difference between preaching and teaching, between a sermon and a lesson? Any supposed difference is not very easy to define apart from our own cultural understandings. Is the supposed difference based on the seating arrangement of the room, the bodily posture of the teacher or preacher, the use of voice, the degree and nature of the audience's participation, the way the passage of Scripture is being handled, the sex of the person doing the talking, or the formality or informality of the setting?

Surely, each of these is arbitrary. Preachers in first century synagogues sat down to address their audiences (see Luke 4:20-21). Does this make them teachers instead of preachers? Some pastors speak to their congregations with great fire and enthusiasm, while others use the pulpit to explain and apply the Word of God calmly and rationally. Must we arbitrarily assign the former to the category of "preacher" and the latter to the category of "teacher"? Suppose that a pastor shares his understanding of a passage and its application with one other person in a discipling situation and then shares exactly the same message with the entire congregation. Is it the difference in setting that makes the initial message "teaching" and the second one "preaching"? J. I. Packer shows that *euaggelizo* is used of Paul when he speaks to a synagogue gathering in Pisidian Antioch and to groups gathered in the marketplace at Athens. It is also used of Philip speaking to the Ethiopian eunuch in a chariot.[5]

Obviously, arriving at a clear distinction between preaching and teaching is difficult, if a distinction does in fact exist. It seems that every attempt to show a difference between the two concepts ends in inconsistency. While using the term *teaching* to refer to classroom situations may be helpful, particularly where there is verbal interaction among the participants, the use of both *preaching* and *teaching* rightly characterizes the pulpit.

It is preferable to think of both preaching and teaching as the communication of the Word of God—the giving of a message based on the Bible and applied to life today. When that is being done before an audience (can we realistically limit the size?) with the speaker having taken the initiative in formulating what he is saying, it can be called preaching.

Traditionally, preaching has been carried out in the mode of speech making. The word *sermon* comes from the Latin *sermo*, meaning "a speech or a talk." Most preaching, therefore, will be carried out in a monologue with some measure of formality. Remember that this recognition is more cultural than biblical.

We return to the larger question under consideration: What is preaching? In his Lyman Beecher lectures delivered at Yale more than 100 years ago, Phillips Brooks said: "Preaching is the communication of truth by man to men. It has in it two essential elements: truth and personality."[6] Though Brooks probably never intended for this statement to be understood as a formal definition of preaching, it is probably the most oft-quoted definition of preaching. He is often paraphrased as saying that "preaching is truth through personality," and this expression is quoted by many from a wide variety of backgrounds.

A variation of Brooks' definition comes from J. Daniel Baumann: "Preaching is the communication of biblical truth by man to men with the explicit purpose of eliciting behavioral change."[7] This is an improvement on the former definition, for it includes the concepts of "biblical truth" and specific purpose ("behavioral change"). Although Baumann's definition is somewhat brief, it includes several important concepts.

Haddon Robinson offers a very thorough statement about expository preaching which can be applied to other kinds of sermons as well:

> Expository preaching is the communication of a biblical concept, arrived from and transmitted through a historical, grammatical, and literary study of a passage in its context, which the Holy Spirit first applies to the personality and experience of the preacher, then through him to his hearers.[8]

A definition can only say so much about a subject without becoming awkward and too complicated. Other things must be added to mere definition. In regard to preaching, Packer highlights the following truths:[9]

1. Its *content* is God's message to man, presented as such.
2. The *purpose* of preaching is to inform, persuade, and call forth an appropriate response to the God whose message and instruction are being delivered.
3. The *perspective* of preaching is always applicatory. . . .
4. *Authority* is also integral to the notion of what preaching is. . . .
5. Preaching mediates not only God's authority, but also His *presence* and His *power.* . . .

Even a casual reflection on the preceding definitions and truths should convince us that preaching really is quite unique. As Pitt-Watson said, "It is *sui generis*—in a class by itself."[10]

Why Preach?

Having now discussed the nature of preaching, let us turn our attention to the question: "Why preach?" As Packer correctly points out, there is both an objective and a subjective response to the question.[11] The objective issue is whether God intends for preaching to continue to be a part of the life and work of the church. This issue is usually discussed in the context of the great communication advances made in the 20th century. Is not pulpit monologue at least slightly out-of-date in comparison to television and film? Are not techniques such as small-group dialogues or multimedia presentations more likely to be effective? Even if it is granted that preaching has had a tremendous effect on church history, and subsequently on world history, has it not lived beyond its real usefulness?

The Objective Response

Actually, this is not a question uniquely new to the present generation. James W. Alexander, a pastor and professor at Princeton Theological Seminary, expressed concerns about the demise of preaching well over one hundred years ago:

> I fear none of us apprehend as we ought to do the value of the preacher's office. Our young men do not gird themselves for it with the spirit of those who are on the eve of a great conflict; nor do they prepare as those who are to lay hands upon the springs of the mightiest passions, and stir up to their depths the ocean of human feelings. Where this estimate of the work prevails, men even of inferior training accomplish much. . . . The pulpit will remain the grand means of effecting the mass of men. It is God's own method, and he will honour [sic] it. . . . In every age, great reformers have been great preachers.[12]

In fact, throughout church history, the pulpit has had its detractors. It appears that almost every generation has wrestled with the seeming lack of effectiveness of its preaching, even in the so-called "golden age of preaching" in the 19th century.[13] Yet, preaching persists with only minor changes in methods. As Fant states: "Preaching, then, has a double stubbornness: it is stubbornly the same, and it is stubbornly there."[14]

Still, one may argue that the late 20th century is different from all preceding eras of history. That is certainly true. The advent of technology has changed life radically. Certainly television, film, and other advances should be used to enhance the communication of the gospel. The issue before us, however, is whether the traditional monological sermon is obsolete. The answer is found in the very nature of God as One who has primarily revealed Himself verbally.

> The religion of Israel is very much a matter of hearing rather than of seeing. Even God's actions are spoken of by the prophets as his word. No man can see God and live, but he is known by his speaking. By contrast, it is the gods of the nations that are mute, and their visible images are dumb. As we read in Psalm 115:7, 'They do not make a sound in their throat.' Throughout Scripture, revelation is identified above all with speaking and hearing . . . rather than with the imagery of the visual arts.' . . . Of course, like all religions Christianity has its sacred

actions and spectacles, sacred places and times, sacred arts and objects, but it is in connection with God's speaking that they are sacred. . . . Language, then, is more fundamental than graphic representation, except where the latter is itself a transcript in some sense of the word of God.[15]

God has revealed Himself nonverbally, as in nature; but even the greatest nonverbal revelation, the incarnation of Christ, was limited by space and time factors. We know of it only by verbal revelation. Even the incarnate Lord communicated almost all of His message verbally, not just bodily. The most important of His actions, the crucifixion and the resurrection, would be unintelligible apart from verbal revelation.

Apparently, words *are* important to God. If that is the case, does this not serve as a basis for justifying preaching as a necessary means of communicating the truth of God? Is preaching rendered irrelevant merely because of scientific advancement? (Perhaps all of this has taken God by surprise!) Or is verbal communication—even the monological sermon—still a relevant means of declaring the complete counsel of God? Consider the biblical response to the following rhetorical questions:

1. *Does good preaching differ from good public speaking?* Yes! The Christian preaching tradition owes much to the tradition of public speaking, rooted in the rhetoric of the ancient Greeks. It goes far beyond that heritage, though, being related to the Old Testament prophet and, perhaps even more closely, to the preaching and teaching of the synagogue. The apostle Paul was assuredly aware of the well-known methods of the itinerant public speakers of his day when he reminded the believers at Corinth that "My message and my preaching were not with wise and persuasive words, but with a demonstration of the Spirit's power, so that your faith might not rest on men's wisdom, but on God's power" (1 Cor. 2:4-5, NIV).

2. *Does the preacher have a special status or divine calling?* Yes! Without doing harm to the teaching of the priesthood and ministry of all believers, one must admit that the Bible indicates that God has a role in choosing certain persons to minister the Word. Ephesians 4:11 indicates that it was the ascended Christ "who gave some to be apostles, some to be prophets, some to be evangelists, and some to be pastors and teachers" (NIV). The Book of 1 Peter tells us that "Each one should use whatever gift he has received to serve others, faithfully administering God's grace in its various forms. If anyone speaks, he should do it as one speaking the very words of God" (4:10-11, NIV). In Acts 20:28, Paul reminded the Ephesian elders (pastors) that they were appointed to this position by the Holy Spirit.

3. *Is there a unique authority in the Word of God?* Yes! Public speaking relies on human cleverness and, therefore, has very limited authority.

Authentic preaching, however, relies on the truth of the Word of God and has an authority inherent in the Word. The final commission of the Lord included a reminder of His authority and His continuing presence with those who would spread His message (Matt. 28:18-20). Second Timothy 3:16 claims that "All Scripture is God-breathed and is useful for teaching, rebuking, correcting and training in righteousness" (NIV). It should not be a surprise when, a few verses later, the apostle charges the young pastor to "Preach the Word; be prepared in season and out of season; correct, rebuke and encourage—with great patience and careful instruction" (2 Tim. 4:2, NIV).

4. *Is the Word of God dead or dormant, or dynamically alive?* We do not ordinarily think of words as possessing life, yet Scripture says of itself that "The word of God is living and active. Sharper than any double-edged sword, it penetrates even to dividing soul and spirit, joints and marrow; it judges the thoughts and attitudes of the heart" (Heb. 4:12, NIV). Paul told Timothy that "God's word is not chained" (2 Tim. 2:9, NIV). Both of these texts affirm what God said about His Word long ago through the ancient prophet: "It will not return to me empty,/ but will accomplish what I desire/ and achieve the purpose for which I sent it" (Isa. 55:11, NIV). This is why Paul could write confidently to the church at Thessalonica, "We also thank God continually because, when you received the word of God, which you heard from us, you accepted it not as the word of men, but as it actually is, the word of God, which is at work in you who believe" (1 Thess. 2:13, NIV).

5. *Is true preaching only the product of man, or is it attended by the Holy Spirit?* The age of the New Testament church was initiated with the promise and coming of the Spirit. Jesus told His early followers that they would be given power when the Holy Spirit came upon them, and in that power they would be witnesses (Acts 1:8). Thus, years later, Paul could remind his Corinthian readers that his preaching was in "demonstration" of the Spirit's power (1 Cor. 2:4). Likewise, he could tell the ThesHsalonian believers, "We know, brothers loved by God, that he has chosen you, because our gospel came to you not simply with words, but also with power, with the Holy Spirit and with deep conviction" (1 Thess. 1:4-5, NIV). In every age, the faithful presence of the Holy Spirit has accompanied true Christian preaching. The Spirit applies the Word of God with conviction to the individual.

All this indicates that God still intends for preaching to be a part of the church's ministry. The theological realities which saw the first-century church stress the preaching/teaching of the Word have not changed. God still reveals Himself and His will for people through verbal propositions. God still sovereignly places persons in positions of church leadership in which the preaching/teaching of the Word is a high priority. God's Word is still authoritative and dynamically alive, and God's Spirit still empowers the authentic spokesman. None of these realities is dependent on modern technologies or rendered obsolete by them. Again, that is not to say that the church should not make proper use of any legitimate tool. It is simply to recognize that objectively, God can and does use the "foolishness of preaching" to accomplish His purposes.

The Subjective Response

What about the subjective response to the question: "Why preach?" Why should a particular individual become a preacher or teacher of the Word? As with the objective question, the subjective question must be addressed theologically.

The matter of "a call to ministry" is seen in both the Old and New Testaments. Whether one considers Amos, Isaiah, and Jeremiah, or Peter, John, and Paul, the sense of call is there. Sometimes these calls were quite dramatic (as in the cases of Isaiah and Paul); in other instances they were relatively simple (as in the cases of Amos and John). The circumstances of the call are not important. The assurance of the call is. It is this assurance that gives a sense of steadfastness and stick-to-itiveness when unjustified criticism comes or failure seems likely.

In the New Testament, the call to ministry leadership seems to be both internal and external. The called ones have a strong sense that this is what they must be doing. At the same time, the church confirms the call. We see this happening throughout the Book of Acts. Those who are called never act in a "lone ranger" manner but are always seen as accountable to the larger body.

The "internal call" cannot be separated from the called one's understanding of some basic theological truths. These would include the truth and power of the gospel, the authority of Scripture, the giving of spiritual gifts, and the Lord's sovereign right to call whomever He chooses. If these are missing, the *felt* call may be shallow and the product of one's own thinking. The counsel of the church is important in this regard.

The called must have their theological understanding of the concept of call in order and must have an abiding conviction that they *must* be involved personally in a preaching or teaching ministry. Then the *why* issue has been resolved. The called will echo the sentiment of Jeremiah, who said:

> So the word of the Lord has brought me
>   insult and reproach all day long.
> But if I say, "I will not mention him
>   or speak any more in his name,"
> his word is in my heart like a fire,
>   a fire shut up in my bones.
> I am weary of holding it in;
>   indeed, I cannot (Jer. 20:8-9, NIV).

Notes

1. Haddon Robinson, "A Profile of the American Clergyman," *Christianity Today,* 23 May 1980, 27.

2. Ian Pitt-Watson, *A Primer for Preachers* (Grand Rapids, Mich.: Baker Book House, 1986), 11.

3. His views are set forth in C. H. Dodd, *Apostolic Preaching and Its Developments* (New York: Harper, 1936).

4. Two major works which interact with Dodd, often taking exception to his opinions, are Robert Mounce, *The Essential Nature of New Testament Preaching* (Grand Rapids, Mich.: Wm. B. Eerdmans Publishing Co., 1960); and Robert C. Worley, *Preaching and Teaching in the Earliest Church* (Philadelphia: Westminster, 1967).

5. J. I. Packer, "Introduction: Why Preach?" in *The Preacher and Preaching: Reviving the Art in the Twentieth Century,* ed. Samuel T. Logan, Jr. (Phillipsburg, N.J.: Presbyterian and Reformed Publishing Co., 1986), 8.

6. Phillips Brooks, *Lectures on Preaching*, 2nd ed. (Grand Rapids, Mich.: Baker Book House, 1978), 5.

7. J. Daniel Baumann, *An Introduction to Contemporary Preaching* (Grand Rapids, Mich.: Baker Book House, 1972), 13.

8. Haddon W. Robinson, *Biblical Preaching* (Grand Rapids, Mich.: Baker Book House, 1980), 20. This is an excellent volume on expository preaching and is highly recommended.

9. Packer, 8-13.

10. Pitt-Watson, 13.

11. Packer, 14.

12. Quoted in John R. W. Stott, *Between Two Worlds: The Art of Preaching in the Twentieth Century* (Grand Rapids, Mich.: Wm. B. Eerdmans Publishing Co., 1982), 37.

13. See Clyde E. Fant, *Preaching for Today* (New York: Harper and Row, 1975), 1-10. This author spends the bulk of his first chapter relating a history of the pulpit's weaknesses and the criticisms of preaching which were voiced because of them.

14. Fant, 1.

15. Amos N. Wilder, *The Language of the Gospel* (New York: Harper and Row, 1964), 18-19.

2

A RATIONALE FOR SERMON STRUCTURE

The words *preaching* and *homiletics* are often used interchangeably, yet technically they are not identical. *Preaching* is the "larger" of the terms. It refers more to the total task of preparing and delivering sermons. Homiletics, on the other hand, is only one part of the total preaching task.

Homiletics is that part of preaching involved with preparing sermons rather than delivering them, although the latter would always be the goal in mind. (A "sermon" written only for the printed media would not truly be a sermon, but an essay. Preaching presupposes that oral communication of the message will take place. Some would suggest, in fact, that the true *sermon* exists only while it is actually being delivered. That may be an arbitrary opinion, but it does help us better understand the nature of preaching.)

Lloyd Perry defines homiletics as "the science of sermon construction. It is the systematic setting forth of the body of laws and principles on which all art must rest."[1] This does not mean that sermon construction is an absolute science with inflexible rules. It does mean that as a discipline homiletics draws from a large body of knowledge dating back to the time of the ancient Greeks and including not only their views on rhetoric, but also the findings of subsequent generations of public speakers and Christian preachers up to the present day.

Preaching is both a science and an art. Some teachers have emphasized the former. Others, like Grady Davis, have argued for the latter:

> The communication of the gospel . . . is an art rather than a science. It is a way of doing rather than a complicated theory of what to do and how to do it. In this, speech is like any true art. Art is skill in doing, controlled by an inner sense of rightness, a sense that is nearer to feeling than to calculation, nearer to intuition than to deliberation. Skill in doing may be helped by study, but basically it must be acquired and perfected by practice. The inner sense of rightness, too, can be awakened and sensitized by a study of theory, and still more by exposure to fine work; but it remains a kind of feeling or intuition.[2]

Since preaching is an art, there must of necessity be some way to limit and control its subjective nature. Otherwise, the objective truth to be presented could be obscured:

If preaching is an art, can there not be free-form sermons? Contemporary arts are trying to escape from pattern and rational design. There is nonrepresentational painting, abstract sculpture, poetry beyond meaning, and music that is nonrhythmic and atonal. If there can be a theater of the absurd, should there not be a pulpit of the absurd? Some ministers have found a good deal of satisfaction in an awareness-evoking style of preaching that transcends the ordinary limits of reason and speech. It has attracted some attention, but not many hearers.

Some arts have their purposes in themselves, but others are means to an end. An attorney's presentation to a court could be art, but it could not be abstract art. A sermon is like an editorial, a speech to the Senate, or a football coach's pregame exhortation—it has a function and it must be carefully designed for just this purpose. It is to inform, to elevate, to reprove, to incite, to open a way for the Spirit who makes young men see visions and old men dream dreams.[3]

The tension between preaching as art or science lies in the middle (as even Davis hinted). Preaching is both a science and an art. According to Perry, "Homiletics is the science which treats the nature, classification, analysis, construction and composition of the sermon. 'It is the science of which preaching is the art of which the sermon is the product.'"[4]

This handbook is intended to emphasize the homiletical aspect of preaching. It will especially discuss sermon structuring and how to apply the structuring methods learned to the various kinds of literature found in Scripture. It may appear at times that the methods presented are too rigid in form—that artistic freedom is being stifled. That is not the intention. Instead, it is believed that an awareness of basic rules and processes will help the preacher, especially the novice, build a solid methodological foundation. When these are well in hand, the preacher is encouraged to experiment with other forms and methods. The advice of James Braga is helpful:

> But while the student is learning homiletics, it would not be wise for him to exercise this liberty. On the contrary, the beginner should apply himself rigidly to the rules until he has mastered them thoroughly. There will come a time later in his ministry when, under the leading of the Spirit of God, he may disregard some of these principles.[5]

Warren Wiersbe gives the same kind of advice, with a view toward the delivery aspect of preaching:

> If your personality doesn't shine through your preaching, you're only a robot. You could be replaced by a cassette player and perhaps nobody would know the difference. Do not confuse the art and the science of preaching. Homiletics is the science of preaching, and it has basic laws and principles that every preacher ought to study and practice. Once you've learned how to obey these principles, then you can adapt them, modify them, and tailor them to your own personality.[6]

The Importance of Structure

Every teacher of preaching has heard the questions: "Why do we spend so much time worrying about sermon structure? Why can't we just stand up and tell them what is on our hearts?" In fact, every teacher of preaching has probably asked the same questions!

Preachers do spend a lot of time dealing with sermon structure. Some of them probably spend too much time structuring their sermons; for example, they are overly concerned about precise alliteration or too careful about an equal number of subpoints under each main point. As a result, valuable time is taken away from exegetical study, attention-grabbing introductions, convicting conclusions, or even pastoral work other than preaching! J. Daniel Baumann asserts:

> A preacher, therefore, ought to be a good craftsman, but never a mere technician. He has only so much time for preparation, and it is never enough time. If he devotes too much time to form and too little to content, if he studies the use of form as something apart from content, he may become a rhetorician, an attractive speaker, but he will turn out to be something less than a preacher of the gospel.[7]

Does this mean, then, that structuring sermons is unnecessary? Hardly! It means that the role of sermon structure should be understood properly so that it is neither overemphasized nor ignored. If it is overemphasized, it becomes the proverbial "cart before the horse." If it is underemphasized, the sermon becomes a shapeless mass that exerts itself in any convenient direction and deprives the audience of a fair chance at following a progression of ideas.

At the very least, structure will help the preacher avoid talking in circles or rambling on without apparent purpose. The anonymous essay on "Pigs" quoted by Baumann speaks louder than words:

> A pig is a funny animal, but it has some uses [the uses are not mentioned]. Our dog don't like pigs—our dog's name is Nero. Our teacher read a piece one day about a wicked man called Nero. My daddy is a good man. Men are very useful. Men are different than women, and my mom ain't like my daddy. My mom says that a ring around the sun means that a storm is coming. And that is all I know about pigs.[8]

Unfortunately, many sermons seem to progress in about the same way. Listeners are left to fend for themselves as far as the organization of ideas is concerned. Too many sermons resemble a broken string of pearls that has scattered "little jewels" in no particular pattern or arrangement. The pearls may be "real gems," but their ultimate value is realized only when they are properly strung together. Likewise, the sermon that is a rambling collection of spiritual gems falls short of its ultimate potential. Each individual thought or insight may be good, but corporately, if they are arranged in proper form, they can be great!

Charles Koller felt strongly that good structure is a key to freedom in the pulpit.[9] He compared the art of structuring sermons to the art of crafting arrows, carried on by the American Indian:

> He realized that his very survival might depend upon the excellence of his arrow. The shaft must therefore be absolutely straight, lest it wobble in flight; the point must be sharp enough to penetrate; the feathers must be in just the right amount to steady the arrow in flight, yet not to retard its flight or dull its thrust. Similarly, the sermon must have a clear thought running straight through the length of it, a sharp point at the end, and just enough 'feathers' to cope with the atmosphere through which it must pass on its way to the target.[10]

Every sermon will have a structure of some sort. Even the previous essay on pigs has a distinguishable form as each new idea leads to a further tangential item. The issue is whether the structure chosen will benefit or hinder the communication process.

It must be understood that structure is not what preaching is all about. It is a vehicle meant to allow the substance—the content—of the sermon to be more effectively communicated. It is a means to an end:

> The plan must not call attention to itself as clever or profound. The purpose of the plan is to help the people see past it to the truth being set forth. The structure is the frame of the painting, which contains and draws attention to the beautiful without distracting from it. Frames help us to focus our attention to separate the art from all else. So structure aids hearers by setting the revelation of God in an orderly and limited arrangement with which they can deal on a given occasion.[11]

Benefits of Good Structure

A well-conceived structural plan will be of significant benefit to both the preacher and the audience.

Benefits for the Preacher
1. Good structuring confirms and solidifies the preacher's grasp of the material being presented in the sermon. (Conversely, the lack of a good structure may indicate that the preacher is still struggling to understand fully the relationship of the various concepts with which he is dealing.)
2. Good structuring helps the preacher emphasize one central idea in a sermon, rather than dabble in several minor ones.
3. Good structuring encourages the preacher to know his target clearly and not digress from it.

4. Good structuring results in good sermonic movement toward an appropriate climax.
5. Good structuring results in a "balanced attack," avoiding the error of overloading certain parts of the sermon and underloading other parts.
6. Good structuring helps the preacher in delivery, for each time the next idea will flow naturally from the last one.
7. Good structuring enhances the preacher's credibility with the audience, making the total force of the presentation more effective.

Benefits for the Audience

1. Good structuring helps the listener follow the argument being presented. Thus, persuasion is enhanced.
2. Good structuring gives the listener a feel for where the sermon is headed.
3. Good structuring helps the listener remember the thrust of the sermon, and not just isolated or unrelated parts.
4. Good structure helps attention span, for it gives the audience periodic psychological breaks at the right times rather than encouraging the listeners arbitrarily to take needed breaks at the wrong times.

Characteristics of Good Structure

Since sermons are enhanced by a carefully arranged structure, what should this structure be like? Four things should characterize it:
1. A well-structured sermon is *unified*. It deals with one subject and only one aspect of that subject.
2. A well-structured sermon has a *discernible order,* beginning with an appropriate introduction, moving through necessary parts, points, or movements, and finally reaching a fitting conclusion.
3. A well-structured sermon has a *balanced arrangement,* with the main points usually being about the same length.
4. A well-structured sermon *moves toward a specific target* and arrives there climactically.

Basic Components of Sermon Structure

Details about how to structure sermons will be given later in this handbook when various homiletical arrangements are discussed. Now some basic components of structuring will be mentioned so that a broad frame of reference may be established.
1. Every sermon should be rooted in at least one Scripture text. The text(s) should have a bearing on structure.
2. Every sermon should be reduced to one propositional sentence.

(This is sometimes called the central idea, the big idea, the theme statement, or the thesis.) John Henry Jowett made a statement often quoted in this regard:

> No sermon is ready for preaching . . . until we can express its theme in a short, pregnant sentence as clear as crystal. I find the getting of that sentence is the hardest, the most exacting, and the most fruitful labor in my study."[12]

It is this proposition that holds the sermon together in a thematic unity. (Some preachers prefer a theme stated in the form of a phrase as the integrating center of the sermon. This writer believes that a phrase is usually too broad and can allow the sermon to lack clarity in direction. A complete sentence, on the other hand, is more specific than a phrase and provides more clearly defined limits on the broader subject being discussed.)

3. The proposition is supported by two or more subordinate ideas or truths. These are usually called the main points, but are sometimes called the romans, divisions, or even sermon moves. These main points should be equal in value. One of them should not be subordinate to another. They should also be clearly distinct from one another. These are, in effect, subtheses of the main thesis. If they can be established, and if they are adequate in strength or number, the main thesis will stand firm.

4. The main points are supported, clarified, illustrated, and proven by subpoints, sometimes called supporting material.

5. While it is sometimes thought that each main point and its own subpoints form "miniature sermons," great care should be exercised that a three-point sermon, for example, does not come across like three unrelated sermonettes. Appropriate transitions that remind the listeners of the sermon's proposition or theme are usually given between the main points.

6. An appropriate introduction and conclusion should be added only after the body of the sermon (proposition, main points, and subpoints) has been completed.

Traditional Methods of Structuring

While books on preaching have varied throughout the years on structural matters, such as how to move from a central idea to a main point outline, most of them have one thing in common. They usually place sermons in three traditional categories: topical, textual, and expository. While these categories are somewhat arbitrary, especially the second and third, the preacher should be aware of them because they will appear repeatedly in his reading on preaching.

Topical Sermons

Sermons whose subject (topic) is based on a given Scripture text while the main points and the subpoints are *not* based on that text are commonly called topical sermons. Sometimes the main points and subpoints are based on related texts, and sometimes they are not based on any text but are arrived at by other means such as questioning (who, what, when, where, why?), faceting (looking at a subject from various angles or perspectives), or formal reasoning (deduction or induction). The sermon text from which the subject is taken should, at the very least, clearly speak to the subject being explored in the sermon. Otherwise, the text can be a pretext for the preacher's own agenda.

The following are sometimes suggested as advantages of topical preaching:

1. It enables a thorough examination of any one topic.
2. It trains the mind of the preacher to a breadth of view.
3. It lends itself to great oratorical preaching.
4. It ensures sermonic unity.

Topical preaching also has some possible disadvantages of which the preacher should be aware:

1. There is a limited number of topics (when using that term in the sense of broad subject as compared to a more narrow defining of the theme).
2. It is sometimes, though not necessarily, biblically shallow. There is a danger of failing to deal with contextual matters. When this is the case, a steady diet of topical preaching will do little to enhance a congregation's understanding and integration of the Bible and theology.
3. It leads to sermonic unity only in the sense of keeping on a broad topic. Generally, a given topic is too broad to handle in one sermon without a further narrowing of its scope. (If this is done by means of a thematic or propositional statement, then this criticism is not valid.)

It is sometimes thought that the greatest sermons in history have been topical and that the best preachers have preached topically. While it is true that the various collections of "great" sermons lean heavily toward topical preaching, it should be remembered that the issue of "cause and effect" is not clear. Are those whose works are included in these anthologies great preachers *because* they preached topically? It may well be that they would have been outstanding preachers regardless of the homiletical method chosen. Many of them preached predominantly topical sermons because that was the common practice of their time and sphere of ministry. In many eras of the church's history, topical preaching has been more widespread than other methods.[13]

While topical preaching is ignored or disdained by many theological conservatives, it should be remembered that many doctrinal and ethical subjects can be handled in this way. Some, indeed, must be! One would be hard-pressed, for example, to preach expositorally (in the traditional sense of that term) on contemporary issues like abortion, homosexuality, or capital punishment. Doctrinally, subject matter such as the divine attributes would seem to require a topical treatment.

When the subject is handled topically, the preacher must make certain that he is basing his ideas on scriptural truth, for that is the basis of the authority of any sermon.

Textual Sermons

Textual sermons are based on one or two verses of Scripture, with the main points of the message coming from the text itself, often from phrases or clauses that are of somewhat equal weight in importance. The main points are built around the central theme found in the text. Sub-points are sometimes inferred from the text but are usually taken from parallel passages or from outside of Scripture.

Some homileticians believe that relatively few single verses or brief Bible passages lend themselves to textual preaching. Ilion Jones counted not more than one hundred or so.[14] This writer believes that Jones and others who hold this opinion underestimate the potential usefulness of the textual method of preaching. Many texts are appropriate. Consider the Book of Psalms. Dozens, if not scores, of verses in this part of Scripture alone seem to be capable of being treated in this fashion without any hermeneutical or exegetical misuse. Charles Spurgeon found numerous texts throughout the Bible to which he applied this method.

When a verse or two contains two or more distinct ideas related to a single theme and when this text reflects the thrust of the larger context, then it may very well serve as the basis of a textual sermon. When handled properly, such sermons carry biblical authority and provide sound instruction.

Expository Sermons

Expository preaching has traditionally been understood to refer to sermons based on texts longer than two verses or so. Beyond that, differences of opinion seem to prevail.

Some have understood expository preaching as a verse-by-verse treatment of the passage under consideration without any theme or central idea to hold the sermon together. Thus, "exposition" becomes a running commentary on the passage rather than a sermon per se. While this approach may have merit in certain settings, it is not recommended for regular pulpit fare. A sermon needs to have thematic unity and a particular purpose in mind.

Others insist that main points and subpoints, based on parts of the text, should be used (in true sermonic fashion) and that every part of the text—every sentence, clause, and phrase—be used in the homiletical structure. This can become quite a formidable task for most preachers, though there may be merit in this approach for the listener.

Still others advocate that the entire text should be understood thematically and that the main points and subpoints (based on parts of the text) should support that theme. It is unnecessary, however, to use every textual detail in the sermon. Most expository preachers follow this approach.

Many books on homiletics, particularly those written in the first half of the 20th century, say relatively little about expository preaching. There seems to be an underlying assumption that sermons will be mostly topical with a few textual ones added for variety's sake. Expository preaching has certain strengths which should be considered:

1. It is a powerful way of presenting and reinforcing scriptural truth.
2. It motivates in-depth Bible study both on the part of the preacher and the hearer.
3. If done well, expository preaching serves as an effective model for the interpretation of Scripture.
4. If done in series, it prevents the neglect of some themes.
5. It allows tremendous variety thematically and structurally.
6. It allows the Scriptures to speak authoritatively.

This is not to suggest that expository preaching alone is characterized by these benefits. It does seem, however, that these strengths can be enhanced by this approach. Charles Koller speaks wisely:

> Textual preaching has much to commend it; likewise, topical preaching. No one method should be employed exclusively. But as a prevailing method, for year-round ministering, expository preaching has the greater potential for the blessing and enrichment of both pastor and people.[15]

Evaluation

While these traditional categories may be somewhat helpful in our efforts to distinguish between kinds of sermons, it should be understood that they are rather arbitrary. The distinctions between them are not always hard distinctions, as can be seen when comparing the textual approach with the expository approach. Furthermore, some would add additional categories such as the textual-topical, though the difference between this approach and the textual approach is somewhat unclear when one understands that all sermons, including textual ones, should have a unifying topic.

In the final analysis, labels such as those above should not be used to denigrate one approach and exalt another. Every sermon, regardless of arrangement, should allow the text of Scripture to make its own statement about truth and then apply that truth to the lives of the hearers. When this is done, the sermon might be said to be "expository" even if it is arranged topically or textually. It is "expository" in the sense that the meaning of the text is being exposed or expounded. In this sense, "all true preaching is expository preaching."[16]

Further Comments on Structure

Some of the structures discussed in this handbook will be traditional deductive patterns, while others will be less traditional and more inductive in form. No apology is made or considered necessary for the more traditional approaches, even though they are sometimes belittled in some of the newer books on preaching as being too discursive and relying too much on propositional ideas.

It is interesting to note that the same authors who condemn the concept of propositional truth do so almost exclusively through means of propositional argumentation. For example, Eslinger states that "Sermonic trading in ideas, whatever organization they are given, is a static, lifeless, and reductionist enterprise."[17] Yet, the same chapter in which this quotation is found is organized around ideas in the form of propositional statements. Those involved in espousing a "new homiletic" seem to be contradictory in the way they communicate *their* ideas about preaching in comparison to the way they say sermonic ideas themselves must be communicated.[18]

Then there is the matter of structural variety. Many books on preaching are woefully weak in discussing structural methodology. The reader is often told to find a subject or theme and then to break it into its logical or natural parts. These parts become the main points of the sermon. Beyond this rather general kind of instruction, the preacher receives relatively little guidance as to just *how* the division of the whole into parts should be done. There is also little indication of the numerous ways to outline messages, each one legitimate with certain purposes and kinds of texts.

Variety in structure, however, is a key to a well-rounded and well-received pulpit ministry. Killinger remarks:

> Most preachers adapt a single form to their purposes and use it with only slight variations for the remainder of their ministries. But there are many styles and varieties of homiletical form, and a creative preacher while hewing primarily to one form, will occasionally try other forms, if only to enhance the communication process. Periodic experimentation offers freshness and variety to the people who listen to our sermons week after week and, in addition to giving us new perspectives on the material we are preaching, permits us to make value judgments about the forms and methods we ordinarily employ.[19]

This handbook presents eight distinct methods of homiletical structuring, some of which can be done in more than one way.

Finally, the preacher needs to understand that preaching is more than form. Good structure can enhance the communication process, but it will fail by itself:

> Structural soundness can not supply that life of holiness which is basic to pulpit power. There is an eloquence of the lips, and there is an eloquence of the heart. Of Aaron, it was recorded, "He can speak well" (Exod. 4:14); but there is no message of Aaron to be found in the Scriptures. Moses, on the other hand, regarded himself as "not eloquent, . . . slow of speech, and of a slow tongue" (Exod. 4:10). But from Moses we have a legacy of messages mighty in power, reflecting the eloquence which is of the heart.[20]

In addition to structure failing unless it is accompanied by a holy life on the part of the preacher, structure will also fail unless there is solid content in the message. The very best sermon outline is still only a skeletal structure. Without the meat of solid content affixed to it, the sermon will be grotesque. It is better to say something significant in a structurally clumsy way than to speak with great form but say very little of substance.

Structure alone will also fail unless the preacher is an *active* communicator. He must first "own" what is being said, having personally been affected by the truth of the message. He must put himself into the delivery wholeheartedly, communicating to the listener that this truth is vitally important.

Notes

1. Lloyd M. Perry, *A Manual for Biblical Preaching* (Grand Rapids, Mich.: Baker Book House, 1981), 3.

2. Henry Grady Davis, *Design for Preaching* (Philadelphia: Fortress Press, 1958), 12.

3. George E. Sweazey, *Preaching the Good News* (Englewood Cliffs, N.J.: Prentice-Hall, Inc., 1976), 70. It is worth noting that Sweazey's Ph.D. is in the area of philosophy, a discipline that includes concepts like knowing and meaning. These are often discussed by advocates of a "new homiletic" which downgrades the importance of rational form and purpose in favor of a subjective response to symbol and story.

4. Perry, 3.

5. James Braga, *How to Prepare Bible Messages* (Portland, Oreg.: Multnomah Press, 1981), 90.

6. Warren W. Wiersbe, "Your Preaching Is Unique," in *Leadership*, vol. 2 (Summer 1981), 32.

7. Davis, 9.

8. J. Daniel Baumann, *An Introduction to Contemporary Preaching* (Grand Rapids, Mich.: Baker Book House, 1972), 149.

9. Charles W. Koller, *Expository Preaching Without Notes Plus Sermons Preached Without Notes* (Grand Rapids, Mich.: Baker Book House, 1962), 41.

10. Koller, 41.

11. Glen C. Knecht, "Sermon Structure and Flow," in *The Preacher and Preaching: Reviving the Art in the Twentieth Century,* ed. Samuel T. Logan Jr. (Phillipsburg, N.J.: Presbyterian and Reformed Publishing Co., 1986), 278.

12. John Henry Jowett, *The Preacher His Life and Work* (New York: Doran & Co., 1928, 1912), 133.

13. The most extensive survey of preachers and sermons in print today is the 13-volume work by Clyde E. Fant and William M. Pinson, *20 Centuries of Great Preaching* (Waco, Tex.: Word, 1971). Of the 95 highly esteemed preachers whose sermons are featured in this set, the overwhelming majority are topical preachers. Notable exceptions to this include Luther, Calvin, Spurgeon, and Maclaren.

14. Ilion T. Jones, *Principles and Practice of Preaching* (Nashville: Abingdon Press, 1956), 82.

15. Koller, 28.

16. Donald G. Miller, *The Way to Biblical Preaching* (New York: Abingdon Press, 1957), 13.

17. Richard L. Eslinger, *A New Hearing: Living Options in Homiletic Method* (Nashville: Abingdon Press, 1987), 85.

18. Eslinger (*A New Hearing,* 133) states bluntly that "The old rational homiletics is obsolete." Still, Eslinger himself organizes his materials according to a rational structure. At best, his thinking appears to be highly inconsistent.

19. John Killinger, *Fundamentals of Preaching* (Philadelphia: Fortress Press, 1985), 50.

20. Koller, 43.

PART 2

DEVELOPING OUR HOMILETICAL TECHNIQUES

3

PRELIMINARY PROCESSES TO HOMILETICS

Before the preacher becomes involved in outlining and writing his sermon, he must first thoroughly understand the Scripture passage on which the sermon is based. The Scripture text gives real authority to the sermon; therefore, the theological and practical truths of the text must be carefully studied.

The faithful communicator of the Word must carefully follow three processes. Together, they will ordinarily require about one-third of the total sermon preparation time available.

Selection of a Suitable Text

The first process the preacher must follow is to make a decision regarding the choice of the sermon text or texts. Sometimes a text is "discovered," then used on an appropriate occasion. At other times, the specific needs of the audience cause the preacher to seek out a text which speaks to that concern. Whichever happens first, there must be a true thematic agreement between the text and the needs of the hearers.

This blending of text and need comes about more readily as the preacher gains expertise in being a person of "two worlds," as John Stott expressed it.[1] This means that the preacher is deeply knowledgeable in matters of Scripture and matters of society; of ancient culture and modern culture; of the pulpit and the pew. His function is to speak forth the truth of God clearly and powerfully, making it applicable to the needs and experiences of those who hear.

Selection of the text or texts should be a matter of prayer and meditation. Knowing the real needs of the audience requires prayer. The Scriptures must prayerfully be considered. God's help should be sought for direction in bringing the people and the Word together.

While the choice of the preaching portion is being made, several practical guidelines should be kept in mind:

• *The text to be studied for the basis of a sermon should be a complete thematic segment, usually a whole paragraph or more in length.* This does not mean that the sermon must cover the entire segment. It may mean that a topic that will serve as the basis for a topical sermon will be "lifted" from the larger passage. It may mean that a single verse will be set forth and treated textually. It may mean that a sermon structure will be developed in which all or most of the segment will be covered in the course of the sermon. Regardless of homiletical method, it is wise to build on the foundation of a complete thematic segment. This precaution will help assure that the sermon grows out of the authority of Scripture and is not simply a by-product of the preacher's own agenda.

• *The length and/or depth of the text must be considered in view of the preaching occasion.* Some texts cannot be handled adequately in 20 or 30 minutes. It is better to treat a shorter or simpler text adequately in the allotted time than to treat a more substantial text superficially.

• *The passage chosen should be within the abilities of the preacher to research, arrange, and present.* Again, it is far better to do well with a relatively simple text than to do poorly with a difficult one.

• *The words of uninspired men should not be used affirmatively, even though they are truthfully recorded in Scripture.* For example, not everything spoken by Job's "friends" is true. Some of them made false accusations against him. None of them really understood the situation. Treating every assertion they made as though it were the truth of God misuses the Scripture. The same thing is true of parts of Ecclesiastes. In his search for wisdom and understanding, the philosopher draws some false conclusions, as well as some true ones. Great care must be exercised in distinguishing between the two. This guideline is, of course, a part of good hermeneutical practice. The larger context must first be understood before one begins to wrestle with the immediate passage.

• *Spurious or questionable texts should not be used.* Thankfully, our printed Bibles contain relatively few of these. The preacher should understand the nature of textual criticism well enough to refrain from using passages for which there is little textual evidence of authenticity. When one wishes to preach on the Great Commission, for example, Mark 16:9-20 should not be chosen as the text, since there is considerable question about its genuineness. (This passage is not contained in the most reliable early manuscripts of the Scriptures.) The same is true of John 7:53—8:11 and parts of 1 John 5:7-8. It is a good idea either to check several English translations of the passage under consideration or to check in the apparatus of the Greek or Hebrew text. Most modern translations give notes explaining passages with textual questions.

• *A text should not be avoided simply because it is familiar to many in the audience.* The text is probably familiar because it is a great text. Psalm 1, Psalm 23, John 3:16, Philippians 2:5-8, the parable of the prodigal son, the Lord's Prayer, and many similar texts have been used by God in mighty ways over the generations to bring people to Himself and build up the church. John Broadus made the following argument for the inclusion of familiar texts:

What has made some texts familiar to all, but the fact that they are so manifestly good texts? It is a very mistaken desire for novelty which leads a man to shrink from such rich and fruitful passages as "God so loved the world," etc.; "This is a faithful saying," etc., which Luther used to call "little Bibles," as if including in their narrow compass the whole Bible. He who will turn away from the tradition of the pulpit as to the meaning and application of such passages and make personal and earnest study of them will often find much that is new to him and his hearers, as the skillful gold-hunter in California will sometimes follow in the very track of many searchers and gain there his richest harvest.[2]

• *Texts may be chosen according to a preaching series.* This can be done by working one's way through books of the Bible, thematically similar parts of Bible books (such as the seven signs/miracles in John's Gospel or Romans 1—8), or topical series (such as family relationships, prayer, a creedal statement, etc.). Series preaching usually saves considerable time in selecting preaching texts. (Long sermon series should probably be avoided for the most part. A series of eight to ten weeks is about the right length for most congregations.)

• *The text should be chosen as far in advance of the preaching date as possible.* This allows time for familiarization to occur as the preacher takes the next steps toward sermon structuring. It is recommended, in fact, that the preacher set up a sermon plan several months in advance. This allows for a thorough collecting of materials, study, and homiletical reflection before the actual writing of the sermon. If unexpected circumstances arise, the plan can be changed accordingly. A word of caution, however: remember that the plan's purpose is to serve the preacher and God's people, not to be their master.

Contextual Study

The second process that necessarily precedes structuring the sermon is an adequate study of the biblical, historical, literary, and theological context of the preaching passage. The following steps should be done as required by the type of text selected. They are not given in a precise chronological order, because in actual practice, the order will vary from text to text:

1. Intimate familiarity with the wording of the immediate preaching passage and its larger context should be achieved. The passage and the context should be read often in one or more English translations. The use of various translations will provide a better grasp of the flow and sense of the text and its surrounding context.

2. The literary genre (type of literature) of the passage should be noted. Are there special hermeneutical principles that need to be followed? What safeguards are necessary?

3. The speaker or writer of the text should be determined and information gained concerning his background and life. Does this passage fit into a special time in that person's life and, if so, what is the significance of this, if any?

4. The original recipients of the passage should be identified. What is known about them that might have some sermonic significance?

5. The chronology of the text should be fixed. When was it written or spoken, and what is the relationship of this time to other biblical or historical events?

6. Geographic locations related to the passage should be studied. These might include the place(s) of writing or speaking, destination, or other places mentioned in the text. Which of these is incidental, and which might have some sermonic significance?

7. The general theme of the larger context should be determined. How does the theme of the preaching text relate to that of the context?

8. The passage should be compared with any parallel passages in Scripture. These parallels may be historical, thematic, or both.

9. The specific aim of the passage should be determined. Why does it seem to have been included in Scripture by the Holy Spirit?

10. Information from extrabiblical v sources, such as history and archaeology, should be gathered if it has a bearing on the text.

When these steps are completed, a thorough overview of the passage in its biblical, literary, theological, and historical contexts will have been accomplished. The preacher is then ready to study the immediate text in detail.

Textual Study

This process has to do with *exegesis proper*—an in-depth study of the content and meaning of the passage.

1. The passage should be translated from the original language. If the preacher is not skilled in the languages, a careful study and comparison can be made with several good translations. (Some prefer to do this step prior to contextual study.)

2. Textual variants should be checked and a determination made about the correct reading of the preaching passage.

3. A mechanical layout or analytical outline of the passage should be done (see the next section in this chapter). This will help clarify the relationships that exist among various ideas and concepts in the text.

4. Word studies of important words can be done as necessary. (Many fine study helps are available in this regard, even for those who have a limited understanding of the original languages.)

5. The grammar of the passage should be studied. Particular attention should be given to the following:

     a. the kinds and relationships of clauses
     b. the significance of all verbs
     c. all cases and prepositions
     d. the use or nonuse of the definite article

  6. The literary structure of the passage should be studied, noting word order, word play, repetition, and figures of speech.

  7. Special note of parallel (grammatically equal) ideas or forms in the text should be made. These can range from a series of warnings to questions, affirmations, observations, illustrations, promises, duties, privileges, and similar kinds of concepts.

  8. The most inclusive and important broad *subject* of the text should be decided. This can usually be expressed in a single word. (Examples: sin, discipline, salvation, God, prayer, praise, etc.)

  9. The one most important aspect of that subject discussed in this passage should be noted. This is the *theme* of the passage and the sermon. When working with the subject of God, for example, the result of this process might be God's power, God's love, God's faithfulness, what God is like, and so on.

  10. Finally, the practical application of the thrust (theme) of the passage should be considered:

     a. What universal principles are clearly communicated?
     b. What specific applications can be justifiably drawn from these principles for a particular people at a particular time?
     c. What responses are called forth by these applications? (Caution: this step requires a very careful blending of exegetical insight and proper hermeneutics. It is the process in which the preacher faces the greatest danger of reading his own ideas or prejudices into the text.)

Steps in Doing a Mechanical Layout

Whereas grammatical diagramming is concerned with individual sentences, the method of analysis known as the mechanical layout is quite usefully applied to an entire paragraph. When properly done, a mechanical layout of a paragraph indicates visually how the various parts of the paragraph (sentences, clauses, phrases) relate to one another and ultimately to the theme or thrust of the entire paragraph:[3]

  1. The number of sentences in the paragraph about to be diagrammed should be noted. Longer sentences usually indicate a more complex structure than shorter ones.

  2. The main clause (also called independent clause) of the first sentence in the paragraph should be identified. Compound sentences have more than one main clause. This clause (or these clauses) should be written down, beginning at the left margin of the paper. Remember that an independent clause contains the subject of the sentence, the main verb, and perhaps a direct object or predicate adjective.

3. Conjunctions (examples: *and, but, or, nor*), connectives (examples: *although, otherwise, finally, on the contrary*), or nouns of address should be placed above the main clause.

4. Grammatical elements such as modifiers (adverbs and adjectives) and prepositional phrases should be placed below the main clause(s). These can be indented and placed below the elements they modify or describe.

5. The same procedure should be followed with dependent clauses. They can be indented to show that they are subordinate to the main clause.

6. If desired, arrows can be drawn from modifiers to the words or phrases they describe.

7. Steps 3—7 can be repeated for each sentence in the paragraph, with the independent clause in each "secondary" sentence moved to the right of the independent clause of the "primary" sentence.

8. Since the main purpose of a mechanical layout is to indicate visually how the various ideas of a sentence and/or paragraph relate to one another, simplicity and an uncluttered appearance should be strived for as much as possible.

Sample Mechanical Layout: Psalm 1 (NIV)

1. Blessed is the man   I.
      who   1.
          does not walk in the counsel of the wicked,
          or stand in the way of sinners,
          or sit in the seat of mockers.
2.   (but)   2.
          his delight is in the law of the Lord,
           and
          on his law he meditates
           day and night.
3. He is like a tree   3.
          planted by streams of water,
          which yields its fruit in season,
          and whose leaf does not wither.
      Whatever he does prospers.
4. Not so the wicked!   II.
      They are like chaff   1.
          that the wind blows away.
5.   (Therefore)   2.
          the wicked will not stand in the judgment,
          nor sinners in the assembly of the righteous.
6.   (For)   Conclusion:
          the Lord watches over the way of the righteous,   1.
      (but)
          the way of the wicked will perish.   2.

Sample Skeleton Sermon Outline

A very simple keyword-type homiletical approach, based on the parallel ideas which emerged in this mechanical layout, might begin to take shape as follows. (The Keyword method is discussed in detail in the next chapter. What follows is a preview of that method.)

SUBJECT: Humanity

THEME: How God sees humans

PROPOSITION: You can know what God thinks of you personally.

INTERROGATIVE: How can you know what God thinks of you personally?

TRANSITIONAL SENTENCE: By studying the categories of humankind described in Psalm 1, you can know what God thinks of you personally.
  I. Some people are pleasing to God (1:1).
  II. Some people are displeasing to God (1:4).

CONCLUSION: Therefore, you should know what God thinks of you personally.

This is a sort of "first-run" approach to a skeletal outline. It can be refined and reworded, as long as any revision is in keeping with the subject, theme, and emphasis (as seen in the mechanical layout) of the text itself. Thus, the shape of the sermon outline is determined to a large extent by the shape of the text itself.

In the case of this particular psalm, the subject of the sermon will probably need to be either humanity, God, or perhaps an ethical concept like choices. The theme, then, will be a narrowing down of the broader subject. If the preacher decides to pursue God as the subject of this text, then the theme might be something such as "how God deals with people." If this is the case, then there would be two main points, based on the contrasting ideas of verse 6. The preceding verses would serve as the basis for subpoints under the main points.

Several attempts at tentative outlines may be necessary before one seems entirely suitable. Other homiletical methods might be usable as well. It is at this point that the decision regarding homiletical methodology needs to be made.

Notes

1. John R. W. Stott, *Between Two Worlds: The Art of Preaching in the Twentieth Century* (Grand Rapids, Mich.: Wm. B. Eerdmans Publishing Co., 1982).

2. John A. Broadus, *A Treatise on the Preparation and Delivery of Sermons*, rev. by Jesse Burton Weatherspoon (New York: Harper and Row, 1944), 20.

3. Additional insights into this method of structural diagramming can be found in Walter C. Kaiser's *Toward an Exegetical Theology* (Grand Rapids, Mich.: Baker Book House, 1981) on pages 95-104, 165-181.

4

THE KEYWORD
METHOD

The Keyword method[1] of sermon outlining can be used with those sermons traditionally called expository, as well as with those called textual. It can also be used with so-called topical preaching with some modification.[2]

Of all the homiletical methods presented in this handbook, the Keyword method will prove to be the most useful, once it is mastered. When the preaching text is a minimum of a paragraph and deals with something other than a parable, miracle, or figure of speech, this method will be usable most of the time.[3]

To determine whether the Keyword method is the correct method to use with a given text, the preacher should carefully study his mechanical layout of the passage. Are there two or more *parallel ideas* in the text that relate in the same way to the same theme? If so, the text can probably be developed sermonically using the Keyword method. If not, another homiletical method will be necessary.[4]

The parallel ideas in a text are possible main points when the Keyword method is being used. A given paragraph (or more) of text may well have several sets of parallel ideas. On one level there may be two or three independent clauses; on a second level, there may two or three dependent clauses related to one independent clause. There may even be a series of prepositional phrases, each related to the same clause. The homiletician will need to choose which set of parallel ideas he wishes to use as the basis of his main points. Usually, the main points will be based on the independent clauses of one or more paragraphs. The remaining subordinate clauses or phrases can then be used for subpoints. It is this method of arriving at the main ideas of a sermon which is the distinguishing feature of the Keyword approach.

The Keyword method, as presented here, is made up of 12 steps. These steps are structured to ensure that the finished sermon will be unified in its theme, clear in its purpose, followable in its argument, scriptural in its authority, and applicable in its thrust. These steps should ordinarily be followed in the order presented, although in the final analysis chronology is not as important as the logical flow of the finished sermon.

These steps presuppose that the following preparation, discussed in chapter 3, has been carefully completed. Ordinarily, a minimum of one-third of the total sermon preparation time needs to be given to this "prehomiletical" effort: (1) the selection of a suitable text, (2) contextual study, and (3) textual study.

Step 1: Isolate the Subject

This step will usually be done during the textual study mentioned above. The subject of the passage should become the subject of the sermon. The only exception to this is if two subjects are discussed in the same text—one being set in contrast or comparison to the other. (Romans 6:23 would be such a text.) When this is the case, one or the other should be chosen as the sermon subject. Another alternative is to determine the larger subject of which these two lesser topics are a part.

The subject, as stated here, should be very broad. As such, it will usually be stated as one word.

Following is a partial list of subjects which might be encountered in various texts of Scripture:

Advent	Affliction	Agnosticism
Alcohol	Angels	Anxiety
Apologetics	Atonement	Baptism
Bible	Brotherhood	Christ
Christmas	Church	Communion
Compromise	Conscience	Conversion
Courage	Cross	Cults
Death	Discipleship	Discouragement
Divorce	Doubt	Education
Encouragement	Eternity	Ethics
Evangelism	Faith	Family
Fear	Fellowship	Forgiveness
God	God's will	Gospel
Government	Grace	Gratitude
Happiness	Healing	Hell
History	Holy Spirit	Hope
Hospitality	Humility	Idolatry
Joy	Judgment	Justification
Kindness	Law	Legalism
Life	Loneliness	Love
Man	Marriage	Materialism
Ministry	Missions	Obedience
Patience	Peace	Power
Praise	Prayer	Pride
Prophecy	Redemption	Repentance
Resurrection	Righteousness	Salvation
Sanctification	Satan	Second Coming
Sin	Stewardship	Temptation

Thanksgiving	Time	Tongue
Unity	War	Witnessing
Women	Work	Worship

Step 2: Determine the Theme

The subjects listed above are too broad to be covered in a given sermon. Such a sermon, though based on a topic, would lack clear unity and cohesiveness. It is necessary, therefore, to determine how this particular subject is going to be treated; that is, what specific part of the broad subject is going to be covered? The theme, then, is the specific aspect of the subject to be covered in the present sermon. Like the subject, the theme will probably be identified during the study of the text. If not, it must be determined now.

Like the subject, the theme must be based on the Scripture passage. As stated earlier, it represents a narrowing down of the broader subject. As such, it will be stated as a phrase. It should not be stated as a complete sentence, for this will cause a problem when the next step is taken.

If, for example, the text under consideration has as its subject "the Holy Spirit," the preacher will recognize that this concept is too large to cover in one sermon. Further, the text itself does not attempt to cover everything about the subject. The preacher must discover what it is about the Holy Spirit that this particular text emphasizes. Thus, both the subject and the theme will be rooted and grounded in the preaching passage.

Following is a list of possible themes based on the subject of the Holy Spirit. This list is not exhaustive:

The person of the Holy Spirit
The work of the Holy Spirit
The gifts of the Holy Spirit
The filling of the Holy Spirit
The baptism of the Holy Spirit
The helping ministry of the Holy Spirit
The teaching ministry of the Holy Spirit
The praying ministry of the Holy Spirit
The sealing of the Holy Spirit
Grieving the Holy Spirit
Blasphemy against the Holy Spirit
The fruit of the Holy Spirit

It should be noted that each sermon will have only *one* subject and *one* theme. To have more than one subject or theme would result in disunity structurally and confusion on the part of the hearers.

Step 3: Write a Proposition

The proposition of a Keyword sermon is a brief, simple sentence that declares to the hearer what should be known about the theme of the sermon. The proposition can be called "the sermon in a sentence." It embodies the single truth that the preacher hopes to communicate and usually includes an implied response. Everything else in the sermon revolves around, or in some way relates to, the proposition. As Lloyd Perry states, "It is this sentence which is the integrating center of the sermon."[5]

The sermon proposition has been called various names by different writers and preachers. Some have referred to it as the *thesis,* the *central idea,* the *big idea,* or the *central truth,* among other names. Regardless of the label given to it, the proposition is absolutely crucial to a well-done sermon. A sermon without a clear proposition is like a ship without a rudder or an automobile without a steering wheel. Keeping it on course will be very difficult, if not impossible! The result will be an unclear purpose, an unclear direction, and an unclear argument. The audience may feel a sense of frustration, for effective communication has been hindered by a lack of preciseness. The preacher himself may also be frustrated, feeling unable to present clearly that which he desires to present.

Following are some characteristics of a good Keyword sermon proposition. Most of these characteristics are true of propositions for other kinds of sermons as well:

1. It should be stated in one simple sentence, avoiding compound or complex sentences.
2. It should be eight words or less, if possible.
3. It should consist of a personal reference (you, we, each of us), plus a course of action (a suitable verb form), plus the theme of the sermon.
4. It should be a persuasive statement, when possible, rather than being merely factual. The Keyword method is by nature a persuasive structure, and the proposition should reflect this.
5. It usually should reflect, or be stated as, a timeless truth.
6. It should not include proper names, except for Deity.
7. It should reflect the overall purpose of the sermon. The following list of purposes is suggestive:[6]

> To inspire
> To move toward deeper consecration
> To evangelize
> To motivate to action
> To bring comfort
> To instruct
> To bring warning

The Keyword method uses three primary kinds of propositions. They are listed here with sample propositions under each.

1. Proposition of Ability
   a. Every Christian *can* experience effective daily prayer.
   b. The person following Christ *can* be a learner.
   c. Sincere spiritual seekers *can* discover the truth about Jesus Christ.
2. Proposition of Obligation
   a. Every Christian *should* pray daily.
   b. The disciple of Jesus Christ *must* be a learner.
   c. Sincere spiritual seekers *must* investigate the person of Christ.
3. Proposition of Value
   a. *It is better to* pray daily *than to* shoulder the load alone.
   b. *It is better to* grow in the knowledge of Christ *than to* remain childish in our faith.
   c. *It is better to* investigate the person of Christ *than to* look elsewhere for spiritual reality.

Although these kinds of propositions seem to say about the same thing, especially those of ability and obligation, they do not. One word (*can* instead of *should*) leads to an entirely different kind of sermon than the other. The purposes, as well as the basic structures, of the sermons will be different. The only things they have in common are the subject and theme.

As with the subject and the theme, the text must be allowed to determine the kind of proposition to be used. If the text seems to be answering a *why* question, the proposition should likely be an obligatory one. If the text is telling us *how* something is to be done, the proposition should be one of ability. If the text is making a comparison, then a proposition of value may be required. The text should always be allowed to speak for itself. That is the heart of biblical preaching!

Step 4: Compose a Propositional Interrogative

Steps 4, 5, and 6 are unique to the Keyword method and are the steps which lead to identification of the sermon's main points, which will be discussed in detail in Step 7.

The first of these steps is to ask a question of the proposition. The proposition makes an assertion, which should lead naturally to a related question. This question is formulated by simply prefacing the proposition with a suitable interrogative like *why* or *how*. The proper interrogative will depend on the kind of proposition being used (obligation, ability, or value) and the nature of the material in the text (which question does it answer?).

1. With a proposition of ability, the usual interrogative is *how*. (*When, where,* and *what* can also be used.)
   PROPOSITION: Every Christian *can* experience effective daily prayer.

   INTERROGATIVE: *How* can every Christian experience effective daily prayer?

2. With a proposition of obligation, the usual interrogative is *why*. (*When, where,* and *what* can also be used.)

   PROPOSITION: Every Christian *should* pray daily.

   INTERROGATIVE: *Why* should every Christian pray daily?

3. With a proposition of value, the usual interrogative is *why*. (*When* and *where* might also be used.)

   PROPOSITION: *It is better* to pray daily *than to* shoulder the load alone.

   INTERROGATIVE: *Why* is it better to pray daily than to shoulder the load alone?

The interrogative sentence may or may not be stated during delivery, but it is extremely important as a homiletical tool. It will help the preacher remain focused as he prepares to make the transition from the sermon introduction (to be written later) into the sermon body.

Step 5: Choose a Keyword

The keyword is a homiletical device used to identify the main points of the sermon. As mentioned previously, the main points of a Keyword sermon are based on parallel ideas in the text discovered by developing a mechanical layout of the passage. Such a layout will indicate whether true parallel ideas exist. These may be a series (two or more) of independent clauses, or dependent clauses, or modifying phrases. Parallel ideas will always be in the same category. For example, one independent clause and two dependent clauses should not be seen as parallel ideas, for they are not, in fact, parallel in the thrust and meaning of the text.

If the ideas being considered as main points are truly parallel, they will be capable of being identified collectively by a keyword. This keyword will *always* be a *plural* noun, for it is used to identify two or more ideas, or main points. There can be no exceptions to this.

The keyword may or may not actually be found in the text. The text may mention "three lies," or "five woes," or "two promises," but most of the time this will not be the case. Instead, the preacher will need to discover and label the parallel ideas himself. If, for example, the text has a series of "because" statements, the preacher may justifiably choose a keyword like *reasons*. A text may list several *instructions* without ever using that particular word. The Greek word *hina* ("in order that") may be used two or more times to introduce a purpose clause. In such an instance, the keyword *purposes*, or something similar, could be used.[7]

The keyword is a direct response to the propositional interrogative. If the question asked is "how?" the response would be "by [state the action] the [keyword] in [the text]." If the question asked is "why?" the expected response will be "because of the [keyword] in [the text]."

Examples

PROPOSITION: Every Christian can experience effective daily prayer.

INTERROGATIVE: How can every Christian experience effective daily prayer?

RESPONSE: By following the *guidelines* set forth in [the text], every Christian can experience effective daily prayer.

PROPOSITION: Every Christian should pray daily.

INTERROGATIVE: Why should every Christian pray daily?

RESPONSE: Because of the *benefits* seen in [the text], every Christian should pray daily.

Specific, rather than general, words should be chosen. The word *things*, while technically meeting the requirements of a keyword, communicates virtually nothing. The keyword should match the parallel concepts in the preaching text as closely as possible. This will give each sermon a sense of freshness rather than making it sound familiar.

The exact meaning of the keyword should be clear in the preacher's mind. If he is uncertain, he should consult a dictionary. The overall quality of the finished sermon outline will be greatly enhanced if precision is maintained at this point.

Following is a short list of sample keywords. It is intended to be suggestive of the diversity that is possible:

abuses	gains	methods	prescriptions
actions	gifts	ministries	principles
admonitions	guarantees	mistakes	privileges
affairs	guidelines	models	problems
affirmations	habits	motives	proofs
alternatives	hopes	movements	prospects
answers	hurts	names	purposes
arguments	ideals	natures	qualities
attitudes	ideas	necessities	quests

attributes	idols	needs	questions
beliefs	ills	norms	reactions
benefits	impacts	objectives	reasons
blessings	impediments	objects	results
blunders	imperatives	obligations	rewards
burdens	imperfections	observances	rules
causes	implications	observations	sayings
certainties	improvements	obstacles	secrets
changes	incentives	occasions	services
circumstances	incidents	offenses	situations
commands	invitations	options	skills
corrections	issues	paradoxes	solutions
dangers	items	parallels	sources
decisions	joys	particulars	talents
declarations	judgments	parts	tasks
deeds	keys	paths	teachings
details	kinds	patterns	tests
doctrines	laws	penalties	times
duties	lessons	perceptions	truths
effects	levels	perils	uses
elements	liabilities	periods	values
examples	liberties	petitions	virtues
exclamations	limits	phases	visions
facts	losses	pictures	vocations
factors	loyalties	plans	warnings
failures	manifestations	pledges	ways

Each sermon will have only *one* keyword, and each main point of the sermon will be *one* of whatever the keyword is.

Step 6: Formulate a Transitional Sentence

The transitional sentence fully answers the question asked in Step 4. In delivery, it follows the proposition. (The interrogative may be inserted verbally between the proposition and the transitional sentence, but this is not always necessary.) This transitional sentence should consist of the following elements:

1. The response to the propositional interrogative, including the keyword
2. The repeating of the proposition
3. Any additional phrase made necessary by the particular interrogative used:

> "Because of . . ." (*Why?*)
> "By . . ." (*How?*)
> "In" or "in which . . ." (*When?*)
> "At" or "at which . . ." (*Where?*)
> "About which . . ." (*What?*)

Example 1

PROPOSITION: Every Christian *should* pray daily.

(INTERROGATIVE: *Why* should every Christian pray daily?)

(KEYWORD: Benefits.)

TRANSITIONAL SENTENCE: *Because of* the benefits to be gained, as seen in [the text], every Christian should pray daily.

Example 2

PROPOSITION: Every Christian *should* pray daily.

(INTERROGATIVE: *What* should every Christian pray about daily?)

(KEYWORD: Matters.)

TRANSITIONAL SENTENCE: As we see in [the text], there are several matters *about which* we should pray daily.

Example 3

PROPOSITION: Every Christian *can* experience effective daily prayer.

(INTERROGATIVE: *How* can every Christian experience effective daily prayer?)

(KEYWORD: Guidelines.)

TRANSITIONAL SENTENCE: Every Christian can experience effective daily prayer *by following* the guidelines set forth in [the text].

The transitional sentence forms a logical bridge between the proposition and the body (main points) of the sermon. Together with the specific proposition (and the interrogative sentence, if the preacher chooses to verbalize it), it becomes the basis of a "transitional paragraph" between the introduction of the sermon and its body. Using the last example above, this transitional paragraph might be stated something like this:

> From our text, then, we can see that every Christian can experience effective daily prayer. But if you're like me, you may well be asking, "How can I do that? How can I have a daily prayer experience that is really effective?" I would respond by saying that we can experience effective daily prayer by following the guidelines set forth in [the text]. Let's look at these guidelines together.
> The first guideline is . . . [Then follows the statement of the first main point of the sermon.]

This transitional paragraph is like the sermon's homiletical road map—it tells where the sermon is going and how it is going to get there. It informs the hearers of the precise central idea about to be discussed (the proposition), and it tells them how this idea is going to be handled (the keyword and the transitional sentence). Furthermore, the propositional interrogative (if used) can heighten the awareness of the listener to the profitability of "staying tuned" to this particular sermon.

Step 7: Develop the Main Points

The main points of any sermon have the function of establishing the proposition of the sermon. They may help define, explain, impress, or prove that proposition. Since the Keyword pattern is primarily a persuasive one, the main points of a Keyword sermon will ordinarily function as proofs.

Each main point will be one of whatever the keyword is. For example, if the keyword is *guidelines,* each main point will be one guideline and will be stated as such. If the keyword is *commands,* each main point will be one command and will be stated in that form.

This does not mean that the keyword itself must be stated as a part of the main point. Suppose that our text gives a series of commands about prayer and that we choose the word *commands* as our keyword. The main points themselves might be worded:

I. Pray in faith.
II. Pray with humility.
III. Pray about all things.

While the word *command* is not found in this formal statement of the main points, each point is, nevertheless, one command and is stated as a command. In the same way, if a text asked a series of questions, we might use this word as our keyword and state each main point as a question:

I. Can people be trusted?
II. Can wealth be trusted?
III. Can God be trusted?

The following guidelines will be helpful as the preacher formulates the main points:

1. Each main point will be based on a part of the text characterized by the keyword. It *must* have scriptural support, and this scriptural support should be noted immediately after the statement of the main point.
2. Main points should ordinarily be stated in the preacher's own words rather than the words of Scripture. This is not a rigid rule to be followed slavishly, but it has the advantage of allowing the listener to hear the concept twice. The concept will be heard once in the words of Scripture and a second time in the words of the speaker. As a result, the listener's understanding is enhanced.

3. The number of main points will vary from sermon to sermon. The number of main points depends upon the number of parallel ideas in the text. From two to five is usual.

4. Main points should be stated as complete sentences, not as single words or phrases, even on an outline. This is because the preacher will eventually state them orally as complete sentences. Stating these particular concepts precisely is important. It is easier to do this in the solitude of the study than in the pressure of the pulpit.

5. Main points should be stated as simple sentences. Conjunctions like *and* or *but* should be avoided, for they introduce a further idea. Each main point should contain only one concept.

6. Main points should be fresh—"tailor-made" for this specific sermon.

7. Unclear words, abstractions, and figurative language should be avoided unless purposely chosen for effect.

8. Main points should be stated as briefly as possible.

9. As much as possible, each main point of a given sermon should be stated in a parallel manner to the other main points. This will help the preacher recall them more easily and the listener recognize them more readily. Main points should be about the same length, have about the same word order, and be the same grammatically.

Caution: At this point in the preparation process, a basic, skeletal sermon outline has emerged. All of the previous steps should be double-checked to see that they have been done properly. This will help assure that the whole outline [to this point] fits together as a *cohesive unit*, accurately reflecting the meaning and purpose of the Scripture passage.

Step 8: Formulate the Subpoints

Although the skeletal outline is now in place, the major part of the writing of the sermon still remains. The "meat" must now be put on the "bones." This will be done as subpoints are formulated and appropriate illustrations added. When the introduction and conclusion are written, the sermon will then be completed.

Just as the main points establish the sermon's proposition, so the subpoints establish the main points. Baumann suggests three categories of subpoints: explanation, exemplification, and accentuation.[8]

Explanation involves clarifying ideas, words, or concepts. Exemplification means giving understandable examples of the truth being explained. Accentuation entails emphasizing that truth. Baumann says: "Explanation is an attempt to clarify; exemplification is an attempt to prove; and accentuation is an attempt to clinch the idea. It is a form of oral underlining."[9]

Subpointing can be done in several ways. Sometimes a sermon will employ only one method, but on other occasions a sermon may use more:

1. Subpointing can be done by "exposing" the text through:
   a. Exegetical study
   b. Modifiers in the mechanical layout
   c. Definitions and word studies
   d. Contextual considerations
2. Subpointing can be done by "questioning" the text:
   Why? When? Who? Where? What? How? So what?
3. Subpointing can be done by considering the natural relationships between larger concepts and their parts. Perry speaks of these as "thought categories":[10]
   a. If the main point is biographical, the preacher might consider:
      Roots
      Career
      Personality
      Achievements
      Failures
      Name
      Relation to God
   b. If the main point is related to an event, the natural lesser categories might be:
      Time
      Place
      Causes
      Effects
   c. If the main point is related to time, the subpoints might be:
      Past
      Present
      Future

   Other concepts such as relationships, miracles, parables, doctrines, and speeches all have lesser ideas that are natural parts of the whole. In fact, virtually all concepts can be broken down into subideas.[11]
4. Subpointing can be done with formal reasoning:
   a. *Deductive reasoning* (syllogism)—this kind of reasoning moves from a general truth to a specific truth.
   b. *Inductive reasoning*—this kind of reasoning moves from specific examples to a general conclusion.

The following recommendations may prove helpful in this part of the sermon's preparation:

1. If possible, the primary subpoints under each main point should be stated in parallel fashion.

2. The immediate preaching text and context should be gleaned for helpful material before additional Scriptures are searched for further supporting materials.
3. At least one subpoint of application under each main point should be included. These applications should be as specific as possible. (While this recommendation does not apply to some sermon methods, it does fit most Keyword sermons.)
4. During delivery, the subpoints should *not* be numbered aloud. This can create difficulty for the listener in differentiating between subpoints and main points. If there is sufficient reason to present subpoints in the form of a numbered list, care should be taken to ensure that the audience understands what is happening.

Step 9: Include Helpful Illustrations

The word *illustrate* means "to cast light upon something." When used regarding preaching, it refers to those elements in a sermon which by analogy, in a general sense, allow the hearer to grasp more precisely the meaning the preacher intends. Illustrations never stand alone. A story or figure of speech does not become an illustration until it is actually used to clarify an idea that is being communicated. The idea is the master in this process, while the illustration is merely a servant.

Although every preacher has heard about the value of illustrations and is aware of books consisting of illustrative material, relatively little has been written on the rationale and process of illustrating. Most material of this nature will be found in books on the general topic of preaching or homiletics.[12]

The purposes and advantages of sermon illustrations are more numerous than is usually thought. Ian Macpherson v mentions no less than 17, although his list is somewhat repetitive.[13] Following are some general functions of illustrations in sermons:

1. They can be used to clarify main points, subpoints, applications, and even introductions and conclusions.
2. They help make abstract truth become concrete by making it visual.
3. They add variety to sermons, for they can be drawn from every arena of life.
4. They vary the pace of a sermon by giving listeners needed psychological breaks, thus aiding their attention span.
5. They impress the truth on the mind of the hearer.
6. They help persuasion because they are a form of inductive reasoning.
7. They make repetition possible without a sense of redundancy.
8. They attract attention.

9. They can bring a sense of relevancy to messages.
10. They help build bridges to a variety of audience members.
11. They help memory.
12. They can touch the hearer on both an intellectual and an emotional level.

When we hear the term *illustration*, we often think immediately of some kind of story that has a moral. This is only one of many kinds of illustrative material. Consider the following:

1. Single words or phrases (visual language)
2. Short figures of speech, such as similes or metaphors
3. Analogies and parables
4. Allegories
5. Fables, myths, and legends
6. Biographical incidents
7. Personal experiences
8. Testimonies
9. Anecdotes—short stories, often with humor, not necessarily true. (They should not be passed off as true if they are not.)
10. Quotations—quips, prose, and poetry. (Poetry should be used sparingly with most congregations. Poems that are brief and plain communicate better than complicated ones.)
11. Statistics
12. Hymns
13. Current events
14. Visual aids and object lessons

Illustrations are available from many sources. The preacher needs to learn to keep eyes and ears open and to have a pen and paper handy to record illustrations. Many preachers set up their own topical file of illustrations gleaned from numerous places. To do this well, the preacher needs to devise some system of retrieval, especially in regard to his personal reading and study. Sources of illustrative material include, but are not limited to, the following:

1. The Bible (Two things are accomplished: the point in the sermon is illustrated, and some Bible content is taught indirectly.)
2. The preacher's imagination
3. The preacher's observation of life experiences
4. Serious reading (A good method for retrieval is essential.)
5. Light reading (Articles from newspapers and magazines can be clipped or copied.)
6. Biography
7. Fiction
8. Radio and television (Notable quotes or other materials may be useful.)
9. The fine arts

10. History
11. Nature
12. Pastoral work (The preacher should be careful not to betray confidences!)
13. Hymnals and hymn concordances
14. Personal experiences (These are often the best illustrations if they are not used too often.)
15. As a general rule, books of illustrations should be used with caution. Too many "canned" illustrations make a sermon sound "used" or "secondhand." Perhaps the greatest value of these books is that they can sometimes stimulate the preacher's mind to create his own illustrations.[14]

One final word: illustrations should not be viewed as things which are "tacked on" to sermons. Discovering or creating good illustrational material is an integral part of the sermon-writing process. As the preacher outlines and writes his messages, he should constantly ask himself whether each idea is conceptually clear. Will the hearers understand it? Is there a better way to say it? Can it be verbally visualized or explained better by using some analogy? This is the natural time to incorporate illustrations.

Step 10: Devise an Introduction

Although the sermon introduction is obviously presented first in delivery, it should not be prepared until after the body of the sermon has been completed. Until the preacher has a sermon body, he has nothing to introduce. This does not mean that the preacher should avoid all thought about the introduction until this point in the preparation. It simply means that the formal preparation of the introduction is best done after the body of the sermon is finished.

From a practical point of view, the introduction is usually the most important part of the sermon. If we fail to capture the hearer at this point, the sermon as a whole, in all likelihood, will fail. W. E. Sangster addressed this issue wisely:

> It is impossible to exaggerate the importance of the beginning of the sermon. Most of our hearers give us their attention at the start. However convinced they may be that preaching is boring, hope springs eternal and the thought lingers in the mind of the most blasé that perhaps on *this* occasion something of the awful majesty and arresting power they would associate with a message from God may be evident in what the preacher has to say. If he does not take firm grip of their attention in the first few minutes, how can he hope to hold it to the end?[15]

An introduction has five basic functions:

1. It must arouse interest.

2. It must inform the audience of the subject.
3. It shows the hearers their need to listen to the development of this particular subject (personal relevance).
4. It should promote the respect of the audience toward the speaker (ethos).
5. It should give some indication as to how the sermon is going to be developed.

Although sermon introductions vary considerably, they do share some basic characteristics:

1. They should not exceed about 10 to 15 percent of the total speaking time. This means that the introduction to a 25-minute sermon should not exceed about 3½ minutes. A long introduction discourages listeners, for they interpret this to mean that the sermon itself will be unusually long.
2. The very first sentence (*the approach sentence*) should point in the direction of the sermon subject but not necessarily in a "religious" sense. Introductions that begin with a story should still usually be prefaced with a suitable approach sentence, for this gives the hearer a frame of reference. This sentence should attract the hearer, arousing curiosity as to what might follow.
3. The introduction should progress from the general subject to the specific theme. From the theme, it should move to a brief encounter with the biblical context. Following this, the *transitional paragraph* (consisting of the proposition, the propositional interrogative [if used], and the transitional sentence) should be stated.
4. Numerous kinds of materials and rhetorical methods can be used in sermon introductions. The ideas mentioned in the section on illustrations (Step 9 of the Keyword method) may also be applied here. In addition, the preacher could use methods such as a startling statement of fact or opinion, a rhetorical question, or a reference to the particular occasion.
5. The introduction should be unique to its particular sermon. Henry Grady Davis states: "No two sermons are alike, and no two should begin the same way. If the introduction could possibly be used for any other sermon than this, it is not a good introduction to this sermon."[16] While this opinion may be slightly exaggerated, its intention is certainly true.

A preacher should avoid some things in sermon introductions. These will lower rapport with the audience or cause confusion about the subject being addressed. Avoid:

1. Apologies for the preacher or the subject.
2. Beginning indecisively. (Careful work in preparing the introduction should help the preacher begin with bold certainty.)

3. Big words and long sentences. (Both the preacher and the audience need time to "get in gear.")
4. Material not related to the sermon subject. (Otherwise, the listeners will receive mixed thematic signals.)
5. Sameness. (Sermons should not all begin the same way. The Scripture reading, if done as part of the sermon, can be placed differently at times. A variety of kinds of materials can also be used.)

Step 11: Prepare the Conclusion

Homileticians as diverse as John A. Broadus, Ilion T. Jones, and J. Daniel Baumann agree that conclusions are the most consistently weak parts of sermons. Many sermons just stop without warning, while others drone on and on, to the dismay of tired and confused listeners.

The Conclusion

Like the introduction, the conclusion is a crucial part of the sermon, the importance of which is sometimes underestimated. Preachers often spend only minutes on the conclusion, compared with the many hours spent on the other parts. The conclusion is frequently prepared hastily as the preacher plans to "play it by ear" during the actual delivery. After all, many preachers rationalize, "We must be in tune with the leading of the Spirit when we conclude our sermons." Such an attitude actually dishonors the Spirit! It limits His functioning to the last few minutes of sermon delivery, rather than recognizing His help in all facets of preparation.

The sermon's conclusion serves three general purposes:

1. *The factual purpose.* The conclusion should remind the audience of the most important idea(s) in the sermon. Sometimes this is done by formally restating each main point, but at other times it may simply involve restating or paraphrasing the proposition.
2. *The conceptual purpose.* The conclusion should help the audience understand that the major truth claims of the sermon have a bearing on their moral judgments and volitions.
3. *The applicational purpose.* Every sermon should strive to bring about a change in either the behavior or the attitude of each listener. The conclusion should assist in this by responding to the "so what?" question.

The conclusion should begin with a carefully worded sentence that will serve as a *final transition*. This sentence consists of the sermon proposition, prefaced by a transitional word or phrase such as "therefore" or "now that we have seen." This sentence helps the sermon maintain a sense of unity and alerts the listener that a major shift in direction is taking place. The following examples show the slight but important difference between the proposition and the final transition:

PROPOSITION: Every Christian should pray daily.

FINAL TRANSITION: Therefore, every Christian should pray daily.

PROPOSITION: Every Christian can experience effective daily prayer.

FINAL TRANSITION: So you see, every Christian can indeed experience effective daily prayer.

PROPOSITION: It is better to pray daily than to shoulder the load alone.

FINAL TRANSITION: We have now seen that it is better to pray daily than to shoulder the load alone.

In addition to the final transition, the conclusion should ordinarily include the following kinds of material:

1. A brief review of the major idea(s) in the sermon.
2. A challenge that motivates the listener to respond properly.
3. A specific course of action suggested for the listener to take. This should be made personal, when possible, rather than corporate.
4. A carefully worded closing sentence that is climactic in nature. Preciseness is important at this point.

Effective conclusions will ordinarily avoid:
1. Abruptness
2. Multiple conclusions (Words like *in conclusion* or *and finally* should be avoided, for they sometimes give false expectations.)
3. Apologies for the speaker, his performance, or the subject
4. Irrelevance (New ideas should not be introduced.)
5. Indecisiveness (Speech should be forthright and specific.)
6. Humor

Materials sometimes used in conclusions (such as stories, poems, quotations, and projections of future success) should be selected with great care. If used, they should be kept reasonably brief.

Effective conclusions should be done with thorough preparation of the ideas to be used. This material should be thoroughly known and delivered without the use of notes, even if notes are used elsewhere in the delivery of the sermon. Eye contact with the audience is crucial at this stage.

Further, the conclusion should be prepared and presented with a sense of positiveness and expectation. What is it that the speaker desires the Lord to do in the lives of people as a result of this particular message? He must prayerfully work toward that end with a sense of excitement.

Finally, the conclusion should be kept quite brief, usually not exceeding 5 percent of the total preaching time. If the rest of the sermon was presented clearly and convincingly, the preacher will not need to belabor the conclusion.

Step 12: Choose a Title

Sermon titles usually function in one of two ways. Some homileticians identify and use the title in much the same way as the theme or proposition of the sermon. It is the essence of what the sermon is about. With this approach, the title must be done very early in the homiletical process and must surely reflect the thrust of the sermon.

Others view the title more as an advertising slogan rather than a sermon part with inherent homiletical function. In this case, the title is not usually a matter of great concern. It may be useful for the bulletin, announcements, and advertising. The following guidelines will be helpful when considering sermon titles:

1. Titles should be creative, but not sensational.
2. Titles should be contemporary, but not faddish.
3. Titles should be brief, but not vague.
4. Titles should arouse interest or curiosity, but should not overstate what the sermon will actually accomplish.

* * * * *

Following these 12 steps of sermon construction carefully allows a thematically unified sermon based on the preaching text to emerge. The preacher must then commit the material to some form of writing for use during the actual preaching event and/or for filing for future reference. During this process, particular attention should be given to matters of vocabulary and style. If the preacher chooses to write a complete manuscript, he should remember that a sermon is intended for preaching, not reading. Therefore, the manuscript should be written in an oral style rather than a literary one.

Finally, the preacher must allow sufficient time to internalize the sermon's content thoroughly so that an effective delivery can be achieved. This ordinarily requires at least two hours of concerted effort. Some preachers rehearse the sermon aloud two or three times, while others talk their way through it silently. Still others pray their way through the sermon point by point, asking God to apply its truths to their own lives first and then to those who will hear. Whatever the method, this phase of preparation is extremely important to assure that the work done previously will have a positive impact on those who will listen.

Notes

1. The Keyword method might well be called the "Kollerian" method, for it is based on the work of Charles W. Koller, *Expository Preaching Without Notes*

(Grand Rapids, Mich.: Baker Book House, 1962). Koller used the method long before publishing it. The approach has been modified and popularized by Lloyd M. Perry, Faris D. Whitesell, Raymond W. McLaughlin, and other students of Koller, as well as their students. This method was doubtless used before Koller, but he seems to have been the first to systematize and publish it.

2. As discussed in chapter 2, these traditional categories of sermons are somewhat misleading, for they imply that only expository sermons really "expose" the text and that textual and topical sermons are necessarily less biblical. Every authentic sermon must find its authority in Scripture, whether the preaching text is long, short, in one passage, or based on several texts. If the sermon lays bare the meaning of the text(s), resting in the authority of Scripture, then it is expository in the proper sense of that word. Conversely, dealing with a long text of Scripture does not automatically result in an expository sermon in the best sense of that term.

3. Because of its wide usefulness, Lloyd M. Perry originally called the Keyword method the Foundational Pattern. See *A Manual for Biblical Preaching* (Grand Rapids, Mich.: Baker Book House, 1981), 65.

4. A helpful discussion of the process of clarifying and using the parallel ideas in a text is found in Walter L. Liefeld, *New Testament Exposition: From Text to Sermon* (Grand Rapids, Mich.: Ministry Resources Library [Zondervan], 1984), 45-55, especially 50-52.

5. Lloyd M. Perry, *Biblical Sermon Guide* (Grand Rapids, Mich.: Baker Book House, 1979), 32.

6. An excellent discussion of the purpose of preaching is found in J. Daniel Baumann, *An Introduction to Contemporary Preaching* (Grand Rapids, Mich.: Baker Book House, 1972), chapter 13. Baumann discusses four kinds of purposes: kerygmatic, didactic, therapeutic, and prophetic.

7. See Liefeld, 51-52.

8. Baumann, 152.

9. Baumann, 153.

10. Perry, *Manual*, 75.

11. R. C. H. Lenski discusses "groups of cleavage marks," presenting 12 different ones. These are, in effect, the same as categories of thought. Lenski's discussion concerns dividing the sermon theme into main points, but the principles are the same for subpointing. See *The Sermon: Its Homiletical Construction* (Grand Rapids, Mich.: Baker Book House, 1968; reprint), 164-183.

12. An enduring work on the subject of illustrating sermons is Ian MacPherson, *The Art of Illustrating Sermons* (Nashville: Abingdon, 1964). When he wrote this book, he had discovered only six other "slim volumes" on the subject (p. 7).

13. MacPherson, *The Art of Illustrating Sermons*, 13-31.

14. See, for example, Herschel H. Hobbs, *My Favorite Illustrations* (Nashville: Broadman Press, 1990).

15. W. E. Sangster, *The Craft of Sermon Construction* (Philadelphia: Westminster Press, 1951), 119.

16. Henry Grady Davis, *Design for Preaching* (Philadelphia: Fortress Press, 1958), 187.

5

THE ANALYTICAL
METHOD

The Analytical method of homiletics is a method closely identified with so-called expository preaching.[1] While it is not the only approach to expository preaching, it is a very useful method, particularly when the preaching text is long. The method is most easily adapted to passages that are two or more paragraphs, but it can also be used with shorter texts, depending on the nature of the text itself.

Along with the Keyword method, the Analytical approach to sermon building can be used in a great majority of preaching situations. It can often be used with relatively long passages as well as with sermons presented from multiple texts. With these two methods well in hand, the preacher should be able to develop a sermon on almost any passage in the Bible, with the exception of very short texts such as proverbs, parables, and pithy sayings. Even these can be handled with some modification to the methods. (Additional homiletical methods will, of course, be helpful for flexibility and variety, and this is the reason for the inclusion of six additional methods in this handbook.)

Generally speaking, the Analytical method is more didactic (designed to teach) than persuasive, whereas the Keyword method is primarily persuasive. This is not to say that an Analytical sermon is only information apart from application. The essential purpose of preaching requires that the factual basis of any sermon be accompanied by application, and this method is no exception. Nevertheless, what follows is a method closely linked with the teaching ministry of the pulpit, for "the basic purpose of the analytical sermonic pattern . . . is to impart information."[2]

The Analytical approach is useful with several different kinds of sermon subjects. It can be used to preach on: (1) the life of a character in the Bible, (2) a theological concept, (3) a specific event or narrative, and (4) an ethical concept. Thus, it is a method of sermon construction with wide potential usefulness.

The process for developing an Analytical sermon, explained in the following pages, is, in some ways, similar to the Keyword method. The nine steps will be presented in the same order followed in the Keyword approach. Steps 4, 5, and 6 of the Keyword method are unnecessary for this approach because the Analytical method does not use a keyword device. These steps are useful only for the purpose of establishing a keyword.

Step 1: Determine the Subject

The subject of the sermon is the specific thing to be analyzed. As stated earlier, it may be the life of a Bible character, a doctrine, an event, or an ethical concept. The sample subjects below will be developed step by step in this chapter:

• The life of Jeremiah (Jer. 1—51),
• The doctrine of salvation (Eph. 1:4-14)
• The turnabout of Nineveh (Jonah 3)
• The concept of love (1 Cor. 13)

Step 2: Determine the Precise Theme

The theme begins with a phrase like "the analysis of" or "a study of." It includes the subject and concludes with the Scripture passage that serves as the basis for the analysis. This latter element communicates helpful limitations to the hearer and keeps the subject from being too broad.

Sample Analytical Themes

1. A study of the life of Jeremiah in that book
2. An analysis of the doctrine of salvation in Ephesians 1:4-14
3. An analysis of the turnabout of Nineveh in Jonah 3
4. A study of the concept of love in 1 Corinthians 13

The fourth theme, for example, indicates that the preacher is not attempting to cover everything in the Bible concerning love. He will not discuss this concept as found in some writings of John or in the Book of Hosea, at least not in any detail. To make his subject manageable, the preacher has chosen to focus his attention on the subject of love as presented by Paul in this particular text.

Step 3: State a Clear Proposition

The general rules for the proposition of a Keyword sermon are applicable here, except that the Analytical approach results in a longer-than-usual proposition. It does need to be kept as short as possible, however, so that the hearer will understand that this is the central idea of the sermon and will be able to grasp its essence.

The Analytical proposition consists of two parts. First, it repeats the theme; and, second, it summarizes the anticipated results of the analysis about to take place. The homiletician must ask himself: "What will this analysis accomplish for the hearer?" He must answer this question precisely and verbalize it with the theme so that a proposal (proposition) is actually being made to the audience. Examples of this second part of the sermon proposition (the *anticipated result*) follow:

"An analysis of (the subject) . . .

> ". . . will inform us of our privilege to pray regularly."
> ". . . will motivate us toward more faithful discipleship."
> ". . . will clarify the meaning of this important Christian truth."
> ". . . will persuade us that God can use us too."
> ". . . will help us see that we must practice biblical love."

Complete Analytical propositions based on the themes previously presented would be stated similarly to the following examples:

> A study of the life of Jeremiah in that book will encourage us to be true to our task as he was to his.

> An analysis of the doctrine of salvation, as found in Ephesians 1, will persuade us of its God-centeredness.

> An analysis of the turnabout of Nineveh in Jonah 3 will show us that God works when people change.

> A study of the concept of love in 1 Corinthians 13 will convince us that love is the most important virtue in life.

Step 4: Formulate the Main Points

In Keyword sermons, the main points are arrived at by means of the interrogative sentence (step 4 of the Keyword method). The Analytical approach, however, has neither an interrogative sentence nor a keyword. Instead, the main points are based on the various parts into which the subject can be divided for analysis. In other words, each main point is one aspect or facet of the subject.

The preacher discovers main points by using either the mechanical layout or a traditional topical outline of the preaching text. If multiple texts are used, each one will ordinarily serve as the basis for one main point. Thus, the main points are based on *thematic segments* in the preaching passage(s). This differs from the Keyword approach, in which main points are found in parallel ideas in the text. As a result of this important difference, the scriptural undergirding for the main points of Analytical sermons usually covers several verses, and often consists of a paragraph or more.

Outlining 1 Corinthians 13, for example, reveals that while the subject of the entire passage is love, the chapter easily divides into three paragraphs (thematic segments), each presenting something unique about love in comparison to the other two. On the basis of this, the main points of an Analytical sermon on this text might first begin to take shape as follows:

> (vv. 1-3) How love is seen to be important
> (vv. 4-7) How love behaves, or what it looks like
> (vv. 8-13) How love lasts

Then, the points can be restated as phrases that will soon be incorporated in formal main points:

> I. The preeminence of love (1-3)
> II. The patterns of love (4-7)
> III. The permanence of love (8-13)

Since each main point of an Analytical sermon consists of *one part of the whole subject*, it will be helpful to word the main points according to the following "formula." This will help assure that the process of analysis is taking place:

"The _____ of [the subject] is seen in [text]."

If each main point of the sermon follows this formula, the only difference in them would be the unique aspect of the subject which each specific point addresses. This unique aspect will be stated in the underlined portion of the "formula" as given above. Again, using the text of 1 Corinthians 13 as an example, the unique aspects of love as presented in 1 Corinthians 13 are its preeminence, its patterns, and its permanence.

The use of the preposition *of* in the statement of the main points is not absolutely necessary, but this will be the preposition used most often. *Of* should be considered normative because it naturally identifies the concept being presented as a part of a larger whole. This is seen, for instance, when we speak of the core *of* an apple, the peel *of* an apple, and the meat *of* an apple. In some cases, however, main points may require prepositions like *for* or *to*.

Other than the differences discussed above, the main points of an Analytical sermon should follow the guidelines discussed in the chapter dealing with the Keyword approach. This includes such things as complete sentences, exclusivity, brevity, and parallelism.

Complete propositions and main points reflecting the four texts and subjects specified earlier are given below:

PROPOSITION: A study of the life of Jeremiah in that book will encourage us to be true to our task as he was to his.
    I. The call of Jeremiah is seen in Jeremiah 1:4-10.
    II. The ministry of Jeremiah is seen in Jeremiah 1:11-16.
    III. The difficulties Jeremiah faced are seen throughout the book (12:6; 16:2; 20:1-9; 23:11; 37:13-16; and 38:6 BSSB style uses and in series).

IV. The divine promise to Jeremiah is seen in Jeremiah 1:17-19.

PROPOSITION: An analysis of the doctrine of salvation, as found in Ephesians 1, will persuade us of its God-centeredness.
  I. The Father's anticipation of salvation is seen in Ephesians 1:4-6.
  II. The Son's acquisition of salvation is seen in Ephesians 1:7-13a.
  III. The Holy Spirit's affirmation of salvation is seen in Ephesians 1:13b-14.

PROPOSITION: An analysis of the turnabout of Nineveh in Jonah 3 will show us that God works when people change.
  I. The prerequisite of Nineveh's turnabout was Jonah's change of mind in Jonah 3:1-4.
  II. The events of Nineveh's turnabout occurred as the people had a change of mind in Jonah 3:5-9.
  III. The result of Nineveh's turnabout was God's gracious change of mind in Jonah 3:10.

PROPOSITION: A study of the concept of love in 1 Corinthians 13 will convince us that love is the most important virtue in the Christian life.
  I. The preeminence of love is set forth in verses 1-3.
  II. The patterns of love are set forth in verses 4-7.
  III. The permanence of love is set forth in verses 8-13.

Step 5: Prepare the Subpoints

In general, the same procedures followed in the Keyword method apply here. Two things which are true of almost all sermons need to be especially emphasized with this pattern because of its unique didactic nature:

  1. Subpoints should be based on the "peculiar" word or phrase of each main point. In this way, the preacher thoroughly exposes the thematic segment on which each main point is based. At the same time, he avoids overlap with the other main points. This is important to maintain a sense of forward movement in the sermon, rather than a sense of moving in circles.
  2. Subpoints of application under each main point should be clear and forceful so that the sermon moves beyond being a mere presentation of facts. While this is an important need for almost all sermon methods, it is especially crucial for those which are heavily didactic.

It should also be noted that Analytical sermons tend to be rather "wooden" or formal in their statement of the main points. A conscious attempt to state the subpointing material less formally will help make the entire sermon more pleasant to the listener.

Step 6: Include Illustrations

The general guidelines for illustrations discussed in the chapter on the Keyword method should be followed. Keep in mind, however, that didactic sermons tend to require more illustrations than usual. This is especially true of doctrinal and ethical themes which, by their very nature, often consist of abstract truths or principles. Illustrations can be quite helpful in allowing these abstractions to be understood in concrete ways.

Step 7: Prepare the Introduction

The introduction needs to raise some practical questions and issues in the minds of the audience. While the theme must be discussed in the introduction, it is also vital that the practical relevance of the theme (its relation to daily living) be clear in the hearers' minds. The preacher must convince them that they need to listen.

The transition from the introduction to the sermon body, especially the first main point, must be carefully planned in advance. The common tendency is to drift into a "keyword mode." After announcing the proposition, the careless preacher will grasp after some keyword to identify the main points collectively. Keyword devices such as "things" or "aspects" are sometimes used, but this is neither necessary nor advisable.

The keyword selected (usually on the spur of the moment) will ordinarily not be very helpful because the main points of an Analytical sermon are not usually the same in kind. This is because they are not based on parallel concepts as are the main points of a true Keyword sermon. A study of the sample outlines above, under Step 4, shows the difficulty of finding accurate, yet descriptive, keywords for Analytical sermons. (The word *things* as a keyword device should normally be avoided in sermons, as it communicates virtually nothing.)

A clear and helpful transition from the sermon's introduction to its body can be enhanced if these recommendations are kept in mind:

1. The proposition should be stated at least twice. It should be stated verbatim one time and slightly paraphrased the other. Analytical propositions are relatively long, and the audience needs to hear a proposition at least twice to begin to grasp it.
2. The proposition should be announced the first time immediately before the scriptural background part of the introduction. It can be announced the second time after this background has been given.
3. After the second statement of the proposition, the first main point can be prefaced with "first, we see that . . ." Then the preacher can announce that point, repeating the heart of it for

emphasis. The following model begins with the last sentence of the formal introduction and repeats it just before the background of the text:

(*Proposition*)   "Yes, love is something in which we all are interested. In fact, a survey of the concept of love in 1 Corinthians 13 will convince us that love is the most important virtue in the Christian life.

(*Background*)   "You may be surprised to learn that love is not the primary topic about which Paul was writing. He was writing to a church that was troubled by several problems, including the misuse of spiritual gifts. In chapter 12, Paul gave some basic descriptions of spiritual gifts. He wrote about their origin and their purpose. He continued that teaching in chapter 14, including some warnings about their misuse.

"In chapter 13, our text, Paul went off on a slight tangent, although a very important one. In the middle of his teaching about spiritual gifts, Paul put on the brakes to remind his readers that spiritual one-upmanship isn't nearly as important as solid loving relationships. He spoke of love as being 'the more excellent way.'

(*Proposition*)   "As we survey the concept of love in this great chapter, we should become convinced that love really is the most important virtue in the Christian life.

(*First
Main Point*)   "First, we see that the preeminence of love is shown in verses 1-3. The preeminence of love . . ."

    4. As an alternative, the preacher may choose to preview all of the main points before going into detail on the first one. To do this, paraphrase the theme part of the proposition and then add the preview as follows:

(*Proposition:
2nd Statement*)   "And so, Paul directs our attention to the concept of love. A study of the concept of love in 1 Corinthians 13 should convince us that love is the most important virtue in the Christian life.

(*Preview of
Main Points*)   "As we study this concept of love, we'll first look at its preeminence, then we'll discuss its patterns, and, finally, we'll think about its permanence.

(*First
Main Point*)   "First, then, we see that the preeminence of love is set forth in verses 1-3. The preeminence of love . . ."

(This sample assumes that the proposition has been previously announced and that the scriptural background has been given. The first sentence in the sample is a bridge between the background and the restatement of the proposition, the second sentence of the paragraph.)

Since the Analytical method is largely didactic, previewing the main points often helps the listeners. It tells the audience where the sermon will take them and, if the main points are stated well, it can raise some expectations.

Step 8: Complete the Conclusion

The conclusion should begin with a fitting *final transition* sentence. This sentence restates the thrust of the proposition and indicates that the analysis is now complete. The final transition restates the "anticipated result" of the analysis or a slight alteration of that hoped-for result in more specific terms. It is ordinarily stated in an obligatory way—in terms of what the listeners ought to do.

The nature of analysis is to break a whole entity into some smaller parts so that the whole can be better understood. The final transition switches gears. This sentence is one of synthesis. That is, it is intended to put back together the various parts of the single entity being analyzed and to summarize what purpose (or result) this analysis should have accomplished. The transition sentence will consist of the theme (stated in past tense), followed by a statement of this sermon's application to the lives of the hearers. Using the same outlines previously developed (see Step 4), their final transitional sentences could be:

> Therefore, having analyzed the life of Jeremiah, we should indeed be true to our task as he was to his.

> Therefore, since we have grown in our understanding of the meaning of salvation, we should proclaim it boldly to those who are lost.

> Now that we have studied the turnabout of Nineveh, let us determine to have hearts that are receptive to God's works.

> Having therefore analyzed the concept of love in this great chapter, let us vow to practice this virtue consistently.

After this final transition is composed, the guidelines presented in conjunction with the Keyword pattern may be followed. It is important that the sermon's final application or appeal be as specific as possible, especially in view of the didactic flavor of the Analytical approach. The object of the sermon must be to change lives, not simply to give out information. The preacher should make certain that the conclusion reflects the practical direction of the whole sermon without going off on a tangent.

Step 9: Choose a Title

The preacher should keep in mind the general remarks made previously about titles. In addition, he should exercise caution about using the formal subject of the sermon as the sermon title. The nature of these subjects does not usually generate any interest as a title. Instead, a title can often be devised from the "purpose" part of the sermon's proposition.

With the sermon on 1 Corinthians 13, for example, a title like "A Study of Love" is not nearly as effective as "The Most Important Virtue You Can Have." Likewise, "Being True to Our Task" is much better than "The Life of Jeremiah."

Finally, it is better to reflect a personal and present tense flavor in the title than an historical or academic one.

* * * * *

When the preacher desires to do some survey-type teaching about a particular subject, the Analytical approach is a very effective method to use. Care should be taken, however, not to use this method to the exclusion of others. Its tendency toward similarity in the way the proposition and main points are stated causes these sermons to sound somewhat the same if they are the standard fare served to a congregation. They will be more effective if mixed in with the Keyword approach and some of the other methods discussed in the following chapters.

Notes

1. As with virtually all homiletical methods, it is impossible to trace the origin of this method. Lenski devotes a chapter to it, and it is one of the patterns discussed by Perry. See R. C. H. Lenski, *The Sermon: Its Homiletical Construction* (Grand Rapids, Mich.: Baker Book House, 1968; reprint), 90; and Lloyd M. Perry, *A Manual for Biblical Preaching* (Grand Rapids, Mich.: Baker Book House, 1981), 90-95.

2. Perry, *A Manual for Biblical Preaching*, 91.

6

TEXTUAL
METHODS

The three traditional categories of sermons—topical, textual, and expository—might all be called "expository," since each type of sermon "exposes" the meaning of a text. The distinction between the so-called textual and expository sermons is especially arbitrary, since most homiletics books define them as different only in terms of the length of the preaching text. If the passage is one or two verses, the sermon is considered textual; if it is longer than two verses, it is considered expository.

Preaching on a single verse or two does call for some difference in comparison with the methods used for a longer passage, though in some instances, a given sermon method might work well with either length of text. The Keyword method, for example, could be used with a single verse. Some methods are particularly beneficial with shorter texts.

Some short texts are of outstanding preaching value. Each of these can stand on its own merit without doing any disservice to its immediate or larger context. The following list represents many such texts:

Genesis 1:1	John 3:16
Psalm 23:1	Acts 1:8
Lamentations 3:25a	Romans 1:16
Daniel 9:15b	Romans 8:31
Mark 10:45	James 4:14
Luke 15:10	Revelation 19:6b

Further, these verses can be approached in more than one way. Four different methods will be presented here, but since they vary primarily in the arrangement of the main points, the other homiletical steps will be discussed simultaneously. This approach, unlike the other sermon methods presented, begins with the proposition rather than the subject. In fact, with this method, isolating a broad subject is unnecessary, as this step is included in the process of clarifying the sermon theme. Other than this difference, and the possible use of a transitional sentence, this method will follow the usual steps.

Step 1: Determine the Exact Proposition

With the textual approaches being discussed here, the proposition is actually the text itself. This should be fairly brief, being composed of one verse or part of a verse, or in some instances, two very short adjacent verses. If the text is longer than three or four lines, then the preacher will need either to paraphrase or to restate the text. Otherwise, he should use a different method.

The textual proposition can be called a *proposition of impression*. The preacher seeks to impress the words of the proposition (the text itself) firmly upon the minds and hearts of the hearers. This is done through constant repetition and affirmation of the sermon proposition throughout the sermon, driving it home in such a way that the proposition will not be easily forgotten.

The sample propositions to be used in the four textual methods presented here are as follows:

"Our Lord God Almighty reigns" (Rev. 19:6, NIV).

In the beginning God created the heaven and the earth (Gen. 1:1 KJV).

The godly life is always marked by the genuine confession of sin (Dan. 9:15b, paraphrase by R. C. H. Lenski).[1]

Life is a vapor that appears for a little time and then vanishes away (Jas. 4:14b, author's paraphrase).

It should be noted that two of these propositions are quotations taken directly from the Scriptures. The other two are paraphrases that reduce the length of the biblical statements into manageable sermon propositions. They are all fairly brief and easily grasped.

Step 2: Clarify the Theme

In textual sermons, differentiating between the subject and the theme is unnecessary. However, the preacher must be able to articulate the gist of the proposition in a phrase. The theme will be used later in the homiletical process. The theme can be found by asking, "What is this text speaking about?" Applied to the above propositions, the themes might be:

(Rev. 19:6b)	The ultimate outcome of life
(Gen. 1:1a)	The origin of all things
(Dan. 9:15b)	The act of confessing sin
(Jas. 4:14b)	The brevity of life

Step 3: Arrange the Main Points

The preacher can develop the main points of a textual sermon in several ways. We will look at four.

The Implicational Approach

This method seeks to make clear just what the text means by drawing principles or implications from the text. The preacher must take care to avoid reading things into the text; principles must be clearly suggested by the meaning of the text within the context of all Scripture. The sermon builder can use a word like *principles* or *implications* as a keyword device when the transitional sentence is formulated in the next step. This approach and the usual Keyword approach differ. The Keyword main points are stated explicitly in the passage, while with this approach, the main points are only suggested implicitly:

PROPOSITION: "Our Lord God Almighty reigns."
   I. This means that evil will be dealt with.
   II. This means that the righteous will be comforted.
   III. This means that our destiny is in God's hands.

The Telescopic Approach

Several writers, including Ilion Jones,[2] have discussed this kind of sermon structure. A sermon that uses the *telescopic* approach is organized by allowing each succeeding point to add a new idea to the thought of the previous point. When applied to Genesis 1:1, this kind of outline might be developed as follows:

PROPOSITION: "In the beginning God created the heaven and the earth."
   I. In the beginning . . .
   II. In the beginning God . . .
   III. In the beginning God created . . .
   IV. In the beginning God created the heaven and the earth.

The Ladder Method

The third method is called by different names. Halford Luccock referred to it as the ladder method,[3] while R. C. H. Lenski called it the chain method.[4] It is similar to the Telescopic method but is sufficiently different to merit being mentioned by itself.

With this approach, each main point grows out of or builds upon the previous one. Unlike the Telescopic approach, the final thought of the previous point becomes the first thought of the new one. When applied to Daniel 9:15b, the result would be:

PROPOSITION: The godly life is always marked by the genuine confession of sin.
   I. It could not be godly without getting rid of sin.
   II. It could not get rid of sin without confession.
   III. It could not confess without dropping all self-righteousness.
   IV. It could not drop all self-righteousness without casting itself on God's mercy.

The Illustrational Approach

The fourth approach can be called the Illustrational approach. This is a "topical" approach in which each main point consists of one *biblical* illustration of the truth of the proposition. Thus, the body of the sermon consists of two or more illustrations—usually based on narrative texts—that will support the proposition. In determining which illustrations to use, the sermon builder should keep his sermon theme clearly in mind. Each illustration selected must speak directly to that theme.[6]

The illustrations may be selected from various parts of the Bible. When possible, it is preferable to select all of them from the life or lips of the particular person who gave us the proposition. Likewise, it is preferable to find all of the illustrations in one book of the Bible. These things will help give the sermon a greater sense of unity in the mind of the listener.

Each main point should clearly indicate that it is one illustration of the truth of the proposition as abbreviated in the sermon's theme. It is possible to do this in one of two ways. First, it can be done by stating the theme, alluding to the purpose of the point, and identifying the illustration and its biblical reference:

PROPOSITION: Life is a vapor that appears for a little time.
  I. The unexpected brevity of life is evidenced in the death of Herod Agrippa in Acts 12:20-25.
  II. The unexpected brevity of life is evidenced in the death of Stephen in Acts 7.

A second method of wording the main points is to treat the sermon like a Keyword sermon, using "illustrations" as a keyword device. This approach might develop as follows:

PROPOSITION: Life is a vapor that appears for a little time. (*How can we know that life is a vapor soon gone?*)

TRANSITIONAL SENTENCE: We can know that life is a vapor soon gone because of numerous biblical illustrations of this truth.
  I. One illustration of life's unexpected brevity is King Herod Agrippa in Acts 12.
  II. A second illustration of life's unexpected brevity is Stephen in Acts 7.

Since the theme, rather than the proposition, is used in the statement of the main points, the proposition should be stated immediately before or just after the statement of each main point (in delivery). This will suitably impress the proposition on the hearers by the time the sermon is concluded.

Each main point should be based on one *biblical* illustration, not a contemporary one. *Contemporary illustrations* can be used profitably in other parts of the sermon such as the introduction, conclusion, or as an illustration of a main point. Contemporary illustrations help assure a sense of relevance. Scripture-based main points, on the other hand, increase the sermon's authority factor. Both are important.

Step 4: Consider a Transitional Sentence

This step may or may not be necessary, depending on how the main points relate to the proposition. This can be determined as these points are being formulated. If a transitional sentence is deemed necessary, it should be kept brief. Its only function is to serve as a bridge between the introduction (including the proposition) and the body of the sermon by stating what is going to happen next. Note the following examples:

PROPOSITION: "Our Lord God Almighty reigns."

TRANSITIONAL SENTENCE: What important implications can we draw from this tremendous affirmation?

PROPOSITION: "In the beginning God created the heaven and the earth."

TRANSITIONAL SENTENCE: Consider with me just how this verse unfolds.

PROPOSITION: The godly life is always marked by the genuine confession of sin. *(No transitional sentence is necessary in view of the nature of the main points stated on the previous page.)*

PROPOSITION: Life is a vapor that appears for a little time and then vanishes away.

TRANSITIONAL SENTENCE: We can know that this is so because of numerous biblical illustrations of this truth.

Step 5: Develop the Subpoints

The same processes as discussed under the Keyword approach should be used. The preacher must remember to deal primarily with the unique idea that is a part of each main point. With the telescopic outline above, for instance, the unique idea in each respective main point is as follows:

I. Beginnings (origins)
II. The person of God
III. The creative act of God
IV. The product of God's creativity

If the preacher concentrates on unique ideas such as these, the sermon will move forward toward its destination, rather than going in circles or wandering aimlessly. This is important to achieve the overall purpose of the sermon.

The main structure of the illustrational approach is easy to put together, but creating the subpoints may take longer than usual. This is because multiple texts are often used, depending on the source of the main points. Each passage serving as the basis of a main point will have to be thoroughly studied, though not as extensively as when the entire sermon is based on the text. The preacher will need to have a good grasp of its background, context, and basic thrust so that he can be certain that the illustration being used is valid.

As the subpoints are formulated, the general rules for this procedure can be followed. Special care should be given to make the subpoints relate to the overall direction of the sermon. No main divisions should be allowed to become a sermon within a sermon by going off in its own direction.

The preacher should also avoid belaboring the obvious. When main points are familiar to the audience (as is sometimes the case with the illustrational approach), it is unnecessary to tell the story in all of its detail. Too often the preacher will say, "Now you're all familiar with this story . . ." and then he will tell it again anyway! Fresh ways should be found to present the thrust of the main point, or a different illustration should be used.

Step 6: Include Illustrations

The preacher should follow the general guidelines for illustrating, remembering that because textual sermons sometimes interact little with the immediate passage, more than the usual amount of illustrations may be required. This is true of the implicational, telescopic, and ladder methods.

The nature of the illustrational approach means the preacher should avoid including much additional illustrative material. Long stories especially should be avoided. On the other hand, brief quotations, figures of speech, and brief contemporary stories can be used profitably. At least one or two of the latter should be used as deemed appropriate. They usually fit best in the introduction and the conclusion.

Step 7: Prepare the Introduction

The general procedures discussed previously should be followed. The theme of the sermon should be addressed quickly, and the subject matter of the introduction should probe various questions and issues raised by the theme.

Step 8: Finish the Conclusion

Begin with *a final transitional sentence* that includes three main parts: the theme of the sermon, the proposition, and a general application.

Using the Revelation 19:6b text as an example, parts will usually be arranged as follows:

Therefore having seen . . . (*bridge phrase*),
          the ultimate outcome of life . . . (*theme*),
          as presented in our text . . . (*bridge phrase*),
          "the Lord God Almighty reigns," . . . (*proposition*),
          we must learn to trust God's plan patiently (*general application*).

Similarly, the other texts we are considering would lead to purpose sentences as follows:

Now that we have been reminded of the origin of all things, for "God created the heaven and the earth," let us understand that we also are part of His creation.

Now that we have seen the significance of the act of confessing sin, "for the godly life is always marked by the genuine confession of sin," let us continually confess our own sin to God.

Now that we have been reminded of the brevity of life as seen in our text, "Life is a vapor that appears for a little time and then vanishes away," we need to make each day count.

You will notice that each of these examples is fairly long. That will always be the case unless the preacher divides the statement and preHsents it as two or even three sentences. Doing this is suitable, perhaps even preferable, as long as the full thought of the longer single sentence is adequately communicated. If the preacher chooses to use the single sentence, he should be careful that he does not include unnecessary words.

The conclusion of a textual sermon must move beyond the general application suggested in the final transitional sentence to one or more specific applications. In view of the sermon's theme, what specific thing(s) should be done by the hearer?

If this final application is carefully thought out and presented, the listener will leave the preaching setting with two ideas firmly in mind. The first is the proposition itself. The second idea is that specific duty which should now be done because of this truth.

Step 9: Give the Sermon a Title

Generally, with textual sermons, the theme will suggest a title. The title will not necessarily be the theme per se, but should be reflective of it.

Notes

1. R. C. H. Lenski, *The Sermon: Its Homiletical Construction* (Grand Rapids, Mich.: Baker Book House, 1968; reprint), 210.

2. Ilion T. Jones, *Principles and Practice of Preaching* (Nashville: Abingdon Press, 1956), 105.

3. See Halford E. Luccock, *In the Minister's Workshop* (New York: Abingdon-Cokesbury, 1944), 134.

4. Lenski, 209-210.

5. Lenski, 210.

6. This method is similar to that presented by Lloyd M. Perry in his *Biblical Sermon Guide* (Grand Rapids, Mich.: Baker Book House, 1979), 46-48.

7

PROBLEM-SOLVING PATTERNS

All preaching should be related to life, but a special kind of sermon is particularly related to the problems of life any congregation or group of people faces. This type of preaching has sometimes been called life-situation preaching, pastoral preaching, problem-solving preaching, or ethical preaching. When this type of preaching is linked closely with the authority of Scripture, the result can be preaching that is both relevant and theologically accurate.

Various problem-solving patterns, both in secular speech books and homiletics books, have been suggested. One example is the method suggested by a former teacher of preaching, Ilion T. Jones. He suggests a simple, yet effective, interrogative approach:[1]

    I. Where are we?
   II. How did we get here?
  III. Where do we want to go?
  IV. How do we get there?

Another approach is suggested by secular speech teacher Judy L. Haynes, who uses a method that discusses alternate solutions, then settles for the best one.[2]

    I. A serious problem needs fixing:
      A. Background
      B. Effects
      C. Causes
   II. Here are a number of possible solutions:
      A. Solution A
      B. Solution B
      C. Solution C
  III. Solution _____ is the best solution:
      A. It solves the problem.
      B. It is desirable.
      C. It is practical.

Alan H. Monroe, a well-known writer of several books on public speaking, devised an approach he called the "motivated sequence" pattern. His approach to speech outlining has been cited in the vast majority of speech books since he first published it several decades ago.[3]

While this method was not intended to apply only to problem-solving speeches, it can easily be adapted for this purpose. Monroe bypassed the traditional parts of a speech (*introduction, body,* and *conclusion*), substituting the following divisions instead:

I. The attention-gaining step
II. The spell-out-the-need step
III. The spell-out-the-solution step
IV. The visualization-of-success step
V. The take-the-appropriate-action step

Perhaps the simplest arrangement is mentioned by J. Daniel Baumann, a contemporary teacher of preaching whose textbook on the subject has been well received:[4]

I. Statement of the problem (*description, analysis*)
II. Statement of the solution (*description, application*)

Each of the preceding patterns could be useful in preaching on problems, and the preacher is encouraged to experiment with any or all of them. The particular method stressed in this manual is that designed by Lloyd M. Perry.[5] It is quite similar to the approach of Haynes, discussed earlier. In brief, the main structure of the sermon will have three main points:

I. We need to solve this problem.
II. There are several nonbiblical solutions proposed.

PROPOSITION: What is God's solution to this problem?

III. God's solution to this problem

The preacher will note that the sermon's proposition is stated just before the third main point. This is because the sermon pattern is somewhat inductive in nature. The pattern does not state the "answer" at the outset, but instead allows the hearer to discover it during the course of the sermon. The other problem-solving patterns referred to are also inductive in this sense of the word. Since we have surveyed these various methods for outlining problem-solving sermons, let us now enlarge on Perry's method briefly, with some slight alteration.

Step 1: State the Subject

The sermon subject should be a statement of a problem in the form of a question. Any kind of problem could be the subject of a sermon: ethical, psychological, philosophical, or emotional. The scope of the problem can also vary. Some are national or international; others may be of community concern; some may be church-centered; still others may be personal in nature. Examples of subjects include:

• How can we help alleviate the problem of world hunger?
• What should we think about capital punishment?
• How can we solve the problem of worry?
• How can we heal the wounds of church division?
• How can the church move beyond nominalism?

Remember that the broad subject of the sermon should reflect the subject of the preaching passage. This will tend to be more of a problem with this type of sermon than with other kinds, because the preacher often chooses a particular problem to address, then looks for a Scripture passage to build his sermon upon. When this is the case, it needs to be done with great care. A passage should be chosen that deals with the problem thoroughly.

Step 2: State the Theme

The subject of the sermon raises the problem to be discussed; then the theme suggests the direction in which the sermon will ultimately go. The theme will be stated as a phrase and will be similar in form to "God's solution to the problem of _____."

When phrasing the theme, the preacher should make certain that the sermon actually proposes God's solution to the problem, or at least His perspective on it. This kind of sermon is intended to solve problems, not raise additional questions or in some way leave the audience hanging without a definite word from God on the subject. Examples:
• God's perspective on the problem of world hunger
• God's solution to the dilemma of capital punishment
• God's cure for the problem of worry
• God's healing for the wounds of church division
• The biblical answer to nominalism in the church

Step 3: Formulate the Proposition

This proposition varies from the Keyword sermon's proposition in two ways. First, as noted earlier, it fits logically into the sermon just before the third main point. Second, it is stated in the form of a question. In this latter regard, it is akin to the Keyword sermon's interrogative sentence (step 4 of the Keyword approach). More will be said of this when the main point step is discussed.

The proposition is formed by prefacing the theme with *what is*. In some instances a different interrogative may be used, but *what* will be used most of the time. Examples:
• What is God's perspective on the problem of world hunger?
• What is God's answer to the dilemma of capital punishment?
• What is God's cure for the problem of worry?
• How can God heal the wounds of church division?
• What is the biblical answer to nominalism in the church?

Step 4: State the Main Points

Unlike most other sermon patterns, where the number of main points varies, this Problem-solving approach always has three main points. The first point emphasizes that the problem is significant and needs to be solved. The second states that several solutions have been proposed. The third stresses that God Himself has an answer to the problem. Two examples of main pointing are presented here:

I. Society needs to address the issue of capital punishment.
II. Our society approaches the issue in several ways.

PROPOSITION: What is God's answer to the dilemma of capital punishment?

III. God's answer to the dilemma of capital punishment is seen in Genesis 9:6.

I. We need to solve the problem of worry.
II. A number of solutions to the problem of worry have been suggested.

PROPOSITION: What is God's cure for the problem of worry?

III. God's cure for worry is found in Romans 8:28-39.

Because the primary structure of this type of message is similar from sermon to sermon, the wise preacher will avoid using it often. It is a highly effective pattern, though, for it easily involves the audience in dialoguing mentally with the ideas being presented. Therefore, this approach should be used from time to time.

Step 5: Develop the Subpoints

The subpoints for this Problem-solving pattern fit together rather naturally under each of the main points. The preacher will not be hard pressed to outline properly, but he will usually need to do extensive research in nonbiblical sources to develop the subpoints under the first two main points.

The first main heading is largely definitional, so the preacher will devise subpoints dealing with matters like description, analysis, the causes of the problem, its scope, and its direct and indirect results. One subpoint should state that a proposed solution must reflect divine truth if it will have lasting meaning. This subpoint will set the stage for the second and third main points.

Under the second main point, the subpoints will present a series of proposed solutions or answers. While these are, in effect, "straw men"(set up to be easily refuted), the preacher should be fair in choosing suggested solutions that either are held widely or advocated by leading authorities. One by one they should be presented, described, evaluated, and found wanting in part or in whole. Where such solutions may be partially true, this must be noted. Good documentation will enhance the persuasion process, yet the appearance of a mere lecture should be avoided.

Finally, the proposition is stated, and the sermon moves into its most important part. This third main point is actually a miniature sermon in and of itself. The subpoints here can be devised in any logical way that indicates or proves God has a solution to (or perspective on) the problem and discusses what that solution is. For example, these subpoints might be arranged like the main points in a Keyword sermon. They could follow the structure of an Analytical sermon. They might be arranged in the shape of a logical syllogism (see chapter 9). The determining factor here is the Scripture text itself. The preacher should develop the subpoints here structurally in the same way he would develop them if he were doing the main points for an entire sermon. For example, Genesis 9:6 might well be developed using one of the Textual methods discussed in the previous chapter. Romans 8:28-39, on the other hand, might be handled with the Keyword approach.

The subpoints of any sermon contain the bulk of its content. Thus, the balance between points is actually determined by the amount of material in the subpoints. With Problem-solving sermons, the preacher will want to carefully consider how much weight each point will receive. As a general rule, the first main point should receive the lightest treatment, while the last main point should receive the heaviest. Since solving the problem is the chief function of the sermon, it would not be unusual for the last point to be as long as the first two points combined. This is an exception to the general homiletical practice of giving approximately equal time to each main point.

The preacher must make certain that the supporting material under the third main point actually does provide an answer to the problem being discussed. Do not promise what you can not or will not deliver. The purpose of this structure is not only to inform the hearers that the problem exists (they may be well aware of this already) but also to persuade them that God has a solution which they need to appropriate.

Step 6: Add Illustrations

Illustrations are very important parts of Problem-solving sermons. In many instances the problems tend to be abstract, even when the problem is fairly common. Illustrations can "flesh out" how the problem looks and how it behaves. Testimonies, a form of illustration, can be powerful persuaders as they deny proposed solutions or affirm God's solution. Other kinds of illustrations such as statistics, quotations from recognized experts, Scripture quotes, and biblical incidents can all be used effectively. The latter two kinds of illustrations are especially useful in the first two points of the sermon, since those points usually have very little relation to the Scripture.

Step 7: Prepare the Introduction

As he follows the usual guidelines, the preacher should remember that all of the sermon up to the third main point is, in effect, introductory. Therefore, he would be wise to keep the formal introduction as short as possible.

The following items should be included in the introduction, but they should be kept quite brief. The detail can be saved for the first main point:

1. An attention-getting statement of the problem
2. A very brief definition of the problem
3. A statement of any limitations which must be placed on this particular sermon
4. A preview of the three main points of the sermon structure. This will help the listener track the preacher through an unfamiliar structure. It will also assure the hearer that the sermon will eventually deal with biblical truth.

Step 8: Finish the Conclusion

A *final transitional sentence*, as always, will lead the way into the conclusion. It should begin with a transitional word or phrase and state the anticipated result of what the sermon hopefully will have accomplished. Be careful neither to overstate nor understate the result anticipated here. Examples:

> So you see, when the issue of capital punishment is raised, we should advocate God's position as set forth in Genesis 9:6.

> Therefore, when the problem of worry begins to beset us, let us look to God's cure as set forth in Romans 8:28-39.

In the conclusion, the preacher may quickly restate the importance of the problem and remind the audience of futile attempts to solve it. He can then quickly review the solutions he has proposed. Most importantly, he must make some specific suggestions concerning just how the solution(s) should be implemented (if the subject was a personal or local church problem) or what steps the audience should take to try to bring about some necessary changes as advocated in the sermon (if the subject was a community, national, or international problem).

Step 9: Choose a Title

The guidelines stated previously should be followed. The nature of this kind of sermon can be used to arouse the curiosity of people. Care should be taken to see that the title does not promise more than the sermon actually delivers. Generally, it will be best simply to use the subject as articulated in Step 1.

Notes
1. Ilion T. Jones, *Principles and Practice of Preaching* (Nashville: Abingdon Press, 1956), 107.

2. Judy L. Haynes, *Organizing a Speech: A Programmed Guide* (Englewood Cliffs, N.J.: Prentice-Hall, Inc., 1973), 85.

3. See Douglas Ehninger et al., *Principles and Types of Speech*, 9th ed. (Glenview, Ill.: Scott, Foresman and Co., 1982), 144-168.

4. J. Daniel Baumann, *An Introduction to Contemporary Preaching* (Grand Rapids, Mich.: Baker Book House, 1972), 79.

5. Lloyd M. Perry, *A Manual for Biblical Preaching* (Grand Rapids, Mich.: Baker Book House, 1981), 95. Perry presents a somewhat different approach in his *Biblical Sermon Guide* (Grand Rapids, Mich.: Baker Book House, 1979), 51. The former book is actually a reprint of an earlier work, so the method presented in the *Guide* is a revision of an earlier method.

8

THE COMPARATIVE METHOD

The Comparative method of sermon building is intended to be used when the heart of the preaching text is a simile or metaphor.[1] The figures of speech are used when the author or speaker of the text is stating an analogy or comparison between some truth from nature, history, or human events and a corresponding spiritual truth. The sermon develops the spiritual truth by examining various facets of the single truth portrayed in the simile or metaphor.

Comparative sermons usually tend to be more informative than persuasive, since this is the nature of most biblical analogies. As with all informative sermons, the preacher needs to remember that the purpose of preaching is never (or rarely) solely didactic. Rather, the information is used as a vehicle for persuasion. Preaching is intended to gain some sort of response, and Comparative sermons are not exceptions to this general rule.

Numerous analogies in Scripture are suitable for sermonic development. The preacher must exercise caution, however, in determining that a given text and this method are compatible. Some texts may appear to be likely candidates for the Comparative method but are hermeneutically questionable. Parables, for example, should be treated with great care. This method should *not* be applied ordinarily, unless the text itself clearly treats the parable like an analogy with a single point of comparison.[2]

Some of the shorter parables of Jesus, for example, are much the same as similes. (See those in Matt. 13:33,44-45.) These can be preached using the Comparative method. Other parables are closer to allegories; this sermon method should not be used with them. (See Matt. 13:1-9,18-23; and 13:24-30,36-43.) Likewise, many of the so-called "types" are probably not figures of speech at all and should, therefore, not be treated with this method. (To be safe, typology should be limited to those types clearly identified in Scripture as such.)

The homiletician needs to exercise one other major caution. He must not push the comparison beyond its ordinary meaning. A safe rule of thumb is to ask how the original hearer or reader would have understood the figure and to press the analogy only that far. Otherwise, the real danger of eisegesis looms large.

Texts suitable for Comparative sermons are of two types. Some texts include both the figure and some additional explanatory material. With this kind of text, the ideas for main points can be found in the text itself. Let us think of these as Type A texts.

Other texts contain only the figure of speech itself without any other explanation of the figure in the immediate context. These can be thought of as Type B texts. With these texts, main points are found by careful research in the language and culture of the biblical setting. When using this kind of text, the preacher needs to be especially careful to avoid the dangers mentioned in the preceding paragraphs.

Following is a list of sample texts. Those with an asterisk are Type A:

*Jeremiah 17:8	*Psalm 1:3
Isaiah 52:13	Psalm 1:4
Hosea 7:8	*John 10:7,9
*Matthew 5:14-16	2 Corinthians 5:20
Matthew 4:19	*Hebrews 12:1-2

Finally, the preacher must avoid building a sermon on more than one figure of speech. If the text or context contains more than one figure (such as is found in Ps. 1:3-4), then a choice must be made as to which *one* will be used. The other option is to use a different sermon pattern. Using more than one figure with a Comparative sermon will result in disunity either in the sermon subject or in the main points.

Step 1: Determine the Sermon Subject

The subject of a Comparative sermon will always be the broad concept or area of thought for which the figure stands. The subject will never be the figure itself but will always be the idea or concept which the figure represents. The following list shows how some sermon subjects might be stated in view of the figures of speech from which they come:

Figure	Sermon Subject
Tree planted by the water (Ps. 1:3)	The righteous person
The chaff (Ps. 1:4)	The wicked person
The light of the world (Matt. 5:14-16)	The Christian's witness
Running the race (Heb. 12:1-2)	The Christian life
A cake not turned (Hos. 7:8)	Inconsistent spirituality

As we proceed step by step through this method, two texts will be used as examples:

Text	Figure	Subject
John 10:7,9 (Type A)	"I am the door"	Salvation
Matthew 4:19 (Type B)	"Fishers of men"	Soul-winning

Step 2: Focus in on a Precise Theme

In this step the preacher moves from the broad idea to a more definitive aspect of that subject implied in the figure. Again, however, the figure will not be stated as the theme or any part of it.

As with other sermon patterns, the theme will be stated as a phrase in which the subject is found and modified in some way. The theme of John 10:7,9 could be "the role of Christ in our salvation." The theme of Matthew 4:19 might well be stated as "the nature of soul-winning."

Step 3: Write a Clear Proposition

This proposition will be one of clarification and will be worked as a sentence that states the basic comparison the sermon will make. It consists of two main parts: the figure of speech and the theme of the sermon. The proposition basically says that one thing (the figure) is like another (the theme) and that by looking at one we will be better able to understand the other. The purpose of this kind of sermon structure is to clarify the nature of some spiritual concept by drawing comparisons between that concept (the sermon theme) and the figure of speech. The proposition should make clear that this is the approach that is being used.

Unlike the proposition of a Keyword sermon, this proposition tends to be long. The sermonizer must work diligently to keep it as short as possible by removing any words not absolutely necessary to the central thrust of the sentence. This will benefit the hearer greatly.

In formulating the proposition, the preacher should remember to give both the *how* and the *why*. The proposition says a figure of speech is going to be studied or examined and, as a result, some spiritual truth will be clarified or explained. The following examples show how these two parts come together in one propositional statement:

PROPOSITION: A study of the nature of a sheepfold door will clarify the role of Christ in our salvation.

PROPOSITION (*variation*): As we examine the nature of the sheepfold door, the role of Christ in our salvation will become clearer.

PROPOSITION: A study of the nature of fishing will clarify the nature of soul-winning.

PROPOSITION (*variation*): We can better understand soul-winning by examining the nature of fishing.

Step 4: Formulate the Main Points

Each main point should state one point of comparison between the figure of speech and the sermon theme. If the text is a Type A, the points of comparison will be found in the context of the passage itself. When this is the case, the statement of the main point should include its scriptural undergirding. If the text is a Type B, the points of comparison will need to be discovered by researching the meaning of the figure as perceived by the original hearers or readers. The preacher will need to be careful to avoid fanciful or unnatural comparisons.

Remember that a figure of speech usually has only one major point to make as far as spiritual truth is concerned. This primary point of comparison is recognized in the sermon theme. Thus, a "double meaning" approach is avoided, because the theme becomes the unifying factor in the sermon's interpretation of the figure. On the other hand, almost all single truths can be broken into parts. This is what happens with the Comparative approach.

The general rules for main points discussed under the Keyword method should be followed. Brevity is a problem with the main points of this sort of sermon—the preacher should try to state them as briefly as possible. Examples:

PROPOSITION: A study of the nature of a sheepfold door will clarify the role of Christ in our salvation.
   I. Just as a sheepfold door is the means of access into the fold, so Christ is the only means of our salvation (v. 9a).
  II. Just as a sheepfold door serves as a means of security for the sheep, so Christ Himself is the means of our security (v. 10a).

PROPOSITION: A study of the nature of fishing will clarify the nature of soul-winning.
   I. Just as the fisherman clearly understands his central purpose, so the soul-winner must understand the purpose of his task.
  II. Just as the fisherman works to develop necessary skills, so the soul-winner strives to develop needed abilities.
 III. Just as the fisherman gains the reward of his labor, so will the soul-winner.

The number of main points in a Comparative sermon should be few. Two or three main points are ideal. The preacher should avoid the temptation to make too many comparisons. The most obvious and most important comparisons need to be used, but others do not. If these cautions are observed, the figure on which the sermon is based will not be misused.

Step 5: Develop the Subpoints

As in any sermon outline, the purpose of the subpoints in a Comparative sermon is to explain, modify, and apply the main points. In this particular pattern, however, a very natural development can be followed. The first category or set of subpoints can be devoted to explaining the natural or "secular" meaning of the figure. The second category or set of subpoints can emphasize the spiritual meaning of the comparison. Finally, the third set of subpoints makes application.

In the following example, the first two subpoints deal with the figure itself; the next two discuss the spiritual point of comparison made in the particular main point under consideration; and the last two subpoints are applicatory:

I. Just as the fisherman clearly understands his central purpose, so the soul-winner must understand the purpose of his task:
    1. Fishing was more than recreation in Jesus' day. It was a matter of livelihood—a matter of vocation.
    2. The earnest fisherman was not joyriding, surveying the pretty scenery, or making a biological study of fish. He was fishing!
    3. Likewise, soul-winning is at the heart of the Christian's calling.
    4. Other things in the spiritual life may be enjoyable and even necessary, but we have been called to share the gospel.
    5. Where do you put your priorities in this regard?
    6. If you are really following Jesus, you should be fishing!

Step 6: Include Illustrations

Two guidelines should be added to the guidelines for illustration under the Keyword method. First, the sermon text itself is already an illustration; therefore, numerous illustrations are unnecessary with the Comparative method. Also, the nature of the subpoints dictates against using many, if any, illustrations with the first category of subpoints and perhaps only limited illustrations with the second category. Generally, illustrations are best reserved for the applicatory parts of the sermon. Examples of contemporary persons or persons well known in history can be used to help hearers visualize what the application of the sermon will "look like" in actual experience.

The preacher need not confine all of his illustrative materials to the kind of figure being discussed. In other words, a sermon on "fishing for men" need not contain illustrations only from the world of fishing. It is not the figure itself that requires illustration but rather the spiritual point being declared.

Step 7: Prepare the Introduction

Both the figure of speech and the sermon subject should be discussed in the introduction of a Comparative sermon. The background of the figure, including any cultural or linguistic matters, can be presented. The preacher should be careful to avoid referring to the ideas found in the main points. The broad sermon subject should also be presented briefly in the introduction. This can be done before or after the introductory discussion of the figure. Either way, it is important that the actual subject be clear in the mind of the listener.

If, for instance, the preacher is speaking on the Matthew 4:19 text, which deals with "fishing for men," the introduction might begin with a brief presentation about fishing, both in our culture and in the world of the New Testament. It can then be noted that Jesus used the understanding of his contemporaries about fishing to challenge them regarding a fundamental part of the Christian enterprise: soul-winning. A brief discussion makes certain that the audience understands the subject. This can be followed with the statement of the proposition.

Again, caution should be exercised so that material planned for the body is not prematurely "let out of the bag." Comparative sermons are one type of sermon in which it is best *not* to preview the main points.

Step 8: Complete the Conclusion

As in all sermon methods, the conclusion is the time for the preacher to make certain that the sermon moves the listener toward a suitable kind of response. What should happen as a result of the theme having been clarified? How should the hearer respond? What should be thought or done as a result of this sermon?

A *final transitional sentence* should be written. This will make a bridge from the body of the sermon into the sermon's conclusion. The listener will be reminded of the overall direction the sermon has taken thematically and will then be prepared to give the message some final consideration. Examples:

CONCLUSION: Therefore, having clarified Christ's role in our salvation, let us look to Him alone.

CONCLUSION: Therefore, having grown in our understanding of the nature of soul-winning, let us be faithful in seeking to bring others to the Savior.

Stating the figure of speech in the conclusion is unnecessary. The sermon should already have impressed that in the minds of the hearers. At this point, decisive movement toward application is important. Restating the figure does not benefit this direction.

Since the Comparative sermon is largely informational, the conclusion should be made as strongly applicatory as possible. One way to do this is to review, not the main points per se, but the subpoints of application under the main points. This review not only makes the figure clearer, but it reinforces the practical purpose of the sermon.

Step 9: Formulate a Title

The guidelines given in previous chapters should be followed. It is often a good idea to create a title based on the figure of speech being studied rather than the sermon subject or theme. The interest factor is usually higher with the former than with the latter.

Notes
1. This type of preaching is discussed by W. E. Sangster in *The Craft of Sermon Construction* (Philadelphia: Westminster Press, 1951), 162.

2. Parables and types should ordinarily be preached using either the Analytical approach (see chapter 5) or one of the Textual methods discussed in chapter 6. Also, see the section titled "Preaching on Parables," in chapter 21 of this handbook.

9

THE SYLLOGISTIC METHOD

This method of homiletics is based on pure deduction, a form of reasoning that moves from a general truth to a specific truth. As a form of reasoning, the syllogism can be traced to Aristotle's *Organon*.

Although primarily associated with the Greek culture in its origin, syllogistic thinking also appears in the biblical record. The Greek word *sullogizomai* appears in Luke 20:5 where the chief priests, teachers of the law, and elders interrogated Jesus. When Jesus reversed the situation and asked them about the origin of John's baptism, "they *discussed it* among themselves" (NIV, author's italics) and found themselves in a dilemma. The *King James Version* says "they *reasoned* with themselves" (author's italics). Jesus gave a syllogism in John 8:47; R. C. H. Lenski arranged the verse in the following way:[1]

A Test for Divine Childhood

I. He that is of God heareth God's words (*major premise*).
II. Ye therefore hear them not (*minor premise*).
III. Therefore, ye are not of God (*conclusion*).

While pure syllogisms are rare in Scripture, a great deal of argumentation is found there. Such material may serve as the basis for sermons arranged syllogistically.[2]

A simple syllogism consists of three statements: the major premise, the minor premise, and the conclusion. If stated properly, the conclusion will always be true if the two premises are true and are properly related:

MAJOR PREMISE: All men are mortal.

MINOR PREMISE: Socrates is a man.

CONCLUSION: Therefore, Socrates is mortal.

There are three principle kinds of syllogisms: categorical, hypothetical, and disjunctive.

In the *categorical syllogism* (the previous example), a truth about a particular member of the category is deduced because that truth is applicable to the category as a whole. In the example given above, the category spoken of is humanity. The entire category ("all men") is seen as mortal. It follows logically, then, that if this is true of the entire category, it must also be true for any part of the category—in this case, Socrates. Thus the conclusion is true, and Socrates is, indeed, found to be mortal.

The *hypothetical syllogism* is similar to the categorical, except the major premise is stated as a possibility with a certain result if that possibility is indeed true. The minor premise then establishes the truth of that possibility. Then the conclusion states the certainty of the result suggested in the major premise.

MAJOR PREMISE: If Socrates is a man, then he is mortal.

MINOR PREMISE: Socrates is actually a man.

CONCLUSION: Therefore, Socrates is mortal.

The *disjunctive syllogism* deals with an either/or situation. This is introduced in the major premise. The minor premise then rules out one of the options in the major premise. The conclusion affirms the remaining option.

MAJOR PREMISE: Socrates is either mortal or immortal.

MINOR PREMISE: Socrates is not immortal.

CONCLUSION: Therefore, Socrates is mortal.

MAJOR PREMISE: I must either save myself or be saved by another.

MINOR PREMISE: I cannot save myself.

CONCLUSION: Therefore, I must be saved by another.

The numerous Scripture passages that contain argumentation will fit a syllogistic pattern even if the argument is not presented as a clear-cut syllogism in the text (that is, three consecutive statements consisting of a major premise, minor premise, and conclusion). The following steps can be followed to arrange a sermon in this fashion. These steps are arranged more logically than chronologically. With this method, the syllogism itself (the main point structure) may actually be planned first. Nevertheless, when the entire outline is completed, it should be possible to move through these steps, making certain that each one correctly leads into the next.

Step 1: Determine the Subject

Generally, the subject can be stated as one word. The subject of the text, as always, should become the subject of the sermon. The following examples will be used throughout the discussion of this method:

Mark 2:1-12   Subject: Jesus
Romans 3:19-26   Subject: justification
Galatians 5:16-26   Subject: the Holy Spirit

Step 2: Specify the Theme

The theme is stated as a phrase and narrows down the broader subject. The theme should closely reflect the thrust of the passage under consideration.

Mark 2:1-12   Theme: the claim of Jesus
Romans 3:19-26   Theme: justification by faith
Galatians 5:16-26   Theme: being led by the Spirit

Step 3: State the Proposition

The proposition is always the conclusion statement of the syllogism. It is arrived at by using the "bottom line" of the argument presented in the text. This statement should be a natural extension of the theme previously determined. It should be kept as short as possible so confusion in the minds of the hearers is minimized. As with all propositions, the preacher will doubtless find it necessary to word and reword it several times before it is fully satisfactory.

Mark 2:1-12   Proposition: Jesus claimed to be God.
Romans 3:19-26   Proposition: We need to be justified by faith.
Galatians 5:16-26   Proposition: We must choose to be led by the Spirit.

Step 4: State the Main Points

In a Syllogistic sermon, the main points will always be the two premises and the conclusion to which they logically lead. Thus, there will always be three main points.

The preacher should state carefully each premise as well as the conclusion. It is imperative to remember that the premises must be true if the conclusion is to be true. Further, they must be stated properly and in proper order. If there is some doubt as to the proper arrangement of a syllogism, the preacher should consult a book or encyclopedia article dealing with logic and syllogisms. Examples:

Mark 2:1-12 (using a categorical syllogism)
    I. Forgiveness of sin comes from God only (v. 7).
    II. Jesus claimed to forgive sin (vv. 10-12)
    III. Therefore, Jesus claimed to be God.

Romans 3:19-26 (using a hypothetical syllogism)
    I. If we are sinners, we need to be justified by faith (vv. 20,24).

II. We are indeed sinners (v. 23).

III. Therefore, we need to be justified by faith.

Galatians 5:16-26 (using a disjunctive syllogism)

I. We must choose to walk in the flesh or be led by the Spirit (v. 16).

II. As Christians, we must not walk in the flesh (v. 24).

III. Therefore, we must choose to be led by the Spirit.

When possible, include Scripture references with each main point, particularly the first two. These references can be developed in the subpoints.

Step 5: Develop the Subpoints

The preacher can follow the general guidelines for subpointing, but he should also remember the special peculiarities of this sermon method. Under the first two main points, most of the effort will need to be given to proof. Since the conclusion is true only if the premises are true, subpoints here will need to establish their truthfulness. This can be done by citing specific verses of Scripture within the preaching passage itself, or it may be necessary to appeal to the larger truth of Scripture by referring to other texts. Truthfulness can also be established by appealing to other kinds of evidence or forms of reasoning.

If the truthfulness of the two premises (main points I and II) is clearly communicated to the audience, the preacher will not need to belabor the truthfulness of the conclusion (main point III). Its truthfulness should be evident to everyone who is able to think logically. The first two main points should include subpoints of definition, as necessary. Such explanations should be offered here rather than under the third main point. All terms should be clear to the listener before the sermon moves to its final main point.

It is usually unnecessary to make direct applications under the first two main points. Indirect application can sometimes be made through carefully chosen illustrations or examples as the preacher shows what a particular premise "looks like" or what it means in practice.

Subpoints under the third main point should be oriented toward the practical. What does this truth (the conclusion of the syllogism, that is, the proposition) mean? What difference should it make in one's life? What do we need to do about it? These and similar questions should be in the preacher's mind as he develops this part of the sermon.

Step 6: Include Illustrations

The general guidelines for illustrations discussed in previous chapters should be followed. Strong illustrations will help give the sermon a good sense of balance between formal reasoning and practicality. It is better to "overillustrate" this type of sermon than to "underillustrate" it. Otherwise, the sermon might seem to be an intellectual exercise only, appealing only to the mind and not to the heart. This style of preaching might actually be intimidating to those in the audience not used to such reasoning. Illustrations will help make the sermon more palatable to these persons.

Step 7: Write the Introduction

Establish the theme of the sermon early in the introduction. It is best to do this by means of questioning, rather than by assertion, for the latter will tend to "steal the thunder" of the conclusion of the syllogism. In any event, the sermon's proposition should not be disclosed too early, usually only with the actual statement of the third main point (which is, of course, the proposition).

Since the proposition is not declared "up front," the preacher should include a transitional sentence to inform the audience of the sermon's direction. This sentence should come at the conclusion of the introduction, just before the announcement of the first main point. Avoid technical terms such as "syllogism" or "logical reasoning." Examples of transitional sentences based on the three outlines previously considered follow:

> This morning as we consider the person of Christ, I would like to establish two truths and then draw an appropriate conclusion.

> How is it that this concept of "justification by faith" relates to us? Well, notice with me first that . . .

> As we consider the flesh and the Spirit, at least two things appear to be clear.

It should be noted that each of these examples includes the sermon theme without disclosing the proposition. This adds a certain amount of suspense that will be rewarded when the sermon reaches its third main point. Similarly, the second main point (the minor premise) should *not* be mentioned until the first main point (the major premise) has been completed.

Step 8: Complete the Conclusion

The *final transitional sentence* will consist of three parts: (1) a transitional phrase such as "now that we have seen that . . . ," (2) a repeating of the proposition, and (3) some general application suitable to the purpose and thrust of the sermon. Some syllogisms are only factual, while others are oriented toward behavior. This will be reflected in the conclusion of the syllogism (the sermon's proposition). The proposition of the Mark 2:1-12 passage is totally factual, rather than behavioral. Conversely, the other two propositions are oriented toward behavior. A sermon must do more than simply present facts, so it will be necessary to think carefully about how a factual proposition should change people's lives. The application part of the purpose sentence should reflect this anticipated change. Examples:

> Therefore, having seen that Jesus claimed to be God, let us decide whether we will personally make Him our Lord.

> Now that we have seen that we need to be justified by faith, let us make certain that we indeed have been justified.

> Therefore, now that we have seen that we must choose to be led by the Spirit, let us submit to His leadership daily.

If the third main point is nicely developed (see step 5), the formal conclusion can be kept quite brief. The main points of the sermon should *not* be reviewed. This would be redundant as well as awkward. Rather, the final application should be the focus. If this has been done in the third point, then a quick word of warning or encouragement can be given and the sermon finished with a climactic closing statement. If the application under the third point was general, it can be made personal and specific now.

Ordinarily, this latter approach is best with a syllogistic sermon. The truthfulness of the proposition can be settled in the third point. Exactly what this means can be made clear to the audience and perhaps applied generally or by indirect or suggestive means. Then the transition can lead into the sermon's conclusion. The conclusion can spell out in detail the desirable application(s) and then challenge the audience to respond appropriately. (When this approach is taken, the third main point will be unusually brief, while the formal conclusion may be somewhat longer than usual.)

Step 9: Give the Sermon a Title

With a Syllogistic sermon, it may be a good idea to state the title in the form of a question. Care must be taken to assure that the conclusion to which the sermon is leading is not disclosed prematurely. A title in the form of a question can direct attention toward the general subject without doing that.

Notes

1. R. C. H. Lenski, *The Sermon: Its Homiletical Construction* (Grand Rapids, Mich.: Baker Book House, 1968; reprint), 208.

2. Among homileticians who have discussed the use of the logical syllogism for preaching are: John A. Broadus, *A Treatise on the Preparation and*

Delivery of Sermons, revised by Jesse Burton Weatherspoon (New York: Harper and Row, 1944), 181-183; W. E. Sangster, *The Craft of Sermon Construction* (Philadelphia: Westminster Press, 1951), 81-84; George E. Sweazey, *Preaching the Good News* (Englewood Cliffs, N.J.: Prentice-Hall, Inc., 1976), 83-84; Henry Grady Davis, *Design for Preaching* (Philadelphia: Fortress Press, 1958), 174-178; and Lenski. None of these present it in detail, and all give the impression that it is a variation, not a usual method.

10

INDUCTIVE
PATTERNS

With inductive reasoning, the argument moves from specific instances to a general truth; whereas in deductive reasoning, the argument moves from a general truth to a specific truth. Both of these are useful forms of argumentation and can be used in preaching, even in the same sermon.[1] One book entirely devoted to inductive preaching compares a typical deductive outline with an inductive one as follows:[2]

Deductive Approach	Inductive Approach
Introduction	Illustration
Central Idea	Statistics
Main Head A	Main Head A
Statistics	Illustration
Illustration	Instance
	Instance
Main Head B	Main Head B
Instance	Quotation
Instance	Instance
Illustration	Subhead 1
	Illustration
	Subhead 2
Main Head C	Main Head C
Subhead 1	Central Idea
Illustration	
Subhead 2	
Conclusion	

The primary difference between the two approaches is the position of the central idea (the proposition). When the proposition is not fully disclosed until the end of the sermon, the listener has the opportunity to dialogue mentally with the preacher during the sermon. The advantage of this approach is that it can effectively cause the listeners to interact with the preacher's ideas, to come to some tentative opinions on their own, and to feel that they have participated in formulating the proposition (which leads to the drawing of a conclusion with its pertinent application).

Craddock, a leading proponent of inductive preaching, sees this type of sermon as moving in a way that offers a sense of respect for the listener by giving him the "right to participate in that movement and arrive at a conclusion that is his own, not just the speaker's."[3] He feels that this is vitally important to the preaching task because "it is *their* (the listeners') conclusion, and the implication for their own situations is not only clear but personally inescapable."[4]

On the other hand, the congregation that has had a steady diet of deductive preaching will not gravitate easily to a full-blown Inductive approach. Listeners may feel uncertain about the point or direction of the sermon and lose interest because they feel that the sermon has an unclear destination or is going in circles.

Inductive patterns can take two somewhat related shapes: (1) formal reasoning and (2) forms of communication in which the listener enters into the process of discovering truth, rather than having the truth declared "up front" and then having it explained and applied. In this latter sense, some of the sermon methods presented previously can be considered inductive. This is true of the Problem-solving pattern, the Textual/Illustrational approach, and even the Syllogistic method, which logically, of course, is deductive. The formal Inductive sermon will not only follow induction as far as sermonic movement is concerned, but it will also use formal induction as a proof of the sermon's central idea. By presenting a sufficient number of specific instances of the truth, then the general truth is established within the range of *acceptable probability.* This, incidentally, is the so-called "scientific method."[5]

The remainder of this chapter will consider inductive preaching, based on formal inductive reasoning. Four methods will be presented, each slightly different from the others.

Step 1: Determine the Subject

The usual procedure in stating the broad subject to be discussed should be followed. Keep in mind, however, that broadness does not mean lack of preciseness. The preacher should make certain that the subject chosen truly reflects the subject of the passage. Most of the time the subject can be stated in a single word.

Step 2: Narrow the Subject to a Specific Theme

The theme of an Inductive sermon should be stated in the form of a question. The preacher must consider the subject within its immediate context and consider possible questions regarding the subject that might be raised by the skeptic, doubtful person or the uninformed. Select the question which will be most helpful to the anticipated audience, then phrase it as briefly as possible.

The following themes will be used throughout the discussion on the Inductive method of sermon construction. Each of these is stated in a way that will help arouse curiosity in the hearers:

(Heb. 11:1-12)   Why is faith so important?
(Rom. 3:10-18)   Are people inherently good?
(Rom. 8:28-39)   Does God care about life's circumstances?
(1 Cor. 6:9-20)   Does God care about sexual behavior?

Step 3: Write the Proposition

The proposition should be written as a short, very clear statement. Since formal reasoning usually results in establishing a statement of truth or fact, the proposition will often be written as a didactic one rather than as a persuasive or motivational one. This statement will be the direct answer to the question posed in the theme:

(Heb. 11:1-12)   Faith is a necessary means of pleasing God.
(Rom. 3:10-18)   We are all sinners before a holy God.
(Rom. 8:28-39)   God does care about life's circumstances.
(1 Cor. 6:9-20)   Our sexual behavior is extremely important to God.

Unlike other sermon patterns, the proposition for an Inductive sermon is not announced until the last main point has been covered.

Step 4: Develop the Main Points

A preacher has at least four ways to develop a sermon using inductive reasoning.

The first method useful in formulating the main points is to use specific examples cited within a single preaching passage. The proposition may or may not be stated specifically in the passage. If it is not stated, it should be clearly implied:

THEME: Why is faith so important? (Heb. 11).
  I. In faith, Abel worshiped properly (v. 4).
  II. In faith, Enoch walked with God (v. 5).
  III. In faith, Noah practiced blind obedience (v. 7).
  IV. In faith, Abraham gained an inheritance (vv. 8-10).
  V. In faith, Sarah miraculously conceived a nation (vv. 11-12).
PROPOSITION: Faith is a necessary means of pleasing God (v. 6).

The second method is to treat the biblical material topically. This is done when the proposition is based on a particular verse or verses in the primary preaching text, but the main points are taken from various other passages:

THEME: Are people inherently good? (Rom. 3).
  I. Adam recognized his fallen state (Gen. 3:8-19).

II. Abraham was guilty of wrongdoing (Gen. 12:10-20).
III. David confessed his sin before God (Ps. 51).
IV. Peter declared his own wickedness (Luke 5:8).
V. Paul called himself the chief of sinners (1 Tim. 1:15).
PROPOSITION: We are all sinners before a holy God (Rom. 3:10).

This approach is quite similar to the first; the difference is that multiple texts are used. It is also similar to the Textual/Illustrational method presented in chapter 6. With that method, however, the proposition is set forth clearly at the beginning of the sermon body, whereas with the Inductive approach, the proposition is not formally announced until after the sermon body is finished.

The third method of developing an Inductive sermon is the rebuttal method. This can be done either topically or expositorally. Such an outline consists of a series of rhetorical questions which, when given a negative response, affirms the truthfulness of the proposition:

THEME: Does God care about life's circumstances? (Rom. 8:26-39).
I. Do we live outside the scope of His purpose? (v. 28).
II. Are we alone in facing our situations? (v. 29b).
III. Can any circumstance overpower God's love? (vv. 35-39).
IV. Are any circumstances stronger than God? (v. 31).
PROPOSITION: God indeed cares about life's circumstances.

The fourth method is a variation of the rebuttal approach and can be called the affirmation method. Instead of raising questions which call for negative responses, as in the previous example, the questions (main points) are worded to bring forth positive responses, leading to the declaration of the proposition.

THEME: Does God care about sexual behavior? (1 Cor. 6:9-20).
I. Does God have a prior claim on us, including our bodies? (vv. 19b-20a).
II. Does the Holy Spirit reside within our bodies? (v. 19a).
III. Does sexual immorality inflict harm to the Holy Spirit's dwelling place? (v. 18b).
PROPOSITION: Our sexual behavior is extremely important to God (v. 20b).

Step 5: Formulate the Subpoints

The usual processes of subpointing are applicable to Inductive sermon outlines. The nature of the subpoints will largely depend on the direction of the whole outline. For example, the second outline above (Rom. 3:10) would not lend itself to subpoints of application under each main point. The main points are so much alike that attempted applications under each would be redundant. Rather, the final subpoint should point in the direction of the proposition without giving it away. In the outline based on Hebrews 11, however, the main points do suggest various applications.

Step 6: Include Helpful Illustrations

Good illustrations will enhance the effect of Inductive sermons. With some inductive approaches, the main points are based on ancient examples with which the hearer may not readily identify. Contemporary illustrations and applications can bridge this time gap. The first two sermon outlines (above) are good examples of the need for this.

The third and fourth outlines, although not based on ancient examples, also need the help of good contemporary illustrations. These outlines tend to deal with abstract concepts that the hearer may struggle to understand. Illustrations can help make these concepts real and practical to the listener.

Step 7: Write the Introduction

Simply put, the introduction should raise questions in the minds of the listeners related first to the general subject, then finally to the sermon theme. To some extent, this is the purpose of every sermon introduction, but this is especially important in an Inductive sermon. Questions should be raised but not answered.

These questions can be raised directly, or they can be suggested indirectly by means of illustrations of various kinds such as statistics, stories, quotations, and news articles. As these questions are shown to be interesting, relevant, and important, the attention of the audience will be gained.

The sermon theme should be used as the basis of the transition from the introduction into the sermon body. This specific question will serve as the central idea of the sermon until the actual proposition is articulated at the end of the sermon body.

Step 8: Complete the Conclusion

The preacher should remember that the conclusion of the sermon will begin soon after the proposition is affirmed. Thus, unnecessary repetition should be avoided. A *final transitional sentence* should be composed to alert the audience that something different is about to occur. This sentence should include both a restatement of the sermon proposition and some movement toward application. This latter ingredient is particularly important when the proposition is a didactic statement. It is always necessary to move beyond the statement of fact into the area of application. The listener should be encouraged or challenged toward some kind of behavioral or attitudinal change or changes. The previous sample sermon outlines might use final transitional sentences such as the following:

> Because faith is a necessary means of pleasing God, we must learn to exercise it in many areas of life.

> Since we are all sinners before a holy God, what can we do about it?

> Yes, we can see that God cares about our circumstances, but are we really willing to acknowledge His lordship over them?

> If our sexual behavior is extremely important to God, then we must not treat it casually.

Each of these statements includes the sermon proposition and some direction suggesting application. Although the direction at this point is rather general, it should lead to specific suggestions in keeping with the overall thrust of the sermon. Even though induction, as a means of formal reasoning, usually leads to a statement of fact, this is not where the sermon should stop. All preaching should result in doing the Word (Jas. 1:22). The preacher should not assume that the hearer will make his or her own application. The hearer might not make an application at all, or the application made might be an improper one.

As a general rule, restatement of the main points should not be included as a part of the conclusion. Once the proposition has been established, it is best not to regress. To remind the audience of the main points is to involve them in the actual reasoning process once again. Moving ahead is preferable.

Step 9: Choose a Title

As always, the title should be thematic. Stating the title as the theme-question itself may be good, although this is not always necessary. As with the Syllogistic method, the preacher should be careful not to disclose the sermon proposition prematurely.

Notes

1. Two somewhat traditional homileticians who discuss inductive preaching are Henry Grady Davis, *Design for Preaching* (Philadelphia: Fortress Press, 1958), 174-177; and J. Daniel Baumann, *An Introduction to Contemporary Preaching* (Grand Rapids, Mich.: Baker Book House, 1972, 1988). The latter work includes a helpful discussion about various inductive approaches (pp. 79-81).

2. Ralph Lewis and Gregg Lewis, *Inductive Preaching: Helping People Listen* (Westchester, Ill.: Crossway Books, 1983), 82. The authors of this book argue that 20th century people are living in a "right brain" era (creativity, visual memory, feelings, and imagination) rather than the "left brain" period (critical thought, reading, and linear logic) that was initiated by the invention of

the printing press 500 years ago. Our present era is "the age of visual literacy." This change, they say, should affect preaching, making it more visual and participatory and less dependent on linear logic. (See pp. 9-11.) The problem with this conclusion is that traditional deductive homiletical arrangement did not begin at the time of Johann Gutenberg. Rather, it has its roots in ancient Greek rhetoric, which existed several centuries before Christ. It is interesting to note that many Christians of the first century were "bicultural" in terms of communication skills. Greco-Roman culture was very much oriented toward reasoned thinking, while Jewish culture was oriented toward the visual and emotional. Yet, Christians were able to function in both "worlds." Paul, of course, is the prime example in this regard. Likewise, even if our present age is geared toward more visual aspects of communication as the Lewises assert, this does not mean that persons today are incapable of critical thinking or linear logic. Human beings are wonderfully complex creatures whose thinking abilities should not be underestimated.

3. Fred B. Craddock, *As One Without Authority* (Nashville: Abingdon Press, 1979), 62.

4. Craddock, 57.

5. W. E. Sangster, *The Craft of Sermon Construction*, (Philadelphia: Westminster Press, 1951), 84-87.

11

THE NARRATIVE APPROACH

The concept of narrative preaching is not as simple to grasp as one might think. It means different things to different people, and any discussion of this topic must begin by drawing some necessary distinctions.

Some writers use the term to refer to the kind of text being used. If the preaching text is narrative or biographical, then the sermon is called narrative, even if its homiletical structure is traditionally arranged with a central idea (proposition) and two or more main points that explain or otherwise support this idea. This understanding of narrative preaching has been around for many years. John Broadus, writing in the 19th century, discussed preaching on story passages and biographical subjects.[1] More recent authors have also dealt with this style of narrative preaching.[2] Some notable preachers of the past such as Clarence Macartney and Alexander Whyte had reputations as strong narrative preachers.

The term *narrative preaching* is used by others to refer to the repeated usage of long story-type illustrations within a given sermon. This is usually done as a means of impressing the validity of the central truth on the hearers by using contemporary experiences as illustrations of that truth. Norman Vincent Peale often used this approach in his preaching ministry. Preachers in the American black church tradition have made extensive use of this type of narrative approach, often presenting a narrative biblical passage along with a contemporary parallel.[3]

In recent years, narrative preaching has become a term used to describe a sermon that varies from the traditional points-that-explain-a-central-idea homiletical arrangement to one which purposely tells a single story, a story with a spiritual point. This story might simply be the retelling of a biblical narrative in a "story" style, or it might be a modern-day story created by the preacher as a contemporary parable or analogy of some biblical truth, whether the Scripture text itself is narrative.[4] This kind of narrative preaching will be the primary focus of this chapter—preaching as storytelling.

The sermon being done as story is not an entirely new approach to preaching, although in the past it was considered experimental. Over 30 years ago, Ilion Jones wrote of "a number of new approaches" that could be grouped under the heading of *imaginary narratives*. He includes methods such as:

> autobiographical monologue-impersonation, with or without native costume; a story told in the usual manner, or in poetical form, or in the form of an imaginary letter or some other document; a dialogue in the form of an imaginary conversation between two or more characters, or even between a person and an object; or a play with settings and scenes.

He adds that: "The number of this type of sermons has been increasing in recent years."[5]

But something new is developing in homiletical literature as far as narrative is concerned. A new generation of teachers and writers have emerged who advocate narrative as the best way (some seem to think the *only* way) of presenting the truth of Scripture. At the forefront of this movement are seminary teachers and preachers like Charles Rice, Henry Mitchell, and Eugene Lowry.[6]

The concern of strong advocates of narrative preaching is not only homiletical. First, they see the Scriptures as almost exclusively narrative. They often use terms like saga, tale, or folk narrative to describe the biblical accounts:

> Story expresses the Christian tradition so decisively that it becomes the normative mode of biblical revelation. Storytelling, Rice affirms, 'has a close affinity to both the content and form of Christian revelation.' It is, therefore, the hermeneutical key to interpreting Scripture.[7]

Then, they see the narrative form as essential to an understanding of ourselves as well. Charles Rice states: "We need to learn to hear and tell our own stories—not just our individual experience, but the stories we share with a given community and humankind—as much as we need to enter in and follow the Bible's unfolding story of God's ways with us."[8]

Further, strong advocates of narrative preaching see value in narrative from a communications perspective. In response to recent theories of learning and psychology, these homileticians believe that some listeners are "left-brain" thinkers and others are "right-brain" thinkers. Left-brain thinkers usually perceive ideas analytically and logically, while right-brain thinkers usually perceive things more intuitively and imaginatively. The implication for preaching is that the pulpit must address the needs of both groups but usually presents information only propositionally, thus missing the needs of persons who are predominantly right-brain thinkers.

Finally, and most importantly, many narrative homileticians seem to have chosen the narrative method particularly because they wish to divorce themselves from a rationalistic hermeneutic. To these homileticians, propositional truth is seen as largely ineffective, for it communicates abstractly. Storytelling is seen as a more precise method of communication, for it presents situations to which the hearer or reader can relate. Metaphor is seen as the means by which faith comes.[9]

Related to his dislike of a rational hermeneutic, Henry Mitchell argues strongly against the assumption that reason and faith are elicited in the same way. He responds to an assumed question about the biblical narratives:

> The answer lies in how tales impinge upon consciousness. As compared to essays, which type reaches which sector of the mind? The abstract argument reaches rational consciousness, but this is neither the seat of faith nor the source of commitment. Reason is a synonym for what the Bible calls sight, which by very definition is *not* faith. Paul refers to it (Eph. 3:19) as abstract knowledge surpassed by the personal, experiential impact of the love of Christ. On the other hand, tales have an impact upon the total person, and especially the intuitive sector of consciousness, wherein dwells faith. So this is the 'secret' of the Genesis narrative and other narratives: they provide a vicarious *experience* of the truth to be taught, and thus they move persons to identify with and live by that truth.[10]

Those who would take such a position are, of course, suggesting that a person's capacity to think rationally and also believe (that is, trust, make a commitment) should be dichotomized (separated into two usually contradictory parts) rather than viewed holistically. In the matter of spiritual transformation—a primary goal of preaching—this results in a faith that is, by definition, *irrational*. Are reason and faith totally unrelated? Does experiential knowledge have nothing to do with factual knowledge? Is factual knowledge necessarily abstract? (It is highly questionable that Paul is speaking technically about "kinds of knowledge" in Ephesians 3:19. Rather, this text should be understood to mean that Christ's love is so great that earthly understanding cannot fully grasp it.) Furthermore, how can it be known that faith dwells in the "intuitive sector of consciousness"? At the very least, these questions raise cautions about some of the perceived benefits of narrative preaching.

Nevertheless, many narrative homileticians view their endeavors as absolutely crucial to the revitalization of the American pulpit. Mitchell states:

> The dullness of most mainline preaching is due to its being conceived of as argument rather than art—as syllogism rather than symbol. The preacher as inspired artist can easily compel attention to the most profound themes of the gospel, once they are made to live in narrative, picture, and poetry. It has always been so.[11]

Now that we have briefly surveyed narrative preaching by these who are advocating a "new homiletic," what should our response be? Those who take the propositional truth of Scripture seriously may be tempted to "toss out the homiletical baby with the hermeneutical bath water," but is this really necessary? Are there profitable ways of using a narrative kind of structure without moving away from true biblical authority?

As a form of communication, the narrative style has much to offer. For one thing, it may well grab and maintain the attention of listeners better than a traditional deductive sermon. As the popularity of American television attests, people like stories! This is true not only of visual stories but oral ones too. Jay Adams comments:

> It hardly matters what age one is; so long as he can understand what is said, he will give rapt attention and almost immediate response to a well-told story. Persons with the most diverse interests and backgrounds will perk up when they are about to be treated to a story. Why is this? What is this near mystic power that a story possesses?[12]

Furthermore, the story sermon is a natural way to present the truths of narrative texts such as the patriarchal stories, the parables of Jesus, and some miracles of Jesus. It is always proper to fit the form of a sermon to the form of the text.

Finally, narrative can be an effective persuader for it is a form of inductive reasoning. The "proofs" presented through a story are much more subtle than those presented in a syllogism but can be just as effective, and perhaps even more so. The hearers will often be drawn into a story with their guard down, whereas when listening to direct reasoning the hostile or doubtful hearers will become defensive and survey their own arsenal of arguments.

Narrative preaching, that is, the sort of preaching in which the *entire* sermon is cast in the form of a story, is a legitimate kind of preaching when handled properly. It is a new method of proclamation for many, especially for white congregations and preachers, but it is a method with great potential for good if done well. How, then, should one go about preparing this kind of sermon?

The steps presented below are substantially different from those found with the other sermon methods presented in this handbook. The narrative sermon is an entirely different homiletical concept and must be handled accordingly. It is fair to say that this is still an experimental approach and, even more so than with other homiletical approaches, the final word has not yet been written.

These steps are therefore presented with a degree of tentativeness. The preacher should be free to follow them in principle and yet retain some freedom to experiment. Remember, however, that a story sermon is still meant to be a sermon—a message communicating the truth of God in such a way that people are constrained to examine themselves and respond appropriately. The uniqueness or novelty of the approach must not interfere with this overall purpose.

Step 1: Begin with a Text

All Christian preaching, if it is worthy of the name, must be biblical preaching. Narrative sermons, therefore, must clearly have their roots in the Bible. As Richard Jensen states: "Our interest is not in the creative potential of our own storytelling ability. We are concerned with recasting a biblical text so that it might come alive for our hearers in new ways."[13]

Biblical texts that are themselves narratives are perhaps most easily understood and communicated narratively. This is true of the historical accounts of the people of God found so often in Scripture, as well as "created narratives" such as parables and allegories. This does not mean that non-narrative texts should be shunned as texts for story sermons. Indeed, the process for moving from text to sermon is virtually the same with both narrative and non-narrative texts. For those who are novices, however, it will probably be easier to use a narrative text.

Step 2: Identify the Theological Purpose of the Text

At this point in sermon preparation, it is usual to think in terms of subject, theme, and proposition. Every sermon needs a central idea (proposition), and the story sermon is no exception. This central idea is an all-important unifying factor that keeps the sermon from wandering off in several directions at once. With the narrative approach, however, it is helpful to think first in terms of the purpose of the text. If the preacher is basing the sermon on a narrative text, then the question is obvious: What is the purpose of the story?

The historical narratives in the Bible are not only history. They are not merely a succession of people, events, and times—fact followed by fact followed by fact—but are, instead, the story of God and His people. Each story has not only historical significance but theological significance as well. The trite approach is to dwell merely on the historical, to recite the facts. The purpose of preaching, however, demands that we interact with and communicate the theology of the text.

What, for example, is the theological significance of Abraham's willingness to offer up Isaac in Genesis 22? Merely to restate the historical facts is to fail in two ways: (1) this would make for incredibly dull preaching; and (2) it misses the point of the text. Why, we must ask, is this particular story in the Bible? What would be missing if it were not there? How does this theological concept relate to me and to my listeners? The broad concepts that come from this story include faith, obedience, testing, and God faithfully keeping His covenant promises. From these the preacher can begin to see that the purpose of the account is to help God's people understand that they can obediently trust God even in times of severe testing, for He remains faithful to His word. In effect, this kind of statement becomes the central idea of the sermon.

That which is true of historical narratives is also true of parables and allegories. These are not curiosity pieces to entertain us but stories with theological significance to teach and motivate us. The purpose of a text of this sort must also be determined early in the sermon preparation process. Determining textual purpose is also a basic step when using a text which is non-narrative. The difference will occur in the next step of the process, that of dealing with the plot.

Step 3: Think in Terms of a Plot

Non-narrative sermons are ordinarily arranged with a central idea and main points that help clarify this idea. This is not usually the case with narrative sermons. Instead of a proposition and main points, the preacher needs to think in terms of the sermon plot and the story movements that are necessary to introduce and describe the plot, and finally lead to its resolution. Let us think first of the plot, keeping in mind that a good plot will always have some kind of bind or difficulty needing to be resolved.

In his provocative book titled *The Homiletical Plot: the Sermon as Narrative Art Form,* Eugene Lowry speaks of two different kinds of plots. He compares the first to a movie plot (he uses *High Noon* as an example) in which the issue in the viewer's mind is *what*. What will happen? The second kind of plot is illustrated by a television series. With this kind of plot the viewer knows the star will be back next week. The viewer is not wondering *what* but rather *how*. How will the conflict be resolved? Lowry rightly asserts that this second kind of plot characterizes most narrative sermons, but adds: "In whatever type of narrative plot, the event of the story moves from a bind, a felt discrepancy, an itch born of ambiguity, and moves toward the solution, a release from the ambiguous mystery, the scratch that makes it right."[14]

It is this sense of the unknown that gives narrative its life. The viewers or hearers may have an interest in the various elements of the setting, but it is the bind in the plot that holds their attention. Henry Grady Davis affirms this as well: "A successful story sermon must achieve the unity of a narrative. The unity centers in the crisis, and everything in the sermon must be related to that. That outcome depends on the nature of the crisis and the forces that produce it."[15]

This is seen in the biblical narratives. In Genesis 22, the issue before the reader is: How can Abraham kill his son Isaac (which is itself morally wrong—this becomes a subplot) and still receive the inheritance God promised? Is his faith really that strong? Or will God intervene in some unexpected way? One is compelled to read the entire story to have those questions satisfied.

The parables found in Scripture are similar. Almost all of them have an unexpected twist that calls for resolution. (Those which do not seem to be more allegorical than parabolic, though admittedly the difference is not always easy to tell.) In the parable of the shrewd manager (Luke 16), the reader is quite shocked to find that the rich man commends the manager who cheated him. In the parable of the workers in the vineyard (Matt. 20), we are surprised to discover that all are given the same wages, regardless of the number of hours worked. In the parable of the good Samaritan (Luke 10), Jesus' hearers doubtless struggled with the concept that their own religious leaders refused to get involved with the needs of the suffering, but a Samaritan did.

Sermons on biblical narratives may be primarily a retelling of that story with special emphasis given to this plot twist and its resolution. Or, the preacher may choose to tell a parallel story, one that leads to the same end.

When preparing a story sermon based on a non-narrative text, the preacher must create his own plot and its bind. The Bible text does not have a story that presents the plot, at least not in the narrative sense. Yet, a plot will be necessary if the sermon is to be done as a narrative. In this case, it will be necessary to locate or make up a story that leads the hearer to the same point or concept that the text itself is making. In other words, the story will be analogous to the truth of the text. The purpose of this related or created story will match the purpose of the preaching text.

Step 4: Decide on a Point of View

Stories typically involve more than one character, and this is also true of narrative sermons. However, every character in a story is not of equal importance. In fact, the level of importance may shift from one person to another, depending on the purpose of the sermon. While the main person in the literary classic known as the Book of Jonah is undoubtedly the prophet himself, it might be possible to preach a narrative about "thorough conversion" with the king of Nineveh as the primary character. The same book might yield a story sermon on "finding God in unlikely places" from the perspective of the sailors in chapter 1.

Although Davis' *Design for Preaching* is not primarily a book about story preaching, it contains some helpful insights for those who try it. He includes an abridgment (condensed version) of a sermon he preached from Luke 7:36-50 on the dinner in the house of Simon the Pharisee. While that entire abridgment cannot be repeated here, the beginning and the ending should prove helpful:[16]

> This man Simon was a man not deeply involved in anything.
> He was a Pharisee but not a very good one. He had so little partisan prejudice as to invite Jesus to dinner. He could stand Jesus' strong talk about widow's houses and long prayers, perhaps admitted some truth in it.
> He was broad-minded and Jesus was influential. It would do Simon no harm, he thought, to be decent to this brilliant young teacher. It takes all kinds of men to make a world.

Davis then continues to tell the story, painting in clear pictures what that supper would have been like. He tells about the unexpected interruption of the woman who anointed the feet of Jesus with the costly perfume. Simon never suspected the significance of this, being aware only of the finances involved. Davis concludes:

> Jesus tries to open Simon's eyes, speaks of large debts and small debts, of great love and little love, and of people on whom love is wasted because they do not care enough. . . .
> And so Simon, who had no love at stake, meets the Christ, and it does him no good. For others, not for him, the words: "Thy sins are forgiven. Go in peace."

Davis later added an insightful comment on the "logic" of this same sermon:

> Listening to the story, if it is well told, people will first meet a human being. The truth of existence will confront them not in mental abstractions but in the concrete form of a person so like themselves that they may compare and also identify themselves with him. They can sit with him in the presence of Jesus and go with him to the moment of supreme possibility and supreme testing. The experience is closer to seeing with the eyes than to being told about it.[17]

From this writer, we learn that a story is probably best told from one point of view. In this case, the point of view was Simon's. We also see a twist in the story—the interruption of the woman. This can be called the plot of the sermon, for it gives the sermon its point of truth: Some people, like the woman, love Christ with all their hearts; others only tolerate Him. This *central idea* is never actually articulated in just those words, but the truth is clearly communicated through the medium of story.

When preaching from narrative texts, the preacher will be inclined to tell the story from the perspective of the main character, but the story might be much less predictable (and more interesting) if it is told from another character's point of view.

Step 5: Choose a Specific Storytelling Mode

The preacher must also decide how he wants to tell the story as far as the spokesperson is concerned. Stories can be told in one of three modes.

The usual way, of course, is to tell the story in the third person. Almost all stories in Scripture are told in this way. For the person experimenting with narrative preaching, this way will probably be least intimidating. It can be used when a Bible story is being retold, and it can be used with an extra-biblical story, such as a modern parable written by the preacher.

A story can be told autobiographically in the first person if it is, in fact, about the preacher. This can be effective if the method is not overused and if the story is objectively honest. As long as the story does not appear to be extolling the preacher's virtues, this form of "truth through personality" is valid. This is what Paul did when he stood before King Agrippa in Acts 26.

A story can also be told in the first person when the preacher takes upon himself the role of the person whose point of view is being presented. A Good Friday chapel message in a Christian college is still remembered three decades later because the speaker assumed the role of Barabbas, preaching a gospel message in the first person. A sermon on a well-known text such as Daniel in the Lion's Den (Daniel 6) takes on a whole new perspective when it comes from the "lips" of King Darius. So does a message on the raising of the paralytic in Mark 2 presented as the testimonial of the transformed man himself. Richard Jensen even does this by assuming the role of the lost sheep in Jesus' parable in Luke 15![18]

Whatever mode is chosen, consistency must be maintained throughout the sermon. A sermon that jumps back and forth from first person to third person presents an unnecessary distraction and may be difficult to follow.

Step 6: Plan the Sermon's General Organization

Opinions differ as to the best way to arrange ideas in a narrative sermon. James Cox mentions three possible approaches:

> A narrative sermon unfolds along the lines laid down in the biblical text. It may alternate between narrative detail and application; it may give a simple historical narration and then draw out the lessons; or it may tell the story in such a way that the application is implied.[19]

Most of the writers mentioned previously feel rather strongly that the first two arrangements should be avoided. They believe that members of the audience can draw their own applications from a story sermon. This may be true, but the reader should remember that because of their theological and philosophical positions, some of these writers seem to emphasize subjective, rather than objective, truth. Thus, any "application" drawn or any "faith" that is strengthened is acceptable.

Preachers who believe that a text calls for a certain response should feel free to make this abundantly clear to the hearer. If this can be done without formally spelling out the lesson(s), fine. If not, then the application should be spelled out.

Beyond this issue of whether a narrative sermon should be pure story and assuming that it may well be that, how should such a message begin to take shape? Eugene Lowry, a leading writer and enthusiastic advocate of preaching narratively, suggests that narrative sermons be developed according to the following five "sequential stages." (He strongly dislikes the usual concept of sermon structure, that is, "building a sermon part by part." His distinction seems to be rather arbitrary.)

1. Upsetting the equilibrium (*Oops*)
2. Analyzing the discrepancy (*Ugh*)
3. Disclosing the clue to resolution (*Aha*)
4. Experiencing the gospel (*Whee*)
5. Anticipating the consequences (*Yeah*)[20]

David Buttrick arranges material in a similar fashion. Although Buttrick is not identified as a narrative homiletician, we can glean many helpful ideas from his massive work on preaching. Like Lowry, Buttrick emphasizes sermon movement rather than traditional main points. He also speaks of plot, imagery, and storytelling.[21] An example is Buttrick's sermon on Abraham's offering of Isaac (Gen. 22:1-19).[22] This sermon is not only a worthy model of Buttrick's method, but it is also an excellent sermon from a communications standpoint.

The sermon includes six *moves* plus an introduction and conclusion. It is not as purely narrative as the example from Davis given previously (see step 4), for Buttrick periodically inserts brief illustrations or images from outside the story. The introduction, for instance, begins by discussing an old German woodcut that pictures the sacrifice of Isaac. It then talks about the strangeness of this story.

Following the introduction, the six moves unfold, with each one containing between 13 and 18 lines of content. They can be summarized as follows:

1. For Abraham, all God's promises were riding on Isaac.
2. But God spoke and said, "Kill him off!"
3. Then, of all things, Abraham moves to obey God!
4. But God provides a substitute lamb to sacrifice.
5. God set Abraham free from blind obedience to faith.
6. We are free to trust God, too.

Each of these moves tells the story in graphic, visual language. Brief illustrations and other non-narrative descriptions are added, but the sermon keeps coming back to the story of Abraham and Isaac.

This sermon includes the same kind of plot that Lowry discusses— a plot with a bind, as in seen in moves 2 and 3. Actually, if these two moves are combined, we have something very similar to the five basic stages Lowry presented. The difference is that Lowry sticks pretty closely to straight narrative in his sermon content (he does deviate a bit), while Buttrick is a little more free. Buttrick also includes a formal introduction and conclusion, although the sermon would not have been hurt by the omission of either or both.

Basically, the preacher must arrange his ideas in a way that will present the setting, the plot, the twist in the plot, and the resolution of the plot. The traditional formal introduction should be avoided. It is out of character with a narrative sermon. The sermon should begin with the story itself, setting the stage for what is about to be told. The preacher does not need to inform the audience that this will be a story sermon or offer other explanations. In most instances, a moralizing conclusion should be avoided. If the story is told well, this should not be necessary. It is important, however, that the sermon's central idea (step 2) be clearly communicated during the course of the sermon and stated again during the end of the story. This may be done directly as a declaration, or it may be done indirectly by using a question. Either way, the listener needs to know why this sermon was given and be challenged indirectly to respond in an appropriate way.

Additional Guidelines for Narrative Preaching

• *Give much attention to transitions.* These are important to help the audience sense progress through the story. Pauses, changes of tone, changes in body position, and verbal preciseness are important in this regard.

• *Use visual symbols and other worship aids to enhance the audience's understanding of the story and its setting.* This can be done both before and during the sermon. Thematic hymns or readings, objects, body language, and even the room arrangement are possible ways to do this.

• *Pay attention to the use of language.* Words are the tools of preachers, and some of them are far more effective than others. In this regard, Lowry has some wise words of advice from his own experience.

When in English composition class, I thought "being descriptive" meant using a lot of adjectives and adverbs. But typically, the use of a modifier does what the term suggests—it *modifies*. That is, it alters or shapes. Most of us are not greatly impacted by alteration. We are impacted by a radically new and different image. To do that, one needs the power of nouns and verbs. Moreover, modifiers clutter, complicate the sentence structure, which again tends to dilute the power. They also call attention to the sentence and hence to the speaker.[23]

Lowry reiterates this idea elsewhere: "Passive and subjunctive verbs and prepositional phrases cut the life out of oral speech. No wonder the narratives of the Old Testament preach so easily. They are alive with strong nouns and active verbs."[24]

• *Do not read or memorize the story.* Instead, get the story's content and flow well in mind, then *tell* it. Verbal exactness is not as important as naturalness in the storytelling process. Reading a story will virtually kill it. Memorizing it places both the listener and the preacher in a state of discomfort. Be natural!

* * * * *

While it is possible that narrative preaching is only a passing fad in homiletics, it may be that the emphasis is here to stay, at least as a means of gaining pulpit variety. This may be especially true in mainline denominations, but may be increasingly true in evangelical circles as well.

The narrative method per se is valid. Linguistic, hermeneutical, theological, and exegetical presuppositions may be questionable, however, if certain models are followed. Whatever method is used, the preacher's task is to present the objective truth of the Word in a way that will attract and hold interest. "Faith comes from hearing the message, and the message is heard through the word of Christ" (Rom. 10:17, NIV).

Notes

1. John A. Broadus, *A Treatise on the Preparation and Delivery of Sermons,* revised by Jesse Burton Weatherspoon (New York: Harper and Row, 1944), 159-163.

2. See Henry Grady Davis, *Design for Preaching* (Philadelphia: Fortress Press, 1958), 157-162,180-181; James W. Cox, *A Guide to Biblical Preaching* (Nashville: Abingdon Press, 1976), 70-72; Lloyd M. Perry, *Biblical Preaching for Today's World* (Chicago: Moody Press, 1973), 84-86; and Andrew W. Blackwood, *Biographical Preaching for Today* (New York: Abingdon Press, 1954).

3. Some examples of this are seen in Henry H. Mitchell, *Black Preaching: An Analysis of the Black Homiletic Tradition* (San Francisco: Harper and Row Publishers, Inc., 1979), 112-147.

4. Some helpful examples of this approach to preaching are found in Richard A. Jensen's *Telling the Story: Variety and Imagination in Preaching* (Minneapolis: Augsburg Press, 1980), 162-182. Jensen's book is a scholarly discussion of communication theory as it relates to three basic kinds of sermon approaches: the didactic, the proclamatory, and the story. While Jensen fairly discusses the worth of the first two methods, he is clearly more enthusiastic about the third. This is possibly the best book currently in print on the subject. See also H. Stephen Shoemaker, *Retelling the Biblical Story* (Nashville: Broadman Press, 1985).

5. Ilion T. Jones, *Principles and Practice of Preaching* (Nashville: Abingdon Press, 1956), 114. Jones mentions Henry Van Dyke's "The Other Wise Man" as an older model of a story sermon. Another example is "Acres of Dia-

monds" by the Baptist pastor and founder of Temple University, Russell Conwell. This sermon/lecture was delivered some six thousand times and raised the initial funding for that university.

6. See Edmund A. Steimle, Morris J. Niedenthal, and Charles Rice, *Preaching the Story* (Philadelphia: Fortress Press, 1980); Henry H. Mitchell, "Preaching on the Patriarchs," *Biblical Preaching,* ed. James W. Cox (Philadelphia: Westminster, 1983); Henry H. Mitchell, *Black Preaching: An Analysis of the Black Homiletic Tradition* (San Francisco: Harper and Row, Publishers, Inc., 1979); Eugene L. Lowry, *The Homiletical Plot: The Sermon as Narrative Art Form* (Atlanta: John Knox Press, 1980); and Eugene L. Lowry, *How to Preach a Parable: Designs for Narrative Sermons* (Nashville: Abingdon Press, 1989). A helpful summary of the recent proponents of narrative preaching is found in Richard Eslinger's book, *A New Hearing: Living Options in Homiletic Method* (Nashville: Abingdon Press, 1987).

7. Eslinger, 20. He takes both Rice and Mitchell to task for ignoring non-narrative portions of the Bible in their discussions, creating, in effect, a new "homiletical canon." (See pp. 29,55 also.)

8. Cited in Eslinger, 20.

9. Eslinger, 56. The hermeneutic these homileticians employ is existentialist in its roots. Objective meaning has given way to a subjective search for meaningful experience. For help in understanding this "new hermeneutic," the reader is directed to J. I. Packer, "Infallible Scripture and the Role of Hermeneutics," in *Scripture and Truth,* eds. D. A. Carson and John D. Woodbridge (Grand Rapids, Mich.: Zondervan Publishing House, 1983), 340-344. Also, see Walter C. Kaiser, Jr., *Toward an Exegetical Theology* (Grand Rapids, Mich.: Baker Book House, 1981), 17-40. Kaiser's introductory chapter includes a discussion of hermeneutics and exegesis. A newer and very thorough work on the subject is William J. Larkin, *Culture and Biblical Hermeneutics: Interpreting and Applying the Authoritative Word in a Relativistic Age* (Grand Rapids, Mich.: Baker Book House, 1988).

10. Mitchell, "Preaching on the Patriarchs," 37.

11. Mitchell, 37.

12. Jay E. Adams, "Sense Appeal and Storytelling," *The Preacher and Preaching: Reviving the Art in the Twentieth Century,* ed. Samuel T. Logan, Jr., 350.

13. Jensen, 151.

14. Lowry, *The Homiletical Plot,* 23.

15. Davis, 180.

16. Davis, 159-161.

17. Davis, 181.

18. Jensen, 170-174.

19. Cox, *A Guide to Biblical Preaching,* 70.

20. Lowry, *The Homiletical Plot,* 25. Most of the rest of Lowry's book explains in detail how these five stages should be handled. His discussion is generally helpful and should be suggestive to the person anticipating experimenting with narrative preaching.

21. David Buttrick, *Homiletic: Moves and Structures* (Philadelphia: Fortress Press, 1987). This work has been widely acclaimed as a truly significant book in the field.

22. Buttrick, 357-360. This sermon is also given in Eslinger, 166.

23. Lowry, *How to Preach a Parable,* 163.

24. Lowry, *The Homiletical Plot,* 93.

PART 3

USING OUR
HOMILETICAL
TREASURY

12

PREACHING
FROM EARLIEST
HISTORY

The first 11 chapters of Genesis are properly a part of the section in Scripture known as the Historical Books. These chapters are usually discussed along with the rest of the Pentateuch and the 12 other books of history. Yet, they are unique in some ways and present some special problems and opportunities for the preacher.

Critical Matters

Before considering ideas on preaching from this part of Scripture, it is necessary to consider some introductory matters dealing with the area of biblical studies known as higher criticism. Higher criticism has to do with matters such as authorship, time of composition, sources used in the composition, and the literary forms used. Lower criticism, on the other hand, deals primarily with questions of textual accuracy and is commonly known as textual criticism. The term *criticism* is used in the sense of making reasoned judgments, not in the sense of condemnation.

The use of higher criticism is not unique to the first 11 chapters of Genesis. It is used in the study of all parts of Scripture in both Testaments. Much critical work has produced valuable insights for the understanding of Scripture. However, higher criticism has sometimes been applied to the Bible's earliest history in destructive ways. The result has been that the integrity and authority of these chapters has been severely weakened in the thinking of some nonconservative scholars. The chapters are viewed as Israel's adaptation of a collection of primeval fables passed from one generation of primitive people to another in an attempt to understand origins. If this is the case, these chapters have little preaching value unless the pastor can demonstrate divine authority in the creation and transmission of the stories. Study of the literature of Israel's neighbors can help in understanding the purpose and distinctiveness of Israel's inspired literature.

The preacher must be aware of these issues and understand that they are entwined with the larger issues of authorship, the date of composition, and literary sources. Ultimately, the issue of the inspiration of the Bible and the nature of its authority is involved.

The preacher is therefore advised to have a basic understanding of the matter of higher criticism. This will be helpful as sermon research is carried on in various scholarly resources. That which follows is a brief discussion of the subject. It is meant to motivate the reader to further study in this important area.[1]

Source Criticism

Source critical study tries to determine the oral and literary sources available to Moses in writing Genesis 1—11 and the rest of the Pentateuch. Several theories have emerged:

Fragmentary theories—Literary criticism of the Old Testament, including the Pentateuch, can be traced to the earliest centuries of church history. These attempts were often negative, questioning the traditional views of authorship held by both Jews and Christians. The Neoplatonists, for instance, advocated negative views as early as the second or third century.

By the 18th century, Jean Astruc (1684-1766), a French physician, had proposed a theory that was based on the various names of God used in the Pentateuch. He held that Moses brought together various sources, each of which used a different name for God.

Since various names for God *are* sometimes used in the same passage, even in the same verse (Gen. 6:2-3), this led inevitably to a process of taking the Scripture apart piece by piece in an effort to get to the underlying sources. Sometimes a single verse was fragmented into two or three "original sources." The whole process became extremely speculative, with many different theories about documents, dates of materials, and authorship being espoused. Many of these theories have been contradictory and have, in effect, canceled out one another.

As Gleason Archer has pointed out, there developed a "school" of fragmentary theorists who published their views around the turn of the 19th century. He included Wilhelm De Wette, Alexander Geddes, and Johann Vater in this camp. Vater, for example, concluded that the Book of Genesis was composed from at least 39 different fragments, with some dating from the Mosaic age and final arrangement taking place during the exile.[2] More modern exponents see large literary complexes being joined together to form Genesis through 2 Kings. Such work is seen as exilic or later.

The documentary hypothesis—The best known and most widely accepted higher critical theory is the documentary hypothesis, in its most popular version formulated by K. H. Graf and J. Wellhausen, 19th century German scholars. Their endeavors are described by R. K. Harrison:

> Building on the evolutionary philosophy of Hegel, Wellhausen adapted earlier speculations to isolate four allegedly underlying "documents" in the Pentateuch, as expounded in his book *Die*

Komposition des Hexateuchs, published in the *Jahrbucher fur Deutsche Theologie* in 1877. These were the Jehovistic (J), Elohistic (E), Deuteronomic (D), and Priestly (P) sources respectively. The first was dated in the ninth century B.C., not long after writing was supposed to have been invented; the second about a century later; the third about the time of Josiah (640-609); the fourth from perhaps the fifth century B.C. Wellhausen also rewrote Hebrew history to conform to the evolutionary notions of the day, with the results that the Mosaic legislation became the basic code of postexilic Judaism rather than the point from which Israelite religious institutions began.[3]

This documentary hypothesis, as it came to be called, won the day and became the usual framework of Old Testament criticism among all but the most conservative scholars. Though modified and even rejected by many higher critics in the following decades, this theory still seems to be accepted, at least in part, in much of the scholarly literature available today, including commentaries, encyclopedias, and even some books on preaching. Many scholars, however, are turning to study the literary unity and narrative themes of the Pentateuch, admitting the impossibility of agreeing on source isolation and seeing the lack of theological results in such work.

Form Criticism

Source criticism began to share the spotlight with a method known as form criticism:

> Associated with Hermann Gunkel, it was an attempt to trace the fundamental religious ideas of the Old Testament back to their oral form. The method assumed that the Genesis narratives had originally been transmitted orally, and reduced to written form at some period before the eighth century B.C. to form the basis of the alleged "documents" underlying the Pentateuch. Gunkel was endeavoring to recover the spiritual values the Graf-Wellhausen theory had obscured, but at the same time he made it clear that for him the Genesis material was folklore.[4]

Form criticism helped show that much of the Genesis material had oral roots and that Israel preserved the narratives in the memories of gifted storytellers before Moses' time. It also gave valuable information about the Psalms. More recent scholarship has emphasized the theoretical work of form criticism when applied to specific narratives.

Archaeology

The science of archaeology, as related to Old Testament studies, made great strides after the turn of the 20th century. This did much to call into question the previously assumed evolutionary nature of Jewish religious backgrounds. For example, the evolutionists had maintained that monotheism evolved out of polytheism. Archaeology has shown that monotheism coexisted with polytheism in some cultures before 1000 B.C. It has also shown that writing was invented before 3500 B.C., long before the time of Moses; thus Mosaic authorship of the Pentateuch cannot be ruled out *a priori* as had previously been done.

Archaeology led P. J. Wiseman to develop a conservative approach to the Book of Genesis which he published in 1936.[5] He argued that the recurring phrase "these are the generations of" (KJV) was paralleled in tablets found in Mesopotamia and that Moses might well have written the book by using tablets from patriarchal times preserved by the patriarchs and their descendants. Subsequent findings such as the Dead Sea Scrolls have given strong support to the inherent unity of the Pentateuch and its existence as canonical literature long before the sources of the documentary hypothesis were supposedly written.[6]

Redaction Criticism

Redaction criticism has its roots in New Testament scholarship in which the purpose of each of the Gospels was sought. Applied to the Old Testament, it sought to study the purposes of editors in adding materials to earlier compositions. This was especially the need found by source critics who suddenly found a need to study the whole rather than simply look at the parts. Such study led to fruitful results in the Psalms and Prophets, where all Bible students agree that originally independent units have been joined to form the literature we now have.

Canonical Criticism

A reaction against the lack of theological results produced by extreme source criticism led scholars like James Sanders and Brevard Childs to introduce canonical criticism, an effort to study the Scriptures in their final form and determine the theological structure, meaning, and message of the canon of Scripture.

Conclusion Concerning Critical Matters

Whereas hypercritical studies led to unscientific speculation about sources, forms, and uses of forms and materials in producing biblical materials, Wiseman and others (Albright, Kline, Whitcomb, and Yamauchi) have attempted to approach the issue of Old Testament authorship from an objective, scientific basis. Some critics had approached Scripture with their minds made up about matters such as the supernatural and arrived at "conclusions" which supported their presuppositions. The latter group has attempted to look at the evidence first, then draw conclusions.

Throughout the past two centuries, many conservative scholars of outstanding reputation have successfully refuted the claims of the hypercritics. The preacher should be familiar with names like E. W. Hengstenberg (Germany), F. Keil (Germany), J. A. Alexander (U.S.A.), and William Henry Green (U.S.A.). Recent scholars like Gleason Archer, Donald Guthrie, and R. K. Harrison have continued this tradition.

Lest the preacher view these critical issues as irrelevant to the tasks of homiletics and preaching, let him be reminded that the preacher's task is to be a medium, a vehicle, of divinely revealed truth. If that truth does not exist, the preacher's role does not exist either. The preacher has the task of knowing the various theories about the nature of that truth.

Higher criticism is not inherently evil. If used properly, the methods of higher criticism can help the scholar (and the preacher) better understand the biblical text. When used improperly, the methods of higher criticism can leave us with a text which apparently has little, if any, historical basis or divine authority.

Unique Elements in Genesis 1—11 Encountered by the Preacher

Some notable differences distinguish the content of the first 11 chapters of Genesis from that found in the remainder of the Historical Books. These chapters present materials that can intimidate the modern preacher who is aware of secular opinions about the subject matter here. This is particularly true in two general areas.

The Seeming Conflict Between Science and the Bible

Nowhere else in Scripture, with the possible exception of some miracle passages, are there as many seeming conflicts with modern science as found here. Four problem areas especially stand out.

Creation (Gen. 1—2). The explanation of Scripture differs from the process and timing of origins as explained according to evolutionary theories. Yet, what one thinks on this subject has a profound influence on that person's total worldview. The conscientious preacher dare not ignore this extremely important topic. One must be aware of scientific theories, theories of various biblical scholars, and evidence behind the theories.

The fall (Gen. 3). The concept of sin's origin in the human race being attributable to an ultimate progenitor is denied by most behavioral and social scientists. The Scripture clearly affirms this, both in this chapter and in Romans 5. This subject is crucial to our understanding of humanity, sin, and salvation.

The flood (Gen. 6—8). The concept of a judgment in the form of a watery chaos is considered unthinkable among many modern-day scientists, but the Bible treats it as an actual event. Among those who are conservative in their approach to Scripture, the issue is whether the flood was universal or local. In either event, the subject, though scoffed at by most scientists, is a part of the biblical record. It has implications concerning the doctrines of judgment and the unity of the human race.

The genealogies (Gen. 5; 11). These have been used by some to calculate the date of the earth's origin. (In his work *Annales Veteris et Novi Testamenti*, written in the middle of the 17th century, Archbishop James Ussher of Ireland computed that Adam was created by God on October 23, 9:00 a.m., 45th meridian time, in the year 4004 B.C.!) Even allowing for "gaps" in the genealogical record in Genesis, which is not out of character for the Jewish mind (this is done in Matthew 1:1), the Bible seems to favor a relatively late date for the appearance of human beings, as opposed to an early date favored by most anthropologists and paleontologists. Preachers need to have an informed opinion on this as well as other subjects discussed here.

The Dispute Between Myth and History

The second general concern raised by Genesis 1—11 that confronts the preacher is the historicity of the events recorded. Did these remarkable things actually happen? Or did the ancients compose myths to help explain some of humanity's most searching questions? Does Genesis represent theological, inspired narratives about common human problems? The following are those texts in Genesis 1—11 which are most often regarded as myth or parable by scholars who disbelieve or struggle with what this part of Scripture appears to affirm.[7]

Creation (Gen. 1—2). Some scholars regard this as a parallel to the *enuma elish*, or so-called "Babylonian Genesis" and point to a similar course of events. The legend of Tiamat, a Babylonian goddess, is "found" by some in the word *tehom*, which is the Hebrew word for *deep*. Others compare the Atra Hasis epic to the basic plot of Genesis 1—11. Others have argued that these chapters are poetic narrative, not to be taken literally. More conservative scholarship argues that this is not the case at all. These chapters are straightforward prose and are presented as historical.

The fall (Gen. 3). This is often seen as a figurative story meant to explain the origin of evil. Some scholars also think it is an analogy of everyone's personal encounter with sin. As stated above, this text is crucial to an orthodox theology of humanity and redemption.

Enoch (Gen. 5:21—24). The story is sometimes spiritualized rather than taken literally. What hermeneutical principle allows this? Why do we not apply this same principle to other texts of a narrative nature as well?

The flood (Gen. 6—8). Some scholars have seen this account as a Hebrew borrowing of the Gilgamesh epic, the Babylonian flood story, and/or of the Atra Hasis epic.

The curse on Canaan [not Ham!] (Gen 9:25). This text is often seen as a myth to explain Israel's animosity toward the Canaanites. (The "curse on Ham" interpretation has been used by some to justify slavery.)

The genealogies (Gen. 4:17-22; 5; 10; 11:10-32). These are seen as ancient traditions to explain humanity's ancestry in general and Israel's in particular. There is a difficulty in separating those which are personal from those which are tribal or national.

The longevity of the ancients (Gen. 5; 11). Since people today do not live hundreds of years, some scholars think that these numbers were copied in error, symbolic, or purposely inflated.

Babel (Gen. 11:1-9). This is viewed as a legend intended to help explain the origin of the various languages and cultures among the human race.

Approaches to Preaching

Three kinds of texts in Genesis 1—11 are most recommended for preaching. All three categories can be found in several passages, so Genesis 1—11 has much preaching potential. Some examples are given under each kind of text.

Theological Passages

Creation (Gen. 1—2). One must start at the beginning to get a complete picture of anything. The Bible begins here, for this doctrine explains the basics: who we are, where we came from, what our purpose is, and what God expects of us.

The fall (Gen. 3). This completes the creation narrative by introducing the problem of sin. Nothing else in Scripture (or life) is intelligible apart from these basic doctrines of creation and fall.

Pleasing God (Gen. 4:1-16). A discussion of the kind of offering that pleases God, that is, the right way to approach God, has an important application for everyone.

The judgment of God (Gen. 6—8). The flood account shows God's wrath toward sin, His patience with sinners, and His grace toward the righteous.

The doctrine of God. These early chapters say a great deal about the person, attributes, works, and expectations of God. They are really foundational in this regard.

The doctrine of humanity. These chapters also say much about the origin, purpose, and problems of the human race.

Homiletically, the Analytical pattern is often a good method to use when preaching on theological texts, particularly if the text covers two or more paragraphs. The Deductive method of using a formal syllogism may also be useful when preaching on doctrinal passages. The Keyword method may be used, but this method will be more difficult since it assumes that the main points will be based on parallel ideas in the text. Narrative passages (the genre in which this theology is found) do not have parallel ideas suitable for main point construction. A keyword device can be used in arranging a sermon that is topical in nature.

Ethical Texts

This category includes those texts which tell us how we should behave or live. Following are some examples:

1. The Institution of Marriage (2:20-25)
2. Dealing with Temptation (3:1-6)
3. Dealing with Known Sin (3:7-24)
4. How Not to Deal with Anger (4:1-15)

Again, the Analytical pattern could be useful with texts of this type, but there are other possibilities as well. If, for example, an ethical passage states its gist in a verse or a phrase, one of the Textual methods might be used.

Consider Genesis 2:24, a single verse which nicely summarizes the biblical view of marriage. It does not say everything about marriage, but it certainly says enough for a sermon. This verse could be handled textually by using the Telescopic method—the three main ideas of the verse might be used as main points, with each succeeding point building on the previous one:

I. For this reason a man will leave his father and mother
II. and be united to his wife,
III. and they will become one flesh (NIV).

Another possibility is to look for a succinct phrase such as the one in Genesis 4:7: "If you do not do what is right, sin is crouching at your door" (NIV). This is an unusual expression that is picturesque, memorable, and descriptive of the context. It has the makings of a preaching text for a sermon that uses a "proposition of impression." Thus, this text could also be developed using one of the other Textual methods, such as the illustrational or implicational approach.

Biographical Texts

As with all of the historical/narrative passages in Scripture, the opening chapters of Genesis contain some interesting characters about whom sermons (single or in series) could be developed:

1. Adam: "King of the Earth"; "Like Father, Like Son"
2. Eve: "A Woman's Place"; "The Mother of Us All"
3. Cain: "Why Good Boys Go Bad"; "From Heir to Outcast"
4. Abel: "Faith and Religion"; "Pleasing God"
5. Enoch: "Walking with God"; "The Best Road in the World"
6. Noah: "Finding Grace in God's Eyes"; "Stubborn Faith"

Biographical sermons usually follow one of three methods. The Analytical pattern can be used if the preacher's purpose is to present various aspects of the person's life. Example:

I. The *character* of Noah is seen in Genesis 6:8-9.
II. The *deliverance* of Noah is seen in Genesis 6:11-21.
III. The *obedience* of Noah is seen in Genesis 6:22.

This method is suitable if the primary purpose of the sermon is to inform. It is somewhat predictable, even wooden, and not particularly interesting or attention getting. It is advised that the method be used sparingly, especially if a series of biographical sermons is being preached. Two or more consecutive Analytical outlines would be quite undesirable.

The Keyword pattern can also be used with biographical sermons if an appropriate keyword is chosen. Words like the following might be worthwhile considering: *traits, flaws, qualities, principles, strengths, weaknesses, characteristics,* and *experiences.* This approach is usually preferable because it lends itself to less predictability and great variety.

A narrative approach is most useful when the person whose life is being used as the sermon subject did an unusual thing or experienced an unusual turn of events—something of a surprising nature. The plot of the narrative can be built around this surprise. For example, why would Adam and Eve disobey God when they had a paradise to lose? This "twist" in the biblical account can then be applied to today. Why do people today deliberately disobey God?

Things to Avoid

There are several dangers to avoid when dealing with these opening chapters in the Bible. While these cautions are applicable to all kinds of texts, they are particularly relevant here.

• Avoid slipping into a lecture/debate posture. This is especially tempting when dealing with issues like creation and the flood. While the pulpit should not be adverse to apologetics, there is a danger in allowing sermons to become too lecture-oriented. The preacher is advised to consider questions like the following when dealing with these and similar subjects:

1. What is the purpose of preaching? What spiritual purposes will be achieved?
2. Will you be preaching only to the "converted," that is, those who already hold your position?
3. Are you really adequately informed to enable you to discuss the fine points of science in an objective way?
4. Would this approach be better left to the classroom?

• Avoid speculating about unknown details. Genesis 1—11 gives us very limited information in virtually all of its sections. Unnecessary speculation places the preacher at risk over relatively unimportant matters. While preaching truth may sometimes result in division, the wise preacher will not tempt division by preaching dogmatically about something Scripture does not address.

• Avoid spiritualizing. Treat prose as prose; not as allegory, analogy, or type.

• Avoid drawing doctrinal or ethical norms from texts that are narrative. This can only be done inductively, and induction requires more than one "particular" in order to arrive at a general truth.

Notes

1. Two excellent chapters on this subject are found in the first volume of *The Expositor's Bible Commentary*, gen. ed. Frank E. Gaebelein (Grand Rapids, Mich.: Zondervan Publishing House, 1979). See "Historical and Literary Criticism of the Old Testament" by R. K. Harrison (pp. 231-250) and "The Historical and Literary Criticism of the New Testament" by Donald Guthrie (pp. 437-456). Also see R. K. Harrison et al., Chicago Manual of Style *Biblical Criticism: Historical, Literary and Textual* (Grand Rapids, Mich.: Zondervan Publishing House, 1978); Gleason Archer, *A Survey of Old Testament Introduction* (Chicago: Moody Press, 1974); and Donald Guthrie, *New Testament Introduction* (Downers Grove, Ill.: Inter-Varsity Press, 1970).

2. Archer, 75.

3. Harrison, *The Expositor's Bible Commentary*, 240.

4. Harrison, 240.

5. See P. J. Wiseman, *New Discoveries in Babylonia about Genesis* (London: Marshall, Morgan, and Scott, 1958; reprint), 46 ff. This work is cited by Harrison, Ibid., 242.

6. Harrison, 243.

7. An example of this struggle is seen in Clyde T. Francisco, "The Primeval Narratives of Genesis," *Biblical Preaching*, ed. James W. Cox (Philadelphia: Westminster Press, 1983), 18-22. Francisco seems to attempt to straddle the fence on this issue. He downplays the possibility of myth here as "foreign to the Hebrew concept of history." Yet, he states that much in these early chapters in Genesis is "parable" rather than literal history.

Walter C. Kaiser, Jr., in contrast, takes a more conservative approach. He deals with these matters in very helpful ways, respecting the integrity of the text. See Kaiser's *The Old Testament in Contemporary Preaching* (Grand Rapids, Mich.: Baker Book House, 1973), chap. 4.

13

PREACHING
FROM OLD TESTAMENT
HISTORY

When the preacher considers preaching from the historical books of the Old Testament, he comes face to face with the largest and one of the most diverse sections of Scripture. The 17 books in this section comprise about 40 percent of the entire Bible. By contrast, the Prophets cover approximately 22 percent, the Gospels about 10 percent, and the Epistles about 8 percent.

Various Kinds of Preaching Materials

The historical books are diverse in the kinds of material they contain. While they are predominantly narrative, the kind of narrative varies, as we shall see. The books also contain poetry, law statements, ceremonial descriptions, prophecies, and genealogies. Because a relatively short discussion cannot cover everything in these books, this chapter will focus on several kinds of preaching material found most often.

Heroic Narrative
Large parts of the historical books fit a category sometimes called heroic narrative. The story is focused on the personality and activities of an outstanding person, usually of some renown. This protagonist, to use a term from literary circles, is seen as a representative of the general population. He or she is one whose morals and actions are proper, at least as far as the total influence of his/her life is concerned. The story itself follows one or more episodes in the hero's life, usually concluding with some sort of happy ending.[1]

Several outstanding persons in the historical books fall into this literary category. Following is a fairly comprehensive list, beginning with the patriarchs in Genesis and continuing on with persons found in the other historical books. The primary passages are also given:

1. Abraham (Gen. 12:1—25:8)
2. Isaac (Gen. 22:1—35:29)
3. Jacob (Gen. 25:26-34; 27—35; 37; 48—49)
4. Joseph (Gen. 37; 39—47; 50)
5. Moses (Ex. 2—19; Num. 16—17; 20—21; Deut. 1—3; 34)

6. Joshua (Ex. 17; scattered references in Numbers and Deuteronomy; Deut. 31; Josh. 1—11; 23—24)
7. Deborah (Judg. 4:1—5:31)
8. Gideon (Judg. 6:1—8:35)
9. Ruth (Ruth 1—4). Some literary experts would place Ruth in the genre of romance, but for our purpose this distinction is unnecessary.
10. David (1 Sam. 16—31; 2 Sam. 1—24; 1 Kings 1:1—2:11)
11. Elijah (1 Kings 17:1—2 Kings 2:15)
12. Elisha (1 Kings 19:19-21; 2 Kings 2:2—13:20)
13. Ezra (Ezra 7:1—10:14)
14. Nehemiah (Neh. 1—13)
15. Esther (Esth. 2:1—9:32)

In addition to these major personalities who can rightly be described as hero figures, shorter accounts feature many others who exercised a positive influence on the affairs of God's people. Sometimes, only a very brief sketch is given, as in the cases of Shamgar (Judg. 3:31) and Jair (Judg. 10:3-5). Preaching a full sermon on such a person is difficult, and all such attempts should be handled with care. In other instances, more material is given in the text, as in the case of Jehu, discussed primarily in 2 Kings 9—10. (This king is a somewhat ambivalent character who accomplished much good but failed to completely follow the ways of the Lord. He provides a very interesting subject for preaching.)

The Analytical pattern and the Keyword pattern are the usual outlining methods to use with this genre of Scripture. Some "heroes" can be dealt with thoroughly in a single sermon, while with others a series of messages is necessary. With major characters such as Abraham, Moses, or David, it is often a good idea to begin a series with an overview sermon. If done well, this can serve to whet the hearers' appetites toward the remaining messages in the series.

The above persons all made positive contributions toward the purposes and people of God. Obviously, these contributions need to be developed sermonically. The preacher should not stop there, however. Behind these contributions were character traits, standards, and convictions by which these men and women lived. These things can serve as the "backbone" for messages based on these persons.

The preacher should also remember that the Scriptures present these people in a very objective way (unlike much secular literature), including "warts and all." Their faults, failures, and shortcomings should not be ignored. The Spirit of God can use these negatives, as well as the positives, to instruct and build up His people. That is why they are included in sacred writ!

Tragic Narrative

The Bible describes not only heroes but failures as well. The experiences of some Bible characters best fit the literary category of tragedy. Ryken described tragedy as:

> a narrative form that depicts a movement from prosperity to catastrophe. Tragedy presents a fall—a change of fortune.... In tragedy the focus is on the tragic protagonist, who in premodern tragedy is a person of high social standing. Such a conventional tragic hero, usually a king, is greater than common humanity but subject to the natural order and to moral criticism. The important element in his high public position is not simply social eliteness but representative status. Ordinarily a tragic hero possesses something that can be called greatness of spirit. He is usually a good man with some weakness of character.[2]

Literary scholars have discussed whether Christian tragedy is really possible. Can religion and tragedy coexist? Can there be a real tragedy, for example, when salvation or heaven awaits the protagonist? Ryken answers this in the affirmative, but does point out a subtle difference between biblical tragedy and the classical form of the Greeks. In the latter, tragedy is there by necessity, as though willed by the fates. In the Judeo-Christian form, though, the tragic conclusion of the account of a person's life is seen in personal failure—a matter of knowing right, but not acting accordingly.[3]

As Ryken points out, biblical tragedy is seen very early in the events of the fall in Genesis 3:

> This story is, in fact, the archetypal tragedy—the source and model of all later tragedies. As a model, it contains virtually all the ingredients of later biblical tragedies. The characters, Adam and Eve, are prominent and representative figures. They operate in a world that demands moral choice, which is a choice to obey or disobey God. The issues are clearly defined before the test comes.... The tragic choice sets into motion tragic consequences, controlled by a sovereign God and involving big cosmic forces that overwhelm the tragic hero.[4]

Three major tragic figures appear in the historical books. Each of them could have been numbered among the heroes of faith but failed to maintain his spiritual integrity:

1. Samson (Judg. 13:1—16:31)
2. Saul (interspersed between 1 Sam. 8—31)
3. Solomon (1 Kings 2—4; 7—11)

Each of these individuals was an exceptional person with great potential for positive accomplishment. Each was a leader, an unusual representative, of an important group of people. Each made choices which took him down wrong roads. Each ended life as a victim of these bad choices, forfeiting all, or at least most, of the great good he might have accomplished.

Lesser tragedies appear also in these books of history. Other kings and leaders who might have made a positive difference for Israel or Judah failed as well. The ultimate result was the corporate tragedy of the downfall of the Jewish people, seen first in the defeat, deportation, and disappearance of Israel, and then later in Judah's exile. Thus, the overall plot of the Books of Kings and Chronicles can be understood as an example of tragedy in the literary sense of the word.

Homiletically, the Analytical and Keyword patterns will be of greatest usefulness to the preacher who prepares sermons from texts of this type.

Event Narrative

The historical books include many narrative texts that tell the stories of certain events. They are scattered throughout these 17 books. Sometimes the events are quite brief; at other times they are rather detailed. Some are well known (Abraham and Isaac on Mount Moriah, Gen. 22), while others are relatively obscure (Elisha and the floating ax head, 2 Kings 6:1-7).

Every story, whether brief or long, has a point that can be profitable for people today. Otherwise, it would not have been preserved in sacred Scripture. Perhaps the summation of Thomas Long will serve as a helpful reminder of the worth of biblical narrative for the preacher:

> What does a story do to a reader? The answers are virtually infinite. At the risk of oversimplification, though, it can be said that a good story creates its impact in one of two ways: (1) by making the reader one of the characters or (2) by making a claim concerning the nature of life, a claim about which the reader must make a decision.[5]

This is not to say that all stories (or all other texts, for that matter) are of equal importance, nor is it to say that every reported event will serve as the basis of a good sermon. Yet, "All Scripture is inspired by God and profitable" (2 Tim. 3:16, NASB), so even seemingly insignificant events should not be ignored. If they are not of sufficient merit for an entire sermon, they may be useful in other ways, such as for illustrative purposes.

Preaching on events is one of the most difficult tasks the preacher faces. Retelling a story is relatively simple, for virtually everyone likes stories. It is not so simple, however, to move beyond the story to its theological or ethical point and, finally, to the point of the sermon itself. Long suggests that narrative texts be analyzed according to the concept of plot:

> Narrative plots are intricate and complex, but the preacher can expose something of the plot dynamic by exploring the three basic compo-

nents: the beginning, the middle, and the end. What is the need
established in the beginning? How does the end address this need?
What is the path—the middle—by which the narrative moves from
beginning to end?[6]

Understanding the plot of a narrative passage is just part of the
sermon process. The preacher must also gain an understanding of the
text from a theological perspective. To do this, a series of closely
related questions can be posed. These questions might include some
or all of the following:

1. Why is this event recorded in the Bible?
2. What would we be missing if it were not recorded?
3. What is the theological or ethical significance of the story?
4. What was God doing in this event?
5. What did He want His people to know or do as a result?
6. What does this event tell us about God, about humankind, or
   about some other broad area of Christian theology?

By posing questions like these, the preacher is on the way to formulating a subject and theme in keeping with God's purpose for including this account in Scripture in the first place.

As with all narrative texts, the Analytical pattern lends itself to the
preaching of events. The Keyword pattern, on the other hand, will
ordinarily be of little value, since a series of parallel ideas will not
usually be present in the text. A modified version of the Keyword
pattern may occasionally be used to present the various ramifications
of the text in a topical way. It would look something like this:

INTRODUCTION: A brief hook introducing the general subject and why
    it is important.
  I. The telling of the story. (*Sermonizing, theologizing, and application
     would not be included here.*)
 II. The presentation of two or more lessons (*truths, warnings, en-
     couragements, or implications*). This main point would use a
     keyword device in its very statement, and the subpoints would
     be, in effect, a miniature keyword sermon.

CONCLUSION: Application and challenge.

This approach is quite useful, although, as with any approach, a
steady diet will become tedious, boring, and probably too repeti-
tious.[7]

Law, Ceremony, and Civil Instruction

Scattered throughout the historical books are pockets of material in
these categories. Sometimes these passages are quite lengthy, as can
be seen in the following list of principal texts dealing with law (both

moral and civil), religious ceremony, and civil instructions such as the division and settling of the promised land:

1. Exodus 20—40
2. Leviticus
3. Numbers 5—14; 18—19; 28—30; 34—36
4. Deuteronomy 5—26
5. Joshua 13—22

The subject of law and gospel is exceedingly complex, and the way the preacher handles this part of the Bible will depend on personal views on this subject. Which laws are universal in their application? Which are not binding today? Should we go beyond the laws per se and attempt to deal with the spirit of the law, as Jesus did in the Sermon on the Mount? The preacher must face such issues when preaching on texts of this nature.

Perhaps the best homiletical approach is to use the Keyword method on an implicational level. A useful keyword might well be *implications*. This approach allows the preacher to deal with the theology of a certain law or group of laws without necessarily making it or them literally binding. Of course, if the preacher views an Old Testament law as binding, then a more direct Keyword approach could be used.

Passages which contain instructions dealing with the settlement of the promised land tend to be of two kinds. The first kind is that in which instructions are given about territories to be occupied, tribal boundaries, and the like. Joshua 13 and the chapters that follow serve as an example of this. These passages have a very limited preaching value.[8] They were spoken and written for a very limited audience and dealt with very specific issues not easily seen as significant to people today. They are generally best for illustrative purposes rather than sermon texts.

The second kind contains instructions about behavior and beliefs to which the Jews were expected to adhere upon entering the promised land. This kind of text is seen in Deuteronomy 26—29. These passages share some good preaching possibilities on the topics of spiritual commitment, remembering God's faithfulness, and manner of living. Various sermon patterns could be used, including the Keyword and the TexHtual, with the Keyword being the pattern used most often.

Genealogy and Census Texts

Several extended sections of this kind of material are found scattered throughout the historical books. Here are some of the more prominent examples:

1. Genesis 46
2. Numbers 1—4; 26

3. Joshua 12
4. 1 Chronicles 1—11; 23—27
5. Ezra 2; 10
6. Nehemiah 7; 12

For the most part, texts of this nature are not suitable as primary texts for preaching. The observant reader may occasionally spot an interesting detail in a census or genealogy which might have some illustrative or even sermonic value, but this will happen very rarely. (The most noted example is the mentioning of the four unlikely women in the genealogy of Jesus in the Gospel of Matthew: Tamar, Rahab, Ruth, and Bathsheba.)

Things to Avoid

Now that we have discussed several kinds of literature found in the Old Testament historical books, several precautions should be kept in mind.

When preaching on a narrative text, avoid making normal for today the behavior of the people of the past. Their behavior may serve as a worthy example for emulation, but not necessarily. What does the text itself say about their behavior? What does it imply? Is there a later passage in Scripture that discusses this behavior? Getting at the basic principles for godly living implied in the text is more legitimate than emphasizing specific kinds of behavior.

Avoid unnecessary conjecture. Old Testament stories often omit many details, and our minds want to fill in the gaps. Allow your imagination to work on what might have been, but be careful to differentiate between your conjectures and what the text actually says.

Always keep in mind the original hearers or readers. What would they have considered the point of the text to be? If you go beyond that, you may well be steering your homiletical craft into dangerous waters.

Avoid typology except in those instances in which there is good scriptural support. A type suggests that something or someone was intended by God to prefigure a later reality. A few actual types appear in Scripture, but not as many as some would lead us to believe. For example, Scripture does not say that Joseph was a type of Christ. To preach on the life of Joseph Christologically, Webster's is to go out on the sermonic limb. Much typological preaching has been done using the tabernacle as a basis for discussion, and rightly so to a degree. After all, the Book of Hebrews itself does this. However, as some unknown wise person has noted, "at least some of the tent poles and ropes were there just to hold up the tent!"[9]

Avoid allegorizing. The sermon which takes the seven locks of hair cut from Samson's head (Judg. 16:19) and arrives at seven main points, each of which discusses some favorable trait lost by Samson, is badly misusing the Scripture. This kind of hermeneutical method has no logical stopping point, and it leads to sermons which both mislead the hearer and serve as a terrible model for gleaning truth from the Word of God.

Notes

1. A helpful discussion on this topic can be found in Leland Ryken, *The Literature of the Bible* (Grand Rapids, Mich.: Zondervan Publishing House, 1974), chap. 3.

2. Ryken, 95.

3. Ryken, 102 ff.

4. Ryken, 96.

5. Thomas G. Long, *Preaching and the Literary Forms of the Bible* (Philadelphia: Fortress Press, 1989), 74.

6. Long, 80. The concept of narrative plot in Scripture is also discussed in some detail in Sidney Greidanus, *The Modern Preacher and the Ancient Text: Interpreting and Preaching Biblical Literature* (Grand Rapids, Mich.: Wm. B. Eerdmans Publishing Co., 1989), 203-206.

7. For some helpful hints for handling this kind of text, see John D. W. Watts, "Preaching on the Narratives of the Monarchy," in *Biblical Preaching: An Expositor's Treasury,* ed. James W. Cox (Philadelphia: Westminster Press, 1983), 72 ff. Also, see Dan R. Johnson, "Guidelines for the Application of Old Testament Narrative," *Trinity Journal* 7 (Month 78):79-84; and Eugene A. Wilson, "The Homiletical Application of Old Testament Narrative Passages," *Trinity Journal* 7 (Month 78):85-92.

8. Such preaching will demand close study of commentaries such as M. H. Woudstra, *The Book of Joshua* (Grand Rapids, Mich.: Wm. B. Eerdmans Publishing Co., 1981); and Trent C. Butler, *Joshua,* Word Biblical Commentary, vol. 7 (Waco: Word Books, 1983).

9. Berkeley Mickelsen, *Interpreting the Bible* (Grand Rapids, Mich.: Wm. B. Eerdmans Publishing Co., 1963), 236-264, has an excellent discussion of typology. Also, see Robertson McQuilkin, *Understanding and Applying the Bible* (Chicago: Moody Press, 1983), 221-226.

14

PREACHING FROM BIBLICAL POETRY

One cannot have a good working knowledge of the Bible without a clear understanding of biblical poetry. This is because huge sections of Scripture are written in this literary form. The following books, for example, are virtually all poetry:

Psalms	Habakkuk
Proverbs	Zephaniah (except 1:1)
Song of Solomon	Obadiah (except v. 1)
Lamentations	Micah (except 1:1)

Books in which the large majority of the contents are written as poetry include:

Job (all except chaps. 1 and 2)	Hosea
Ecclesiastes	Joel
Isaiah	Amos
Jeremiah	Nahum

Poetry is also scattered throughout other parts of the Bible, in both the Old and New Testaments. For example, poetry is found in the Pentateuch in various places: Ezekiel, Zechariah, Matthew, Luke, Romans, and Hebrews.

Understanding Hebrew Poetry

To preach authentically biblical sermons from poetry passages, the preacher must understand the uniqueness of Hebrew poetry compared with other forms of Hebrew literature. He must also understand that biblical poetry is different from much of the poetry of other cultures and is itself somewhat diverse.[1]

The Nature of Hebrew Poetry

Many languages express poetry in a *balance of sound*. This may be done through rhyme, or it may be done by rhythm. Hebrew poetry, however, uses a *balance of thought*. Poetry takes form as ideas are related to one another in various ways. While this is quite different from the English style of poetry, we are fortunate that this is the case.

In the first place, the translation of Hebrew poetry into English is greatly simplified. Ordinarily, it is no easy task to translate rhyme or rhythm into a different language. Second, translation can take place without the loss of meaning that sometimes occurs with Western forms of poetry. Finally, the redundancies and contrasts of Hebrew poetry aid interpreters as they attempt to gain insight into the meaning of the text.

This balance of thought in Hebrew poetry is called *parallelism* and is found in several different forms. Those which are most common are discussed briefly below.

Synonymous parallelism—This occurs when the thought of the first line is repeated a second and sometimes even a third time:

Blessed is the man
> who does not walk in the counsel of the wicked
> or stand in the way of sinners
> or sit in the seat of mockers
>> (Ps. 1:1, NIV).

The earth is the Lord's, and everything in it,
> the world, and all who live in it
>> (Ps. 24:1, NIV).

Praise him, all his angels,
> praise him, all his heavenly hosts
>> (Ps. 148:2, NIV).

How long will you simple ones love your simple ways?
> How long will mockers delight in mockery
> and fools hate knowledge?
>> (Prov. 1:22, NIV).

Antithetic parallelism—This takes place when the first line is followed by a sharp contrast. This type is found throughout Scripture, but is common in the Book of Proverbs:

For the Lord watches over the way of the righteous,
> but the way of the wicked will perish
>> (Ps. 1:6, NIV).

He who guards his lips guards his life,
> but he who speaks rashly will come to ruin
>> (Prov. 13:3, NIV).

A gentle answer turns away wrath,
> but a harsh word stirs up anger
>> (Prov. 15:1, NIV).

Constructive (or synthetic) parallelism—This form is seen when the second line of a verse adds an idea to the thought of the first, building upon it:

But his delight is in the law of the Lord,
    and on his law he meditates day and night
           (Ps. 1:2, NIV).

Their land teemed with frogs,
    which went up into the bedrooms of their rulers
           (Ps. 105:30, NIV).

Do not answer a fool according to his folly,
    or you will be like him yourself
           (Prov. 26:4, NIV).

    Climactic parallelism—This is similar to the previous form, except that part of the first line is repeated in the second as the idea is completed:

Ascribe to the Lord, O mighty ones,
    ascribe to the Lord glory and strength.
Ascribe to the Lord the glory due his name;
    worship the Lord in the splendor of his holiness
           (Ps. 29:1-2, NIV).

Ascribe to the Lord, O families of nations,
    ascribe to the Lord glory and strength.
Ascribe to the Lord the glory due his name
           (Ps. 96:7-8, NIV).

Praise the Lord.
Praise, O servants of the Lord,
    praise the name of the Lord
           (Ps. 113:1, NIV).

Come back, come back, O Shulammite;
    come back, come back, that we may gaze on you!
           (Song of Sol. 6:13, NIV).

    Figurative parallelism—In this type of poetry, one line makes a figurative statement, and the next line, a literal one.

As the deer pants for streams of water,
    so my soul pants for you, O God
           (Ps. 42:1, NIV).

Like a gold ring in a pig's snout
    is a beautiful woman who shows no discretion
           (Prov. 11:22, NIV).

A ruler who oppresses the poor
    is like a driving rain that leaves no crops
           (Prov. 28:3, NIV).

In addition to parallelism of ideas, some Hebrew poetry has the added characteristic of having been written in an *acrostic* form. In this style, successive verses, half verses, or sections begin with successive letters of the Hebrew alphabet. Artistically, these are superb. The best known is probably Psalm 119, which is written in 22 sections, each consisting of 8 verses. Each verse in each section begins with the same letter of the Hebrew alphabet, with the first eight verses beginning with *aleph,* the second eight with *beth,* and so on. Leland Ryken comments: "This orderliness reinforces the meaning of the poem which is the law of God. The poem thus illustrates on an artistic level the beauty of order that it declares to exist on the moral level."[2]

Other Psalms written in the acrostic style include 9, 10, 25, 34, 37, 111, 112, and 145.

The Book of Lamentations also uses an acrostic style. In that book, chapters 1, 2, and 4 each consist of 22 verses. Each of these chapters forms an acrostic. The third chapter is 66 verses long, and each three-verse stanza uses successive letters at the beginning of each verse. Thus, there are three *aleph* verses in the first stanza, three *beth* verses in the second, and so on. The fifth chapter is not an acrostic, although it has 22 verses. Bruce Waltke suggests that the acrostic form in this book symbolizes a complete (*A* to *Z*) emotional catharsis, for the writer has embraced all possibilities of words.[3] The acrostic style is also used as an aid to memory.

Difficulties in Interpretation

The preacher is advised to have a good grasp on the hermeneutical principles related to interpreting poetry in the Bible. First and foremost, it should be remembered that this *is* poetry. C. S. Lewis' statement concerning the Psalms is applicable to all biblical poetry: "The Psalms must be read as poems; as lyrics, with all the licenses and all the formalities, the hyperboles, the emotional rather than logical connections, which are proper to lyric poetry."[4]

Similarly, Thomas Long remarks:

> Poetry stretches the ordinary uses of words, and places them into unfamiliar relationships with each other, thereby cutting fresh paths across the well-worn grooves of everyday language. Poems change what we think and feel not by piling up facts we did not know or by persuading us through arguments, but by making finely tuned adjustments at deep and critical places in our imaginations.[5]

Practically speaking, this means that poetry must not be pressed too far in its details. It must be understood that what the poetry communicates is being said on an emotional level as well as a factual level. The preacher's responsibility is to discover and tell the truth behind the emotion. In some instances, fact and emotion will be very similar. At other times, there will be more distance.

Another kind of difficulty has to do with particular kinds of passages. The Imprecatory Psalms, for example, are difficult to understand and even more difficult to declare. These psalms consist of prayers for the defeat and overthrow of the wicked. Examples include Psalms 35, 69, 109, and 137, and others as well. The preacher must remember that the psalmist is expressing: (1) a strong abhorrence for sin; (2) a resignation of vengeance into God's hands; and (3) personal feelings in a language that is often hyperbolic. It should also be remembered that some imprecations appear to be prophetic in nature.

Messianic Psalms can also be troublesome. That they exist is seen in Jesus' statement in Luke 24:44 and in various New Testament writings. A helpful policy is to treat texts as messianic only if the New Testament writers do:

Psalm 8:4b-8 is cited in Hebrews 2:5-10.

Psalm 22 is referred to in Matthew 27:35-46.

Psalm 45:6-7 is referred to in Hebrews 1:8-9.

Psalm 110:1-7 is seen in Matthew 22:43-45.

Another difficulty found in Hebrew poetry is the mixing of metaphors. We see this, for example, in the first and last parts of Psalm 23. The preacher must remember to treat these metaphors as means to an end. In other words, the concentration should not be as much on the figure as on the truth it represents.

General Guidelines for Preaching from Poetry

As the preacher approaches the task of preaching on biblical poetry, the uniqueness of poetic language should be respected:

> We need to learn as preachers that when we are working with a psalm we are dealing with language and form which may appear to be simple and compact, but which, in fact, aims at creating a shift in the basic moral perception of the reader. Psalms operate at the level of the imagination, often swiveling the universe on the hinges of a single image. Sermons based on psalms should also seek to work their way into the deep recesses of the hearer's imagination.[6]

Thus, the preacher should attempt to discover as much as possible about the poem-text so his usage of it will be in keeping with its original intent and mood. With that in mind, the following are some usual steps to be taken as the text is being studied and the sermon prepared.

The historical occasion for the particular poem should be determined and studied. Psalm titles often help in this regard.[7]

The psychological mood of the poem should be noted. The Psalms, for example, are highly diverse in this regard. Calvin called the Book of Psalms "an anatomy of all the parts of the soul." The Song of

Solomon and the Book of Lamentations are quite dissimilar psychologically.

The basic theology expressed in or underlying the poem should be ascertained. What does the writer or speaker believe about the particular matter being described?

The kind(s) of parallelism employed should be determined. How does this parallelism help achieve the poet's purpose?

Various figures of speech should be noted and studied. What kind are they? To what do they relate? How far should they be pressed?

The perspective of the speaker or writer needs to be observed. The speeches of Job's friends, though truthfully recorded, are not necessarily truthful.

Note the recurring themes in the poem. Does the poem have one recurring theme? If so, this should be the theme of the sermon.

Homiletical Hints

As a general rule, it is better to preach from whole poems rather than isolated parts. It is dangerous to preach on a single verse unless the preacher is convinced that it adequately states the gist of the whole poem. If the poem is found in a context of prose (such as in Luke or Hebrews), include the prose in the setting of the context.

The homiletical method should be chosen carefully, keeping in mind that each of the following approaches has potential usefulness when a poetical passage is chosen for the preaching text:

The Keyword pattern is suitable *if* the main points are based on segments rather than single lines or short phrases. The main points should be based on single lines or short phrases *only* if they are clearly parallel structurally and yet not the same conceptually, as in the case of synonymous parallelism.

Since it uses a segment-by-segment approach, the preacher may find the Analytical method useful from time to time. It should be remembered that an actual subject is to be analyzed and not just the text itself.

The Textual approach can be used if a single verse clearly states the gist of the entire poem or a major section. Sometimes implications can be drawn. Sometimes contrasts can be seen, especially in the case of antithetic parallelism. In this case, a keyword device might be used. In some instances, single verses may suggest the Illustrational approach.

Since poetry is rooted in personal emotions and the experiences upon which they thrive, it may be possible to use an Inductive approach from time to time. To do this, the preacher would discuss a series of particular experiences or events, then draw a general truth. Psalm 103 is an example of a text that could be preached this way.

The Comparative method may be used on occasion, but only with a great amount of caution. The essential nature of poetry must be kept in mind and care taken not to read too much into a figure of speech.

Notes

1. For a brief discussion, see Donald K. Berry, "Poetry" in *Holman Bible Dictionary* (Nashville: Holman Bible Publishers, 1991), 1121-1123.

2. Leland Ryken, *The Literature of the Bible* (Grand Rapids, Mich.: Zonder van Publishing House, 1974), 153.

3. B. K. Waltke, "Lamentations" in *Zondervan Pictorial Encyclopedia of the Bible*, vol. 3 (Grand Rapids, Mich.: Zondervan Publishing House, 1976), 863.

4. C. S. Lewis, *Reflections on the Psalms* (New York: Harcourt, Brace and World, 1958), 3.

5. Thomas G. Long, *Preaching and the Literary Forms of the Bible* (Philadelphia: Fortress Press, 1989), 45.

6. Long, 47.

7. For a brief discussion of Psalm titles, see Peter C. Craigie, *Psalms 1—50* in Word Biblical Commentary, vol. 19 (Waco: Word Books, 1983), 31-35; and A. A. Anderson, *Psalms I* in New Century Bible (London: Oliphants, 1972), 43-51.

15

PREACHING
FROM WISDOM
LITERATURE

For our purposes, the Books of Job, Proverbs, Ecclesiastes, and the Song of Solomon will be included in this discussion. This is not always the case, for the books categorized as "wisdom literature" vary from scholar to scholar.[1] Everyone includes Proverbs in this genre. Beyond that, agreement stops. Some see the Song of Solomon as a drama, rather than wisdom poetry. Job is also categorized as drama by some. The Book of Psalms does not seem to fit because it is primarily a hymn and prayer book.[2]

When approaching this category, one should keep in mind that most of the wisdom literature in Scripture is written as poetry. Therefore, the descriptions and guidelines stated in the prior chapter on "Preaching from Biblical Poetry" must be understood and applied with this category of Scripture as well.

The underlying characteristic of wisdom literature is twofold: (1) It seeks to impart a proper, wise, and godly view of life ("The fear of the Lord is the beginning of knowledge" Prov. 1:7), and (2) It usually does this by means of short proverbial sayings. Because of this, these books contain some of the most memorable parts of Scripture.

Job

Unlike the Book of Proverbs, which is wisdom literature at its purest, the Book of Job is actually set forth as a long narrative. As a whole, it tells the story of an individual who lost practically everything, wondered why this had happened, evoked the same questions in the minds of others, heard God's point of view, and was then the recipient of material blessing once again. The first two chapters and the end of the last chapter are written as prose. The rest of this lengthy book is poetry of the very highest quality.

> The Book of Job has been recognized as one of the greatest poetic productions of all times. Among the Hebrew writers the author of this book displays the most extensive vocabulary—he is at times referred to as the Shakespeare of Old Testament times. Exhibited in this book are vast resources of knowledge, a superb style of forceful expression, profundity of thought, excellent command of language, noble ideals, a high standard of ethics, and a genuine love for nature. The religious

and philosophical ideas have claimed the consideration of the greatest
theologians and philosophers down to the present day.[3]

This book must be handled and understood as a whole before
attempts are made to preach on smaller sections. Great care must be
exercised in the preaching of individual verses in the book, even if
they are well known (for example, "I know that my Redeemer lives,"
Job 19:25, NIV). The context is extremely important when this book is
being considered.

After the initial devastation by Satan, the content of the book
consists of six spokesmen, each interacting with the others and
each stating his own opinions about the calamity that has come.
The spokesmen are Job, Eliphaz, Bildad, Zophar, Elihu, and God. The
first five (or at least the middle four) say some wonderful things,
but not everything they say is truth. This is why the larger context
is so important.

The Book of Job deals with some of the most serious questions
humans can ask. People still face evil and suffering, and this book is
always contemporary. The most natural sermon pattern to use with
this book, it seems, is the Problem-Solving method. While this pattern can be used, the preacher should be aware that the book does not
give pat answers to the problem of evil and suffering. Those
"solutions" will have to come on an implicational level.

It is best to preach on the Book of Job as a whole or in a very brief
series. When this is done, the Problem-solving pattern may be used,
or the preacher may choose to try the Keyword or Analytical patterns.
The problem, of course, is that the book is very long (42 chapters).
Covering that much material in one sermon or even in a short series is
difficult. Nevertheless, the preacher runs the risk of faulty interpretation if short texts are used as part of individual sermons. If short texts
are used as part of a long series, the preacher risks redundancy.

Proverbs

The Book of Proverbs, on the other hand, is best preached in
shorter sections. This is because many of its materials are independent statements which are not tied in with the surrounding context
except in very general ways. While understanding a text's background is desirable, this is often difficult or even impossible with
single proverbs.

The proverbs in Scripture seem, for the most part, to be handy
pieces of practical information, but not particularly heavy as far as
theological content is concerned. Furthermore, they sometimes seem
to contradict one another as well as to contradict reality. Proverbs 26:4
states, "Do not answer a fool according to his folly,/ or you will be like
him yourself" (NIV). The very next verse, however, says, "Answer a

fool according to his folly,/ or he will be wise in his own eyes" (NIV). Other sayings such as "The fear of the Lord adds length to life,/ but the years of the wicked are cut short" (Prov. 10:27) can be considered problematic as well. These "head scratchers" are the reasons why Thomas Long says that for most preachers, this book "is nothing more than a deserted stretch of highway between Psalms and Ecclesiastes."[4]

Hermeneutically, it should be remembered that a proverb is just that: a statement of a general truth. We are supposed to meditate on Proverbs, seeking to discover the principle of truth they contain. We should not view them in a slavish, mechanical, behavioristic way that implies that if certain "behavioral buttons" are pushed, the results will always be the same. To do so is to have a robotic worldview.

As an example, consider Proverbs 22:6: "Train a child in the way he should go,/ and when he is old he will not turn from it" (NIV). Assuming that this verse is speaking of child rearing, rather than vocational training as some have suggested, is this proverb expressing an absolute promise? Or, is it giving a principle by which parents should live and which usually results in offspring who follow the ways of the Lord? (A similar question must be addressed to the Fifth Commandment as mentioned in Ephesians 6:3. Does honoring one's parents automatically result in long life?)

This book is somewhat varied in its contents. The first nine chapters are a discussion of wisdom and foolishness. The discussion is done in a father-son or teacher-student kind of format, though it is not in any way a dialogue. This section is more thematic and unified than the rest of the book. Subthemes are also found, sometimes in stanzas containing several verses. When this is the case, sermon methods such as the Keyword and Analytical methods might be used.

The heart of the book is found in 10:1—22:16. This section contains about 375 individual proverbs, each capable of standing on its own merit. Most of these are written in the poetic form of antithetic parallelism, but other poetic forms are also used. Many kinds of behavior are referred to in these proverbs, and they have quite a contemporary ring to them. The preacher should usually handle these individually. The single text (proverb) should become a proposition of impression, and this can be done by using a Textual method like the illustrational approach. The implicational approach may also be used to arrive at the main points.

The next section is found in 22:17—24:34. This section is similar to the first nine chapters of the book, as it assumes a teacher-student posture. The wise sayings are sometimes in forms other than couplets.

Chapters 25—29 were collected by the men of Hezekiah but attributed to Solomon. Most of these proverbs are in couplet form, but some have three lines and even four. Many are similes—they state that one thing is like something else. Proverbs 25:28 is a typical example: "Like a city whose walls are broken down/ is a man who lacks self-control" (NIV).

The last two chapters stand alone, with chapter 30 attributed to Agur, an unknown writer, and chapter 31 to King Lemuel, also unknown. Chapter 30 speaks of human limitations apart from the help of God's guidance. The final chapter begins with some instructions to the king and then concludes with an acrostic poem lauding the ideal wife. This closing section could be preached using the Keyword method, although each main point would have to be a summary of several verses. Otherwise, the number of main points would be far too excessive.

Ecclesiastes

Whereas Job is a book that searches for hope in the midst of hurt and Proverbs is a book of principles by which to live, Ecclesiastes is a book of frustration and pessimism, at least for the most part. It is a discussion of philosophical concerns based on the writer's observations of life and the conclusions which he draws.

At first glance, it may seem that this book runs counter to the rest of written revelation as well as to itself. It is often accused of containing contradictions within its own pages, and so it does! Certainly, some points of view expressed in the book contradict the general view of the Judeo-Christian tradition, but that is not the whole story! Contrary to what some may think, the theme and message of this book are not unlike that of the rest of Scripture. Leland Ryken said, "This book espouses the most basic theme of biblical literature—that life lived by purely earthly or human values, without faith in God and supernatural values, is meaningless and futile."[5]

This being the case, why are large sections of the book so pessimistic? Is there an evident structure in the book that explains this? The answer, according to Ryken, is seen in the book's dialectical arrangement of ideas. He suggests that the book follows one of the oldest literary devices, the quest motif. The author pictures himself as a wise man in search of the good life. He does this by searching, evaluating, and recording his findings in a dialectical juxtaposition of positive and negative passages. His search covers all the main spheres of human existence: the city, fields, gardens, the temple, a house, a bedroom, courts of justice, seats of power, and even warfare. He examines wealth, power, religion, relationships, work, and play. He comes to the conclusion that life has meaning only as a person properly relates to God.[6]

When understood as a whole, this book has a tremendous message for today's world. As long as the overall message of the book is clearly understood, the preacher can deal with the book section by section. Those passages which are positive in nature (true) can be preached as such. Those which are negative (pessimistic and inaccurate) can be compared to the positions of mistaken philosophies in today's world. Each message, of course, should conclude by speaking of the meaning of life from God's perspective.

Special caution should be used when isolated texts are chosen. Just as with the Book of Job, not everything recorded in this book is true, though everything is truthfully recorded. Single verses should be used as sermon texts only when they accurately reflect the theme of the immediate context.

The Problem-solving method can be used with a variation when preaching from this book. When this method is applied to most texts, only the third point interacts with the Scripture. In Ecclesiastes, however, both the second and third points can be found in certain longer texts. For example, 4:1-16 gives some negative descriptions of life "under the sun." This has potential for a second main point. Ecclesiastes 5:1-7 gives a positive response that could be the basis for the third main point of the same sermon.

The Song of Solomon

Through the years scholars have expressed many different opinions about the purpose and proper interpretation of the Song of Solomon. Some have seen the book as an allegory, expressing the loving relationship that exists between God and His people. (The early church father Origen preached a long series on this book in which he took this position.) Others have seen the book as a drama or love story—an interpretation that Ryken dismisses with solid reasoning.[7] Still others understand the book to be a collection of love poems reflecting a single relationship, but not telling a story per se. The book has also been viewed as a miscellaneous collection of love poems, but not about anyone in particular. Finally, some scholars hold that the book is both historical (reflecting the love of Solomon for his Shulamite bride) and typical (a type, or foreshadowing, of God's love for His people, His bride). These viewpoints are all ably discussed by R. K. Harrison.[8]

Preaching on this book is extremely difficult. One runs the risk of improperly allegorizing its contents, especially if the typological view is maintained. Yet, the book has a practical value in communicating the goodness of erotic love. It can be valuable in marital counseling as well.

Notes

1. Gleason Archer, for example, includes only Job and Proverbs in the category. See Archer's *A Survey of Old Testament Introduction* (Chicago: Moody

Press, 1974), 438. H. L. Drumwright includes Proverbs, Job, Ecclesiastes, and a few of the Psalms in his article "Wisdom," vol. 5 in *Zondervan Pictorial Encyclopedia of the Bible* (Grand Rapids, Mich.: Zondervan Publishing House, 1976), 942. Leland Ryken discusses only Proverbs and Ecclesiastes in *The Literature of the Bible* (Grand Rapids, Mich.: Zondervan Publishing House, 1974), 243-258. Ronald Clements includes Proverbs, Job, and Ecclesiastes: "Preaching from the Wisdom Literature" in *Biblical Preaching: An Expositor's Treasury*, ed. James W. Cox (Philadelphia: Westminster Press, 1983), 84.

2. Most scholars consider Psalms 1, 14, 36, 37, 49, 53, 73, 78, 112, 119, 127, 128, and 133 to be wisdom psalms. Canonical critics argue that Psalm 1 sets the pattern to make the whole Psalter a wisdom book, even if the original parts were not wisdom. In addition to the whole books of wisdom literature being considered in this chapter, there are also instances of the wisdom genre scattered throughout Scripture. Examples include Isaiah 28:23-29; Amos 3:3-6; Ezekiel 18:2; 1 Corinthians 15:33; 2 Corinthians 9:6; Galatians 5:9; and Galatians 6:7. See Sidney Greidanus, *The Modern Preacher and the Ancient Text* (Grand Rapids, Mich.: Wm. B. Eerdmans Publishing Co., 1988), 228, 311.

3. Samuel J. Schultz, *The Old Testament Speaks* (New York: Harper and Row, 1960), 280.

4. Thomas G. Long, *Preaching and the Literary Forms of the Bible* (Philadelphia: Fortress Press, 1989), 53.

5. Ryken, 250.

6. Ryken, 251-252.

7. Ryken, 219.

8. R. K. Harrison, "The Song of Songs," vol. 5 in *Zondervan Pictorial Encyclopedia of the Bible* (Grand Rapids, Mich.: Zondervan Publishing House, 1976), 486.

16

PREACHING FROM PROPHETIC LITERATURE

One-fourth of the books in the Bible are books of prophecy, making up approximately 22 percent of Scripture. They cover a period of about 500 years of Israel's history dealing not only with God's people, but with the surrounding nations as well. They are the most diverse books in the Bible, as they present a wide array of styles and topics.

An Overview of the Writing Prophets

Their Identity

It is not unusual for students of Scripture to feel that the prophets and prophetic literature are difficult to grasp. This may be due in part to the fact that some of the prophetic books (especially Isaiah, Jeremiah, and Ezekiel) are very long compositions, sometimes without a clear story line to help the reader follow what is happening.

This difficulty may also be due to the fact that the Old Testament prophets were highly unusual individuals, sometimes bordering on the eccentric. Abraham Heschel, a noted Jewish scholar, begins his volumes on the prophetic literature with these attention-getting words: "This book is about some of the most disturbing people who have ever lived: the men whose inspiration brought the Bible into being—the men whose image is our refuge in distress, and whose voice and vision sustain our faith."[1]

In *The Old Testament in Contemporary Preaching*, Walter Kaiser raises the question of whether the prophets should be considered revolutionaries or conservatives. He goes on to say that they were actually *both*, another indication to us that they were highly unusual people.[2] They were *revolutionaries* in the sense that they were radicals compared to most people of their day. They advocated great change for people individually and for society as a whole. Such change would have caused the upheaval of existing structures, as is seen in the Book of Jonah regarding the city of Nineveh or in the Book of Jeremiah concerning the people of Jerusalem. They were *conservatives* in the sense that they were calling the Jewish people back to the "old-time religion," back to the faith of Moses and Abraham, and away from idolatry and self-indulgence.[3]

Their Role

The word *prophecy* itself invariably conjures up ideas of foretelling the future. (If the pastor announces a series on "prophecy," almost all of the congregation will assume that he will be dealing with "things to come.") Foretelling, however, was not the primary role of the prophet. The prophets were primarily *"forthtellers"* rather than foretellers. Their first concern was their own contemporaries, not some future generation. When predictions did occur, they inevitably contained admonitions to move the people toward holiness. More nonpredictive content is found in the prophetical books than predictive.[4]

The prophets were spokespersons for God. This was basic to their reason for being. Sometimes their message did deal with foretelling the future, but their message was always the message of God, that is, forthtelling. Further, the messages were always delivered with a sense of authority that left little question about their orientation.

> Prophecy is essentially a ministry of disclosure, a stripping bare. Israel's great prophets do not merely lift the veil of the future in order to destroy false expectations; at the same time, they expose the conduct of their contemporaries. . . . Prophets tear the masks away and show the true face of the people behind them.[5]

Their Message

The prophets were essentially communicators of a divine message. As communicators, they exhibited great sensitivity to a number of issues. Their message as a whole will be better understood if we take special note of these sensitivities.

First, the prophets had a great *sensitivity to God*. They had encountered Him themselves and knew His attributes well. They desired to communicate the "person" of God to their hearers, as well as the message that He had given them:

1. They knew Him as the electing, covenant-making God (Hos. 2:16-20; 11:1-4; Hag. 2:24; and Mal. 1:1-3).
2. They knew Him as the God who makes history, using even the enemies of Israel to do His bidding (Jer. 25:9; Hab. 1:5-6; and Isa. 45:1).
3. They recognized the universality of God's domain (Jonah 1; Amos 1-2; and Mal. 1:11).
4. They knew Him as the God of justice (Mal. 3:5; Hos. 5:1; Mic. 3:8; and Amos 5:24).
5. They knew Him as the God of wrath (Nah. 1:6; Hos. 13:7-8; and Mal. 4:1).
6. They knew Him as the God of loving mercy (Jonah 4:11; Hos. 6:1; Mic. 7:18-20; and Mal. 1:2).

Second, the prophets had a great *sensitivity to the depth of sin and unbelief.* Abraham Heschel said: "They speak and act as if the sky were about to collapse because Israel has become unfaithful to God."[6] Heschel even went so far as to say: "The prophets were unfair to the people of Israel. Their sweeping allegations, overstatements, and generalization defied standards of accuracy. Some of their exaggerations reach the unbelievable."[7] He cited Hosea 4:1-2 and 6:8-9 as examples.

Third, the prophets had a great *sensitivity to religion gone awry.* They were concerned with "weightier matters of the law." Religiosity did not impress them; they looked for true religion of the heart (Isa. 1:10-14; Hos. 5:1; 6:6; 7:14; 10:2; and Mal. 1:7; 2:3).

Fourth, the prophets had a great *sensitivity to misplaced values.* They sharply rebuked the materialism, hedonism, idolatry, power grabbing, and various injustices of their day (Isa. 1:17; Jer. 7:1-11; Ezek. 22:6-16; Hos. 10:13-14; 12:8; Hag. 1:2-11; and Amos 5:10-13).

Fifth, the prophets had a great *sensitivity to God's warnings of coming judgment* (Ezek. 22:17-22; Hos. 13:9,12; Hab. 1:3-6; Hag. 1:9-11; and Mal. 3:5).

Sixth, the prophets had a great *sensitivity to God's promise of mercy* (Hos. 2:15; 14:1-7; Jonah 3:10; Hag. 2:9; and Mal. 4:2).

Seventh, the prophets had a great *sensitivity to their own misery,* that is, their own unenviable position as God's spokespersons (Jer. 20:14,17,18; 25:3-7; Amos 5:10; and 7:14-15).

Their Literary Style

To say that the writing prophets contain a rich variety of literary material is a vast understatement. The prophetic books are tremendously rich, and this makes possible a great variety of sermon types. Effective preaching on the prophetic literature needs to take seriously this wealth of literary variety and handle it carefully according to sound hermeneutical principles. Homiletical methodology will need to reflect this as well.

Following is a list of various kinds of literary materials found in the writing prophets. Some sample references are also given:

1. *Narrative* (Jonah; Isa. 36—38)—Many of the prophetic writings have narrative portions interwoven with speeches or short pronouncements. The Book of Jeremiah is a further example of this, as is Ezekiel.

2. *Poetry* (Hos. 2; 4—14; Jonah 2:2-9; Obad.)—This is not readily apparent in the KJV, but a glance at the NIV or the NASB will show that a considerable percentage of the material in the writing prophets is in the form of poetry. The preacher needs to handle this genre carefully, understanding the various forms of Hebrew poetry. (See chapter 14 for a discussion of this literary form.)

3. *Sermons, speeches, or synopses of the same*—Haggai consists pri-

marily of four such addresses. Large parts of Isaiah and Jeremiah also are made up of speeches.

4. *Object lessons* (Jer. 18:1-10; Ezek. 4:1-3)—While these are relatively rare in the prophets, those found are rich in imagery and meaning.

5. *Reports of visions* (Isa. 6; Ezek. 37)—These are some of the best-remembered parts of the prophets, though not always completely understood.

6. *Predictions of the future*—Sometimes these are short-term predictions, as in the case of Habakkuk 1:5-6. At other times, the prophet speaks of something quite distant in time, as in Malachi 4. It seems that the prophets themselves were not fully aware of the amount of time involved.

7. *Dialogical argumentation* (Mal. 1:2; 1:6; 1:12-13; Amos 3:3-6)—Rhetorical questions and similar devices successfully engage the hearer or reader in interaction with the prophet.

8. *Affirmations of faith* (Hab. 3)—Even when uncertainty is present, the prophets have a strong conviction about God's faithfulness. Lamentations is another example of this.

9. *Series of "woes"* (Hab. 2:6,9,12,15,19; Amos 1:3,6,9,13; 2:1,4,6)—Sometimes the word *woe* is used, as in Habakkuk. In Amos, the formula is "For three sins of _____, even for four." Isaiah uses the words "An oracle concerning _____" as a formula (Isa. 13:1, NIV; 15:1; 17:1; 19:1; 21:1,11,13).

10. *Symbolic actions* (Isaiah 20:1-5; Hos. 1—3; Jer. 13:1-11)—These are sometimes quite drastic, as in the cases of Isaiah and Hosea. The example from Jeremiah, on the other hand, is rather ordinary, though still effective.

11. *Figurative language*—The Book of Hosea has a great many similes and metaphors. Isaiah 5:1-7 is one of the few parables found in the Old Testament. (Another is found in 2 Samuel 12:1-7, also from the lips of a prophet.) Allegory is found in Ezekiel 17:3-10.

Preaching from the Prophets

The following guidelines are not unique to preaching on texts from the Bible's prophetic books, but are true of preaching in general. Still, because these books of prophecy are so complex in both content and structure, these guidelines are critically important and will help the preacher preach biblically.

• Choose a text that is a self-contained thematic segment. If the same theme runs on for an extended time, choose a segment that accurately represents the larger passage.

• Choose a text that is a complete literary unit. Do not cut off portions of poetry, narratives, dialogue, or parables unless the length is prohibitive.

• Honor the original oral form of the prophecy. Although we speak of the "writing prophets," in reality most, if not all, of their messages (except for symbolic actions) were given in oral form. This means that a particular audience was present and that the message was intended for them. The modern preacher must find parallels between that audience and today's. This will greatly enhance the relevance of the ancient text for today's hearers. Berkeley Mikelsen says: "To lose sight of the original hearers and to focus our attention on what may tickle the fancy of the curious minded in the present day is to lose sight of the very reason for the message."[8]
Likewise, regarding these oracles, Stephen Winward states:

> The message was event-plus-prophet; it was history interpreted. The revelation was for the contemporaries of the prophet who received it; it was communicated in their language and thought forms, related to their needs, relevant to the situation in which they lived. That is why it is always necessary to look at a given message against the background of the historical situation in which it was delivered. Only when it is studied in its original context can any message be rightly understood, and be rightly re-applied to the changed circumstances of our own times.[9]

• Exercise caution in interpreting the text. Sound hermeneutical principles should be applied to historical, grammatical, and contextual matters.
• Study the theology of the text. If the prophet speaks for God, what divine truth did he communicate? The theological issues as understood in that historical context must be dealt with before jumping to theological conclusions based on present-day knowledge. Regarding preaching on messianic prophecy, for example, Sidney Greidanus cautions:

> When preaching on a messianic passage, the tendency may be to draw a direct line from the prophecy to Jesus in the New Testament. But this shortcut does not do full justice to the history of revelation. Messianic prophecies may not be exempted from historical interpretation any more than other kinds of prophecy. Since messianic prophecies, too, were addressed first of all to specific people in the past, we must hear these prophecies first the way these people heard them.[10]

• Adapt the form and mood of the sermon to the form and mood of the text as much as reasonable. To do this is to recognize that even the form of a biblical text communicates as well as the truths in the text.[11]

Using the Homiletical Methods

The prophetic literature is so diverse that practically any legitimate homiletical method will be useful from time to time. This allows the preacher to engage in a rich variety of preaching styles and arrangements even within the scope of a single, brief series of messages. In regard to the different methods discussed in this handbook, the following hints may prove helpful:

The *Keyword method* is especially useful in preaching on the prophetic speeches when they are arranged in a systematic way. Isaiah 1 could serve as a text for one or more Keyword sermons, as God, through the prophet, brings a series of charges against His people. The series of "woes" in Isaiah 5:8-23 is also fertile ground for one or more sermons of this type.

The *Analytical method* can be used with prophetic speeches and the narrative passages found throughout much of the prophetic literature. An example of a prophetic text would be Jeremiah 10:1-16, which deals with the subject of idolatry. A suitable narrative text would be Isaiah's call in Isaiah 6:1-13.

The *Textual method* may be used with the many single verses and short, pithy sayings which capture the essence of the various prophetic themes. Some suitable examples would be: Habakkuk 2:20; Malachi 3:8; Zechariah 4:6; Isaiah 5:20; Isaiah 6:8b; Isaiah 55:8; Amos 5:21-24; and Micah 6:8.

The *Problem-solving pattern* may be usable when extended texts address contemporary concerns. The Book of Habakkuk speaks most eloquently about the problem of evil (1:1—2:4; 3:1-19). Haggai 1 speaks about the problem of misplaced priorities.

The *Comparative method* is quite useful with the many figures of speech found throughout the prophets. The Book of Hosea is full of "preachable" figures (for example, 7:8; 7:11; 8:7). The other prophets also made extensive use of similes, metaphors, and other analogies (Jer. 18:6; Ezek. 22:18; and Amos 7:8).

The *Syllogistic approach* is useful in dealing with certain argumentative texts in which the prophet concludes with a specific truth. The messages in Haggai, especially the first message (1:1-11) and the third one (Hag. 2:10-19), could be presented using this method.

An *Inductive approach* can be used to prove a general truth by citing various examples or specific instances. The first two chapters of Amos, for example, present a series of judgments which collectively lead to the single truth that God judges sin without playing favorites. Malachi raises some rhetorical questions which could also be handled inductively.

A *Narrative sermon* can be preached on a selection from the numerous stories encountered in the prophetic literature. Texts like Isaiah 6; Jeremiah 18; Hosea 1—3; and the Book of Jonah are just a few of the many possibilities. This style of preaching could also be used to preach biographically on the prophets themselves, perhaps in the first person.

Notes

1. Abraham Heschel, *The Prophets*, vol. 1 (New York: Harper and Row, 1962), ix; Randy Hatchett, "Prophecy, Prophets" in *Holman Bible Dictionary* (Nashville: Holman Bible Publishers, 1991), 1141-1143, provides a good overview.

2. Walter C. Kaiser, Jr., *The Old Testament in Contemporary Preaching* (Grand Rapids, Mich.: Baker Book House, 1973), 93 ff.

3. For continuity and wholeness in prophetic literature, see Paul R. House, *Survey of the Old Testament* (Nashville: Broadman Press, 1992).

4. For a further discussion of this matter, see Sidney Greidanus, *The Modern Preacher and the Ancient Text: Interpreting and Preaching Biblical Literature* (Grand Rapids, Mich.: Wm. B. Eerdmans Publishing Co., 1989), 230.

5. Hans Walter Wolff, *Confrontations with Prophets* (Philadelphia: Fortress Press, 1983), 35.

6. Heschel, 4.

7. Heschel, 13.

8. A. Berkeley Mickelsen, *Interpreting the Bible* (Grand Rapids, Mich.: Wm. B. Eerdmans Publishing Co., 1963), 295.

9. Stephen Winward, *A Guide to the Prophets* (Richmond, Va.: John Knox Press, 1969), 29.

10. Greidanus, 237.

11. See Thomas G. Long, *Preaching and the Literary Forms of the Bible* (Philadelphia: Fortress Press, 1989), 12-20.

17

PREACHING FROM APOCALYPTIC LITERATURE

General Introduction to Apocalyptic

Usually associated with the general category of predictive prophecy, the apocalyptic genre is actually quite unique and requires special attention if it is to be properly understood and communicated.[1]

The word *apocalyptic* comes from the Greek *apokalupsis,* meaning "a revelation" or "a disclosing." The word is sometimes used as an alternate title for the Book of Revelation, but this genre of biblical literature includes other books and passages as well. In the Old Testament, the second half of Daniel, and passages in Joel, Amos, and Zechariah are included in this category. In the New Testament, Matthew 24, Mark 13, 1 Thessalonians 4:13-18, and the Book of Revelation are considered apocalyptic by most scholars.

This type of writing is not confined to the Bible, however, but is seen in nonbiblical books such as *Ethiopic Enoch* (1 Enoch), the *Book of Jubilees,* the *Sibylline Oracles,* the *Testaments of the Twelve Patriarchs,* the *Assumption of Moses,* the *Apocalypse of Moses, 2 Enoch, 2 Esdras,* and the Qumran scroll called *The War of the Sons of Light with the Sons of Darkness.* The style is generally dated from about 200 B.C. to about 100 A.D., although the Old Testament examples probably should be dated earlier.

Apocalyptic literature is characterized by several distinctive traits:

1. It is eschatological, that is, concerned primarily with future events.
2. The revelation is often received by a hero figure who is a member of the "in" group. In reality the writings are almost always pseudonymous; in other words, the real author is unknown but has expressed his message through the medium of a well-known person. (For this reason, some conservative scholars argue against the inclusion of Bible books such as Daniel and Revelation in this category.)
3. The revelation is intended only for a special group, God's remnant. Thus, the writings are esoteric in nature.
4. There is usually a strong messianic flavor, that is, a savior is coming to deliver the struggling saints.

5. A strong flavor of pessimism is present. Spiritual and political matters are seen as deteriorating until the final conflict, when the remnant will be delivered.
6. There is a sharp difference between good and evil, and between good people and evil people. (This is a form of dualism.)
7. Much symbolism is used including animals, numbers, colors, and heavenly phenomena. This gives the writings a mysterious character to be understood only by the remnant.
8. There is an emphasis on the spirit world, with angels and demons being involved in a cosmic conflict.
9. The writings speak of the divine wrath and judgment coming upon those outside of the elect (the remnant). They culminate with a final judgment and the ultimate triumph of God and His people.

Not all of these traits will be found in every apocalyptic writing, but several of them will be. In the Book of Revelation, for example, all of these characteristics except the second one are present.

Revelation is different from the noncanonical apocalyptic writings in several ways. First, it expressly claims to be a book of prophecy. Second, it claims (as does Daniel) to be based on visions actually seen by the writer, not simply to be a literary work. Third, it is not ethically passive, blaming others for the plight of God's people. Instead, blame is shared by both the world and the people of God. Finally, while noncanonical apocalypses see the deliverance of God's people as solely future, Revelation sees it as having been accomplished in the past (in a promissory sort of way) through the suffering but victorious Lamb (5:9-14).

For our purposes, some brief introductory matters concerning the Books of Daniel and Revelation will be discussed, followed by some basic guidelines for preaching on apocalyptic literature.

The Book of Daniel

In matters of dating and authorship, no book in the Bible receives more negative criticism than the Book of Daniel. The arguments against its integrity and authenticity have persisted for many years. William Tuck presents a typical nonconservative view in these matters:[2]

It was indicated earlier that the book was most likely written ca. 165 B.C. This is the internal evidence for a second-century date: the writer's vague knowledge of the details about the Babylonian and Persian period, his historical inaccuracies of that time, his precise knowledge of the Ptolemy and Seleucid periods, Greek words, the development of its theology, and its advanced angelology. The author was not attempting to write scientific history but to teach a moral and religious lesson about the presence of God during a time of great crisis.

Conservative scholars are well aware of this type of argumentation against the authorship of the book by the historical Daniel. They have been considered and refuted by able scholars such as Gleason Archer and R. K. Harrison.[3]

Suffice it to say that the kinds of arguments advanced by Tuck display two weaknesses: (1) they do not take into account all of the available evidence; and (2) they have a strong preconceived prejudice against predictive prophecy. These six arguments posed by Tuck sound as if they are quite convincing, but in reality, they are not.

The preacher must remember that the Book of Daniel is more than apocalyptic in its style. The first six chapters, though containing some prophetic material, are really narrative in style, telling of several different events. The first chapter, for instance, tells of the deportation and initial training of Daniel and three other Hebrew young men. Chapter 3 relates the account of three Hebrew young men in their defiance of the king's order and their risk of death in the fiery furnace. Daniel's encounter with the lions is described in chapter 6. All of this is excellent material for preaching and should not be overlooked.

The apocalyptic element enters in chapter 7, where Daniel has a vision of four beasts (creatures). Much of chapters 7—12 reflects the characteristics of this kind of literature.

The Book of Revelation

Revelation is, without doubt, the most difficult book in the Bible to understand and interpret. It sometimes appears difficult to find two commentators who agree on a basic approach to the book, even apart from some of the fine points, about which there are further differences of opinion. Parts of the book are relatively easy to understand (chapters 1—3, for example). It is the overall plan and design of the book about which there is much disagreement. This book is the most intricately structured book in Scripture. Its contents are woven together in a highly organized pattern which makes outlining relatively easy.

To begin with, interpreters hold four different positions.[4] The *preterist* position sees the book as dealing only with the conditions of the church and world at the time of its writing without any predictive element intended. The *historicist* interpretation sees the book as predicting chronologically the various eras of church history up through and including the final events of the ages. The *idealist* approach sees the book as a "drama" or depiction of the conflict between good and evil, without any predictive element. Finally, the *futurist* viewpoint is that all of the book beginning with chapter 4 is a preview, a description, of the events which will occur at the end-of-the-church age.[5]

These four approaches represent a wide diversity of theological positions. Even those who hold to a similar evangelical theology in other areas of doctrine may understand the book differently, depending on their positions concerning postmillennialism, amillennialism, and premillennialism. Even premillennialists evidence strong differences of opinion.

Dispensationalists, for example, often see the letters to the seven churches (chapters 2—3) as both historical and predictive of the seven succeeding eras of church history. Those who fit into the category of "historical premillennialists" do not see the letters as referring to future ages or future churches, but to churches in John's day only. Likewise, dispensationalists see 4:1 as a reference to a pretribulation rapture, and they believe the church is absent from the events discussed in the rest of the book until toward the end. Historical premillennialists see this interpretation of 4:1 as an example of eisegesis based on one's presupposed eschatological viewpoints.

Guidelines for Preaching on Apocalyptic Literature

The preacher should gain an understanding of the book (or section) as a whole. It is important to get and communicate a feel for the whole before trying to deal with the details of the writing. The whole is much more important than the details in this type of literature.

While there surely cannot be a hard rule on this, it is usually better to preach on larger texts rather than smaller ones. Short texts can lead to unnecessary speculation about details if care is not taken.

Preaching texts should be chosen which summarize in plain language the surrounding context. The following texts, for example, all do this well: Matthew 24:36,42,44; Mark 13:35-37; Revelation 1:19; 17:17.

Theological themes should be preached primarily rather than prophetic (predictive) themes. For instance, the Book of Revelation is as much about Jesus Christ as it is about future events. As such, it has a great deal to say about Christology, making mention of Christ some 90 times. The doctrine of God is, likewise, prominent in the book, and other theological concerns are found there as well.

When a series is planned on an apocalyptic book, it is often a good idea to trace a subject or theme through the entire book. This will help unify the writing in the minds of the hearers. For example Revelation might be covered adequately by the following themes:

1. "Images of the Messiah"
2. "Who's in Charge?"
3. "The Ultimate Struggle Between Good and Evil"
4. "What in the World's Going to Happen?"

Great caution should be exercised in interpreting the figures of

speech and the symbols found in this genre. The following procedures should be carefully observed:

1. Let the text interpret itself first (Dan. 2:36-43; 7:17; Rev. 1:20;
   17:9-16).
2. If the immediate context does not explain a symbol or figure, is it
   used elsewhere in Scripture by the same author? If so, how is
   it used?
3. Allow the clear parts of Scripture to serve as a basis for the
   unclear parts.
4. Keep the original hearers or readers in mind. What would they
   have understood the text to be saying? Why would this symbol
   have been effective for them?
5. Do not force symbols or figures into a preconceived mold. Allow
   each context to determine its own meaning.
6. Remember that each symbol or figure does not need to be
   understood fully to get the gist of a passage. The whole flow of
   the text is more important than isolated parts, although these
   details can certainly help amplify its meaning.
7. Be willing to say "I don't know" when it comes to the meaning
   of a given figure, symbol, or even text.

Notes

1. A brief description of the term *apocalyptic* appears in George Beasley-
Murray's "Apocalyptic" in *Holman Bible Dictionary* (Nashville: Holman Bible
Publishers, 1991), 68-69.

2. William P. Tuck, "Preaching from Daniel, Ruth, Esther, and the Song of
Songs" in *Biblical Preaching,* ed. James W. Cox (Philadelphia: Westminster
Press, 1983), 153.

3. See Gleason Archer, *A Survey of Old Testament Introduction* (Chicago:
Moody Press, 1974), 365-388. Also see R. K. Harrison, "Daniel," vol. 2 in
Zondervan Pictorial Encyclopedia of the Bible (Grand Rapids, Mich.: Zondervan
Publishing House, 1976), 12-21; and R. K. Harrison, *Introduction to the Old
Testament* (Grand Rapids, Mich.: Wm. B. Eerdmans Publishing Co., 1969),
1105-1138.

4. An extended introduction to Revelation with charts graphing the various views and interpretations appears in the *Disciple's Study Bible*, New
International Version (Nashville: Holman Bible Publishers, 1988), 1630-1635.

5. See Merrill Tenney, "Revelation, Book of the," vol. 5 in *Zondervan Picto-
rial Encyclopedia of the Bible*, 89-99. Also see Merrill Tenney, *Interpreting
Revelation* (Grand Rapids, Mich.: Wm. B. Eerdmans Publishing Co., 1957).
Both of these works are very sane treatments of a difficult book.

18

PREACHING
FROM NEW TESTAMENT
HISTORY

Unlike Old Testament history, New Testament history covers a relatively small portion of the Bible. Even with the Gospels being considered in addition to the Book of Acts (the Gospels are not usually included in the category of history per se), we are speaking of less than 14 percent of the content of the Bible.

For our purposes, we will discuss preaching on the narrative sections of the four Gospels along with the Book of Acts. Other parts of the Gospels (including the teachings of Jesus, the miracles, and the parables) will be discussed separately.

The Gospels

As mentioned above, the Gospels are not technically considered to have been written in the style of traditional history. Leland Ryken explains:

> The uniqueness of the form known as the gospel ("good news") is obvious at once when we reflect that the form has no real parallel outside of the New Testament writings. Furthermore, none of the usual literary categories does justice to the gospels, although of course they have affinities to a number of conventional forms.[1]

Understanding the Gospel literature is complicated by the fact that these documents are actually a mixture of literary styles:

> We noted earlier that the genres of Hebrew narrative and prophecy contain other genres of literature; similarly, the genre of Gospel does not exist in 'pure' form but also contains a number of other genres. For example, apocalyptic literature is found in Mark 13 (cf. Matt. 24 and Luke 21), songs or hymns in Luke 1 and 2 (the songs of Mary, Zechariah, and Simeon), in Matt. 11:25-30, and in John 1 (the Prologue), and prophecy is found in some of Jesus' speeches.[2]

Further, a comparison of Old Testament heroic narrative with the narratives of the Gospels shows that the latter are more fragmented in their structure than the former. In the heroic narratives of the Old Testament, there is one story line, one plot. All of the various events relate to that plot or its subplots. In the Gospels, especially the Synoptics, we find many unrelated stories which could theoretically be rearranged without doing harm to the overall movement of these documents. John's Gospel has more of a single direction to it. It covers fewer episodes in the life of Jesus but covers them in more detail than the Synoptic Gospels do. Its materials are arranged to lead through a process of thinking to a very definite result, as is mentioned in John's purpose statement in John 20:30-31.

The Gospels also differ from heroic narrative in that they are highly selective in their use of material. Although Jesus is obviously the central figure in these books, huge amounts of biographical information have been ignored by the Gospel writers because their purpose was more theological and evangelical than biographical. As a result, we know very little of "98 percent" of Jesus' life. We do know what is necessary in accordance with the purpose of the writers, namely the importance of faith in Him as the Messiah.[3]

Higher Criticism and the Gospels

It is important for the preacher to be reminded of the major higher critical methods that have been applied to the Gospels in the past and the present. These are *source criticism, form criticism,* and *redaction criticism.* As mentioned previously in the chapter on "Preaching from Earliest History," these methods are not inherently evil but can lead to erroneous conclusions if applied carelessly. An example of the importance of this issue is seen in the work of William Hull.[4]

Hull gives a brief overview of these critical methods from a relatively conservative point of view. The reader should be aware, however, that many of the primary sources he cites are not nearly as conservative. Hull evidently accepts the historicity of the events and sayings in the Gospel documents, but many of the higher critics he cites deny some of these things. (This is not mentioned to label Hull guilty by association but simply to caution the reader that various scholars press higher criticism to various extents.)

Hull discusses source criticism, form criticism, and redaction criticism as "givens" if one desires serious study in the Gospel documents. He discusses what he considers to be the benefits of these higher critical methods from the preacher's standpoint:

> To summarize this entire section: Synoptic criticism is exceedingly complex but not, thereby, irrelevant for the preacher. At its simplest, in treating any Synoptic passage, source criticism demands that we ask, Does it have any parallels and, if so, how are they similar and how are they different? Form criticism demands that we ask, What is the basic unit in which this text was originally transmitted? Redaction criticism demands that we ask, What is the place of this passage in the entire book, and how does it contribute to the purpose for which this particular Gospel was written? Only when these three questions have been

answered as fully as our training and study will permit are we ready to move from text to sermon.[5]

It is difficult to find problems with the conclusions drawn by Hull. In reality, however, they do not adequately address the usual results of these methods. Particularly in the cases of form criticism and redaction criticism, these methods have often resulted in the denial of the traditional views of authorship as well as the basic historicity of the Gospel documents. Form critics have seldom been content to simply categorize the various materials in the Gospels. They have traditionally gone beyond that to speculate about the actual composition of the Gospels (when and by whom?) as well as to speculate about the life setting *(Sitz im Leben)* in which the saying or story originated. Too often the result has been that the Gospels are seen as collections of sayings and stories which are only partly true. That is, some sayings and stories might have actually happened in the life and ministry of Jesus, but others were added by the early church to enhance what was already known. One of the jobs of the critic, then, becomes to differentiate between the authentic happening or saying and later additions. Concerning this sort of higher criticism, F. F. Bruce remarks:

> In its more extreme formulations the doctrine of the life-setting rules that if a saying or action ascribed to Jesus in the Gospels reflects the post-Easter faith of the Church, it should be regarded as a creation within the Church, and that no saying or action ascribed to Him can confidently be taken as authentic if a parallel saying or action is elsewhere ascribed to a Jewish rabbi.[6]

In the redaction criticism method, the emphasis has swung back to the Gospel writers as writers, and this, in and of itself, is good. The writers are seen, however, as theologians whose concern is to communicate their particular viewpoint, rather than also being seen as historians. Thus, Robert Gundry came to the opinion that parts of Matthew's Gospel are not historically accurate, but that Matthew embellished his materials (much the way a preacher uses untrue illustrations in his sermons) to better communicate his theological point.[7]

As Donald Guthrie points out:

> There is no reason, however, to suppose that theological interest must take precedence over historical validity. It is not a question, for example, of Luke's being a theologian or a historian but of his being a theologian as well as a historian. It is difficult to think of the narration of bare facts without some interpretation. But there is no reason to suppose that the interpretation made by each evangelist was his own creation. On the contrary, there is sufficient agreement among them for

us to regard the particular interpretation of each as a variation within a basic unity. There is only one gospel, not a plurality of gospels.[8]

The issue is that of biblical authority. If higher critical methods are applied to the Gospels in a way that eliminates full biblical authority, the preacher has no message to preach. He becomes a speculator engaging in subjective exercises which allow him to stand in judgment of the text, rather than allowing the text to stand in judgment on him. Therefore, higher critical methods must be used quite cautiously.

Preaching on the Gospels

One unique difference in preaching from the Gospels as compared to other parts of Scripture is the large number of parallel passages to be found. In many instances the reader will find that the same event is discussed in all three Synoptics, and sometimes, in John's Gospel as well. As a thorough student of Scripture, the preacher should always study each description of an event or saying. This is not to say that one's text for the feeding of the five thousand, for example, must be based on all four Gospel accounts. Each account tells the story a bit differently; these differences may well have sermonic value.[9] On the other hand, "differences that are inconsequential to the purposes of the sermon . . . should not intrude into the sermon."[10]

As mentioned previously, we will address the majority of texts in the Gospels at a later time. This will include the sayings of Jesus, miracles, and parables. Some other kinds of material in the Gospels should be mentioned here briefly.

Events—These are many and varied. They usually include some kind of verbal material, but the emphasis seems to be on the event itself and not just the words spoken. Following are some examples of this kind of material:

1. The birth narratives (Matt. and Luke)
2. Ministry of John the Baptist (Matt. 3:1-17)
3. The temptation of Jesus (Matt. 4:1-11; Mark 1:12-13)
4. The calling of the disciples (Matt. 4:18-22; Luke 5:1-11; and John 1:35-51)
5. General ministry passages (Matt. 8:14-17)
6. Sending out the twelve (Matt. 10:1-5)
7. Jesus meets John the Baptist (Matt. 11:1-6)
8. Death of John the Baptist (Matt. 14:1-12)
9. The transfiguration (Matt. 17:1-13)
10. The triumphal entry (Matt. 21:1-11)
11. The anointing at Bethany (Matt. 26:6-13; John 12:1-10)
12. The passion narratives (all four Gospels)
13. The resurrection narratives (all four Gospels)

As noted previously, events are usually best handled by using the Analytical approach. Beware of using this method too often, however. Depending on the event, the Keyword method may be usable. If the event can be discussed through parallel ideas, this is a good method. For example, are there several causes, reasons, steps, or results associated with the event? If so, the Keyword method can offer a good alternative to the Analytical approach.

Transitions, comments, and explanations—These are "bridge" texts which help the reader or hearer gain or maintain an understanding of the direction the text has taken or will take. They make clear the flow of the plot. These are usually rather brief passages, but not always. Some examples of these are:

1. The prologue of John's Gospel (John 1:1-18)
2. Matthew's use of the Old Testament (Matt. 1:22-23)
3. Peter's confession of faith (Matt. 16:13-20); this is a key explanation in Matthew's Gospel.
4. Jesus predicts His own death (Matt. 16:21-22); this is a somewhat abrupt transition that follows the previous conversation.
5. Jesus sets "his face" toward Jerusalem (Luke 9:51)
6. The approaching death of Jesus (Matt. 26:1-5); this transition gives two perspectives on the soon-coming death of Christ.
7. Jesus' hour has now come (John 12:23)
8. The purpose of John's Gospel (John 20:30-31)

These "bridges" can often be handled in an interesting way by using an Implicational approach (see "Textual Methods," chapter 6). This can be done using the word *implications* as a keyword device. At other times when the "bridge" consists of a single verse, another of the Textual methods might be used. The preacher must always inquire as to the purpose or function of the particular transition, comment, or explanation being considered. A little time spent at this particular juncture can help assure that the sermon is indeed on target biblically.

The reactions of people to Jesus' ministry—Fewer of these appear in Matthew than in the other three Gospels. They are fairly prominent in John's Gospel. A list of sample passages follows:

1. Mark 1:43-45; 2:12; 12:17; 12:34
2. Luke 5:26; 6:11; 11:53; 20:26
3. John 2:11; 4:39-42; 5:16-18; 6:41-42,52; 7:20,25-52; 8:48

If the text is of sufficient length, it may be possible to use the Analytical method. A keyword like *reasons* may suggest a Keyword approach. Again, an Implicational approach might work as well. Usually, the preacher will have to address the larger context rather than the reaction alone. At times this can be done in the background part of the sermon introduction. At other times, such as when the

Analytical method is used, it will be necessary to include this context in the body of the sermon. Sometimes, it may be best to use a shorter reaction (one verse or so), not as a sermon text by itself, but as the conclusion of a sermon based on the larger passage.

Dialogue—In some instances, Jesus and others engage in this type of confrontation. Often, it is done in a hostile context:

1. Matthew 21:23-27 (Jesus responds to a question about authority.)
2. Matthew 22:15-46 (Several questions are posed to Jesus; He then poses one of his own.)
3. John 3 (Jesus converses with Nicodemus.)
4. John 8:12-59 (Jesus and the Pharisees have a heated discussion about divine sonship and Jesus' identity.)

In addition to the Keyword and Analytical methods, some dialogue texts can be developed through a Problem-solving pattern. As an example, John 3 could be used to address the issue of "How Can a Person Get to Heaven?" The subject of "Being Religious but Lost" in John 8 might also be presented using this pattern.

When preaching from the Gospels, the preacher must remember to do his study with the help of a harmony of the Gospels.[11] These are readily available in both English and Greek and are invaluable for getting the clearest picture possible of a given episode.

The Book of Acts

Technically, the Book of Acts is the only book of history in the New Testament. Even so, it is highly selective history. It is, of course, the second part of the Lukan writings and as such is a continuation of what Luke began discussing in his Gospel, namely, what "Jesus began both to do and teach" (Acts 1:1). In view of the abrupt ending of Acts, some have theorized that Luke intended to write a third part. That, of course, is only conjecture. In any event, Luke chose not to tell the comprehensive story of the early church, but to tell how the church moved beyond Jerusalem to other parts of his civilized world.

As one looks at Acts, one notes that it consists primarily of events (narrative), speeches, and an overall movement as the church expands. One can also ascertain another element in the book. This is not a literary form as such, but is nevertheless a prominent part of the book which should not be overlooked. That is the discussion of the important issues found throughout the book.[12]

The preacher will be able to discover the narrative sections of the book without difficulty. It is unnecessary to repeat the usable homiletical methods at this point, as the previous discussion on events can be noted. Instead, the remainder of this chapter will deal with the speeches in the Book of Acts and some of the issues found there as well.

Speeches—These are very important in Acts, as they disclose the theology and concerns of the early church and their leaders. Note especially the following:

1. Acts 2:14-36 (Peter's sermon on Pentecost)
2. Acts 3:12-26 (Peter's speech in the temple)
3. Acts 4:8-12 (Peter's speech before the Jewish leaders)
4. Acts 7:2-53 (Stephen's speech to the Sanhedrin)
5. Acts 10:34-43 (Peter's speech to those in the house of Cornelius)
6. Acts 15:13-21 (James's address to the council at Jerusalem)
7. Acts 17:22-31 (Paul's sermon on Mars Hill in Athens)
8. Acts 20:18-35 (Paul's farewell message to the Ephesian elders)
9. Acts 22:1-21 (Paul's defense before the mob in Jerusalem)
10. Acts 26:2-29 (Paul's defense before King Agrippa)

These ten speeches are by four different leaders of the early church: Peter, Stephen, James, and Paul. They discuss somewhat different issues but are primarily "apologetic" speeches about the truthfulness of Christianity and the Christian experience.

The Keyword method, Analytical method, and the Problem-solving method are the primary approaches to speech material. The first would, of course, concentrate on presenting parallel concepts in a given speech. The second approach requires that a specific subject in a speech be analyzed. In other words, the speech itself should not be analyzed but, rather, a specific subject in a given speech. Some speeches directly address a problem the early church faced. When this is the case, the Problem-solving method could be used. For example, Acts 10 addresses the problem of racial diversity in the church. Acts 15 discusses a problem rooted in diverse religious backgrounds.

Issues—The careful reader will recognize that although the issues mentioned below are not identified as such in their respective texts, they are clearly issues faced by the church in its early years as well as today. Note these:

1. Missions and church growth (Acts 1:8 and numerous other texts)
2. The nature of the church (Acts 2:42-47; 4:32-35)
3. Spirit baptism and the gift of tongues (Acts 2; 10; 19)
4. Civil disobedience (Acts 4:1-22)
5. Persecution (Acts 5:17-42)
6. Prioritizing ministry (Acts 6:1-7)
7. Racial/cultural barriers (Acts 8; 10; 15)
8. Church disputes (Acts 15:1-35)
9. The gospel meets the secular mind (Acts 17:16-34)

The same three methods used with speeches (see previous section) can be used to address these issues and others in the Book of Acts.

Obviously, the book has much to say to the contemporary church. Caution needs to be exercised hermeneutically so that the narrative emphasis in the book does not lead to seeing the events of the early church as normative for the church today. As with all narrative, principle takes precedence.

Notes

1. Leland Ryken, *The Literature of the Bible* (Grand Rapids, Mich.: Zondervan Publishing House, 1974), 273.

2. Sidney Greidanus, *The Modern Preacher and the Ancient Text: Interpreting and Preaching Biblical Literature* (Grand Rapids, Mich.: Wm. B. Eerdmans Publishing Co., 1989), 264.

3. See P. Joel Snider, "Gospel" in *Holman Bible Dictionary* (Nashville: Holman Bible Publishers, 1991), 567-570.

4. William E. Hull, "Preaching on the Synoptic Gospels," *Biblical Preaching: An Expositor's Treasury*, ed. James W. Cox (Philadelphia: Westminster Press, 1983), 169 ff.

5. Hull, 176.

6. F. F. Bruce, "Form Criticism," vol. 2 in *Zondervan Pictorial Encyclopedia of the Bible* (Grand Rapids, Mich.: Zondervan Publishing House, 1976), 601.

7. Robert Gundry, *Matthew: A Commentary on His Literary and Theological Art* (Grand Rapids, Mich.: Wm. B. Eerdmans Publishing Co., 1982), 623-640. Gundry argues that Matthew used the Jewish method of *midrash*. The *midrashim* were basically commentaries or homiletical expositions of Old Testament history and law. They were transmitted orally before they were committed to writing. Gundry's conclusions have evoked a great deal of criticism and discussion among conservative scholars.

8. Donald Guthrie, "The Historical and Literary Criticism of the New Testament," vol. 1 in *The Expositor's Bible Commentary*, gen. ed. Frank E. Gaebelein (Grand Rapids, Mich.: Zondervan Publishing House, 1979), 448.

9. A helpful discussion of the value of studying Gospel parallels is found in Gordon Fee, *New Testament Exegesis: A Handbook for Students and Pastors* (Philadelphia: Westminster Press, 1983), 103-116.

10. Walter L. Liefeld, *New Testament Exposition: From Text to Sermon* (Grand Rapids, Mich.: Zondervan Publishing House, 1984), 152.

11. John F. Carter, *A Layman's Harmony of the Gospels* (Nashville: Broadman Press, 1961) is one example. Compare *Master Study Bible*, King James Version (Nashville: Holman Bible Publishers, 1983), 1843-1966.

12. See John Polhill, *Acts*, vol. 26 in *The New American Commentary* (Nashville: Broadman Press, 1992).

19

PREACHING FROM THE TEACHINGS OF JESUS

The teachings or sayings of Jesus are unique in many ways and therefore need to be dealt with as a distinct entity in Scripture. These sayings are composed of several different kinds of materials. It will be helpful to examine each of the more prominent kinds individually. Some of these teachings or sayings are quite brief, consisting of only a sentence or two. Others are much longer and may encompass a whole chapter or more. The genre of parable is discussed separately in chapter 21.

Surveying Jesus' Sayings

The Contexts of Jesus' Sayings

Jesus' sayings are found throughout the Gospels and are seen to take place as responses to various stimuli. The Gospel writers always present Jesus in the context of the events which led to His utterances. Thus, His sayings are not just collections of "wisdom" but must be seen in the context of certain events, either verbal or physical or both.

Some of Jesus' teachings, for example, are given in response to questions others pose:

1. The disciples of John, Matthew 9:14. (What about fasting?)
2. The Pharisees and lawyers, Matthew 15:1-2. (What about ceremonial washing in the tradition of the elders?)
3. The Pharisees and Herodians, Matthew 22:15-17. (What about paying taxes to Caesar?)
4. The Sadducees, Matthew 22:23-27. (What about the implications of levirate marriage for the resurrection life?)
5. The Pharisees, Matthew 22:34-36. (Which is the greatest commandment? The three questions in Matthew 22, furthermore, lead to a discourse that takes up all of chapter 23.)
6. Jesus' disciples, Matthew 24:3, NIV. ("When will this happen, and what will be the sign of your coming and of the end of the age?")

Some of Jesus' teachings are in response to direct accusation by His enemies:

1. The Pharisees accuse His disciples of breaking the Sabbath law, Matthew 12:1-2 (His response, 12:3-8).

2. The Pharisees accuse Jesus of casting out demons by the power of Beelzebub, Matthew 12:22-24 (Jesus' response, 12:25-37).

Some of Jesus' teachings are the result of certain events which take place:

1. The departure of John's disciples, Matthew 11:1-7a. (Jesus' response, 11:7b-19).
2. The encounter with the rich young man, Matthew 19:16-22. (Jesus' response, 19:23-30.)
3. The last supper, Matthew 26:17-20. (This event leads to the stating of the New Covenant, 26:26-29.)

A preacher must carefully study the context in which a saying is found. This will shed light on the "why and wherefore" of the teaching and may be useful in the sermon introduction. This step is crucial for the process of making good applications, and it can also suggest illustrations for other parts of the sermon.

The Forms of Jesus' Teachings

As with context, great variety reigns here. We will mention some that are most noteworthy:

Wisdom or pithy sayings—These are sometimes paralleled in the Old Testament or Talmudic literature both in matters of style and content. Yet, with Jesus, they are fresh and authoritative.

1. The Beatitudes, Matthew 5:3-10. (On the basis of parallel structure, there appear to be eight beatitudes, with verses 11-12 providing a summary of the eighth.)
2. "Ask," "seek," and "knock," Matthew 7:7.
3. The "Golden Rule," Matthew 7:12.

Antithesis—This is the kind of teaching that attacks a given position by taking either an opposite point of view or a point of view from a totally different perspective. There are two kinds:

1. Direct antithesis is found in a very straightforward way in the Sermon on the Mount. Jesus often used the formula: "Ye have heard that it was said . . . But I say unto you . . ." (Matt. 5:21,27, 31,33,38,43).
2. Indirect antithesis is seen in the Sermon on the Mount in passages like Matthew 6:2,5,16,19.

Argumentation—Formal reasoning is seen in Matthew 6:25-34 in the passage about worry. Jesus used a form of reasoning called *a fortiori* argumentation: arguing from the lesser to the greater. (If God cares for birds and flowers, things of lesser importance, He will care for people, things of greater importance.)

Jesus also used argument by placing His opponents on the horns of a dilemma so they withdrew their question. Matthew 21:23-29 is the passage in which the chief priests and elders asked Him about the source of His authority. He responded by asking about the source of John the Baptist's authority, thus placing His accusers in a dilemma.

Debate or dialogue—This is seen in several passages in the Gospel of John, but is found in the Synoptics as well:

1. John 6:35-71: Both the Jews and some of Jesus' disciples took issue with His teachings about being the Bread of life.
2. John 7:14-44; 8:12-59: Jesus debated with the Pharisees and others about His identity and mission.

The "Upper Room" discourse—This takes the form of a "farewell address" which is a relatively common Hebraic literary form. It is, of course, a bit dangerous to try to press all of Jesus' teachings into preconceived forms. Yet, there are similarities between this address and many others as far as form is concerned, as Leland Ryken has pointed out:[1]

• The speaker's announcement of His soon departure
• The listeners' sorrow
• Words of comfort from the speaker
• A directive to keep God's commandments
• A prediction of what will happen to the listeners in the future
• An invocation of peace upon the listeners
• The naming of a successor (the Holy Spirit)
• A prayer for the listeners

Figures of speech—Jesus' speech is full of extremely vivid expressions, including many figures of speech:

1. Metaphor and simile
   Matthew 9:36
   > "Sheep without a shepherd"
   Matthew 9:37
   > "The harvest is plentiful but the workers are few" (NIV).
   Matthew 10:16
   > "I am sending you out like sheep among wolves. Therefore be as shrewd as snakes and as innocent as doves" (NIV).
   Matthew 23:27
   > "You are like whitewashed tombs" (NIV).

2. Paradox
   Matthew 16:25
   > "For whoever wants to save his life will lose it, but whoever loses his life for me will find it" (NIV).
   Matthew 20:26
   > "Whoever wants to become great among you must be your servant" (NIV).

3. Hyperbole
   Matthew 7:3
        "Why do you look at the speck of sawdust in your
        brother's eye and pay no attention to the plank in
        your own eye?" (NIV).
   Matthew 19:24
        "It is easier for a camel to go through the eye of a
        needle than for a rich man to enter the kingdom
        of God" (NIV).

The Content of Jesus' Teachings

Numerous books have been written on the subject of Jesus' teachings which will inform the student of the details regarding content.[2] For our purpose, the following broad categories of content, as given by Guthrie, can be noted.[3]

Teachings about God—These include the following three subcategories:

1. God as Creator (Mark 10:6; 13:19)
2. God as Father (Matt. 7:11; 11:25-27; John 5:36-37)
3. God as King (Matt. 6:10; 11:25)

Teachings about the Kingdom—The Kingdom is seen as both present and future. It is a dynamic power over the spiritual forces of darkness (Luke 10:18; 11:21-22). Further, the concept of salvation is linked closely with that of the Kingdom.

Teachings about Himself—This has to do with Jesus' understanding of who He was, that is, questions of self-identity. It is clear that Jesus had no illusions about Himself, for He clearly stated His own relationship to and identification with God.

Teachings about the work of the Messiah—Jesus saw Himself as the Suffering Servant of the Old Testament and understood that the Messiah would suffer an atoning, sacrificial, substitutionary death for the sin of God's people.

Teachings about the Holy Spirit—John's Gospel, particularly, emphasizes Jesus' teachings about the role of the Spirit in the lives of the disciples. Yet, there are also references in the Synoptic Gospels about the Holy Spirit's role (Matt. 10:19-20; 12:28; Mark 12:36; 13:11; and Luke 11:13).

Teachings about personal ethics—These cover a wide variety of topics related to Christian living. Included are issues such as prayer, stewardship, marriage and divorce, loving one's neighbor, loving God, persecution, moral purity, anxiety, wealth, hypocrisy, false teachers, discipleship, evangelism, faith, real authority versus tradition, church discipline, spiritual preparedness, and servanthood.

Preaching on the Teachings of Jesus

The teachings of Jesus are of such a broad variety that virtually every known sermon pattern can be used from time to time. This is certainly true of the eight methods presented in this handbook. In fact, some texts might fit more than one pattern:

A. The *Keyword pattern* is often useful with a statement or teaching when several parallel ideas are inherent in the structure.

Matthew 6:9-13 (keyword: *petitions*)
1. Be sovereign, Lord.
2. Provide our needs, Lord.
3. Deal with us mercifully, Lord.
4. Protect us, Lord.

John 6:35-40 (keyword: *benefits*)
1. Spiritual desires will be satisfied (v. 35).
2. All will be welcome (v. 37).
3. All will be preserved (vv. 39-40).

B. The *Analytical pattern* is useful when a long text has been selected.

John 3:1-18 (the doctrine of the new birth)
1. The need of the new birth (vv. 3,7,18b)
2. The process of the new birth (vv. 5-6,16)
3. The result of the new birth (vv. 15-16)

Matthew 28:16-20 (the Great Commission)
1. The basis for the commission (v. 18)
2. The duties of the commission (vv. 19-20a)
3. The promise for the commission (v. 20b)

C. *Textual patterns* are helpful, for many of Jesus' sayings are only a verse or so in length.

Matthew 16:26 *(Implicational method)*
1. This implies that a person is of utmost value.
2. This implies that the utmost values can be lost.
3. This implies that such a loss would be the ultimate tragedy.

Matthew 16:24 *(Telescopic approach)*
"If anyone would come after me . . .
1. "He must deny himself.
2. "He must deny himself and take up his cross.
3. "He must deny himself and take up his cross and follow me" (NIV).

Matthew 6:21 *(Illustrational method)*
"For where your treasure is, there your heart will be also" (NIV).

    1. This is illustrated in the life of Amos's contemporaries (Amos 6:1-6).
    2. This is illustrated in the life of Haggai's contemporaries (Hag. 1).
    3. This is illustrated in the life of the rich young ruler (Matt. 19:16-22).

D. The *Problem-solving pattern* is useful when a text tells us how to overcome a difficulty.

    Matthew 6:25-34 (the problem of anxiety)
    1. There is a need to deal with this problem.
    2. Suggestions for dealing with this problem are of many kinds.
    3. Jesus says that we can be helped with this problem if we take the following steps:
        a. Observe God's care for His creation.
        b. Keep life's issues in proper perspective.
        c. Learn to live life on a daily basis.
        d. Acknowledge God's rightful priority.

E. The *Comparative method* can be used with the many figures of speech Jesus uttered.

    John 10:11 ("I am the good shepherd")
    1. Just as a shepherd gives the flock his protection, so Jesus provides for us.
    2. Just as a shepherd gives the flock his protection, so Jesus protects us.
    3. Just as a shepherd makes the flock his priority, so Jesus makes us His.

F. The *Syllogistic pattern* can be used when a conclusion is stated or implied in a text.

    John 6:35-51 ("the bread of life" text)
    1. God's nourishment satisfies spiritual hunger.
    2. Jesus is God's nourishment.
    3. Jesus satisfies spiritual hunger.

G. *Inductive patterns* are useful when the text ends with a general truth based on certain examples.

    Matthew 6:25-34 (Do we need to worry?)
    1. God provides for the fauna (v. 26).
    2. God provides for the flora (vv. 28-29).
    3. God will provide for the crown of His creation (vv. 26b,30).

PROPOSITION: Therefore, we need not worry (vv. 31-34).

Matthew 16:17-20 (Will the church emerge triumphant?)
1. Is the church the product of human effort?
2. Does Jesus establish failure?
3. Does Jesus fail to provide the necessary resources?
PROPOSITION: The church will emerge triumphant!

H. *Narrative patterns* can be used to preach about the sayings of Jesus from the perspective of those whom Jesus encounters in the Gospels. Examples would include groups like the Pharisees, Sadducees, and scribes; and individuals like the man born blind, NicodeHmus, Mary and Martha, Zacchaeus, the rich young ruler, Jairus, Pilate, and Jesus' disciples. A potentially effective way of doing this would be through the use of the first person. A third-person narrative could also be used.

Notes

1. Leland Ryken, *The Literature of the Bible* (Grand Rapids, Mich.: Zondervan Publishing House, 1974), 289.

2. See the chart on Jesus' teachings in the *Master Study Bible*, King James Version (Nashville: Holman Bible Publishers, 1983), 1967-2018. See also J. Ramsey Michaels, "Jesus, Life and Ministry of" in *Holman Bible Dictionary* (Nashville: Holman Bible Publishers, 1991), 777-788.

3. Donald Guthrie, "Jesus Christ," vol. 3 in *Zondervan Pictorial Encyclopedia of the Bible* (Grand Rapids, Mich.: Zondervan Publishing House, 1976), 497-583. This is an excellent article containing about the same amount of material as a book of about 150-175 pages. See also Guthrie's *Jesus the Messiah* (Grand Rapids, Mich.: Zondervan Publishing House, 1972) and *A Shorter Life of Christ* (Grand Rapids, Mich.: Zondervan Publishing House, 1970).

20

PREACHING FROM MIRACLE PASSAGES

Miracles, as commonly understood, are recorded in Scripture in both the Old and New Testaments. They seem to appear more frequently in the New Testament, especially in the Gospels. The Book of Exodus is the setting for the greatest number of miracles in the Old Testament in a relatively short period of time. Others are scattered throughout both Testaments.

Some Considerations About Miracles

What Is a Miracle?

The location of a "miracle" passage is not always simple. Some events in Scripture may or may not be true miracles, depending on how that word is defined:

1. Is a miracle an event that is an exception to natural law? Thomas Aquinas seemed to say that miracles violate the law of cause and effect—that God can produce effects without secondary causes.
2. Is a miracle the norm for natural laws of which we are ignorant? Augustine of Hippo said that miracles do not violate nature itself but only what we know about nature.
3. Is a miracle any occurrence that is not explainable? (This definition allows virtually anything to be miraculous at a given time in a given place. It must allow for today's "miracles" becoming tomorrow's commonplace occurrences.)
4. Or is a miracle simply a happening that is highly unusual in its means, scope, or result?[1]

Definition and proof of miracles are ultimately matters for philosophers and historians. The preacher faces the different task of understanding, explaining, and applying the texts in which the miraculous seems to be found. If the exegete becomes involved in speculating about whether something miraculous took place or to what extent it took place, then he has ceased being an exegete. Instead, he has turned to philosophical and historical matters. This is not to suggest that matters of philosophy and history are unimportant. They surely are! The preacher/exegete should be committed, however, to dealing with a text on the basis of what it says, not on the basis of what he *thinks* it ought to say.[2]

Biblical Terms for Miracles

The New Testament uses three terms frequently to describe miracles. They are:

1. Sign *(semeion)*—This word speaks of miracle as an indication or signal of something or someone significant. The miracle points to someone or something else. It is a verifier. This is the word John used with great effect (John 2:11; 20:30-31). Paul used it sparingly (for example, Rom. 15:19; 1 Cor. 14:22). Some usages of *semeion* do not carry the meaning of miracle (Luke 2:12; Rom. 4:11).

2. Wonder *(teras)*—This refers to something highly unusual that amazes the spectator. It is always used in the plural and generally is accompanied by "signs," although in Acts 2:19 it stands alone. Usages include: Acts 2:22,43; 4:30; and BSSB style 5:12.

3. Power *(dunamis)*—This speaks of an act of great power, something beyond the ordinary. This word is often translated as "miracle" in the *King James Version* (as is *semeion*) when it is used to refer to some specific supernatural act. It occurs in Acts 2:22; 8:13; 1 Corinthians 12:10; and Galatians 3:5.

All three of these terms are found in Acts 2:22; 2 Corinthians 12:12; and Hebrews 2:4. They are also found in 2 Thessalonians 2:9 in regard to the "lawless one." Each of these terms makes a different emphasis. The first suggests the purpose of the miracle. The second suggests the immediate result or effect of the event. The third speaks of the means by which the event took place.

The first two of the terms just discussed have their Old Testament counterparts:

1. Sign *('oth)*—See Exodus 4:8,9,17; Deuteronomy 4:34; and Isaiah 7:14.
2. Wonder *(mopheth; pala;* and *temah)*—See Exodus 4:21; Joshua 3:5; and Daniel 6:27.

There is no unique word for *miracle* in either Testament. When that word is found in the *King James Version,* it is always a translation of either *'oth, mopheth, pala, dunamis,* or *semeion.* The same thing is true of most other English translations.

The Purposes of the Miracles in Scripture

As the exegetical preacher contemplates preaching on a given miracle in the Bible, he must first inquire as to the purpose of Bible miracles. In general, the following three purposes cover most biblical miracles.

Some miracles are *evidential* in purpose, intended to elicit a favorable response among the observers, specifically faith.

1. This is sometimes intended in the Gospels. (See John 20:30-31; Mark 2:10; and 4:35-41, especially verse 40.)

2. This is also the case with some apostolic miracles (Heb. 2:4).
3. The miracles of Moses fall into this category (Ex. 4:1-9).

Closely related to the previous purpose is that of miracle being an *expression or demonstration of kingdom power.*

1. Jesus casts out demons (Matt. 12:28).
2. The 70 report victory over the demonic (Luke 10:17-20).
3. Elijah confronts the prophets of Baal and Asherah on Mount Carmel (1 Kings 18:16-40).

Some miracles are *acts of compassion.* They demonstrate that God cares about people who suffer various kinds of need.

1. Jesus performed many miracles of healing (Matt. 14:14).
2. Jesus fed the four thousand (Matt. 15:32).

These are not clear-cut categories as much as they are emphases. There is overlap. Nevertheless, the preacher would do well to raise the issue of purpose each time he works with a Bible miracle.

Preaching on Miracles

When preaching on Bible miracles, the preacher's task is the same as with other narrative material. He must describe it, explain it, and apply it. In other words, he must first tell what happened, using both the text and the context. Then, he must tell what this meant to the original participants, observers, and readers. Finally, he must tell what this miracle means today. What practical difference should it make in the lives of his hearers?

To do this, the preacher must catch a "feel" for the actual event. He should put himself, so to speak, into that situation and try to imagine what it was like both from the perspective of the recipient of the miracle (if there was a recipient) as well as from the perspective of those who witnessed the event.

Then, the preacher should examine the text thoroughly to determine the purpose of the actual event. What response, if any, was intended by the doing of the miracle? What actually took place? How should this be paralleled as we "observe" the same miracle today? The goal of the sermon should correspond to these things.

For most miracle texts, the Analytical method is the usual and preferred approach as far as homiletical structure is concerned. This is the method modeled well by Merrill Tenney as he deals with the healing of the man born blind in John 9. Tenney discusses this miracle by dealing with:

  I. The case.
 II. The cure.
III. The confession.
IV. The consequences.[3]

This is essentially the Analytical approach. With a little variation in the statement of the main points, this arrangement offers a good method for presenting many miracle texts. This approach is particularly well suited to longer texts.

If the text is very brief, however, it may be advisable to use the Keyword method and structure it around a keyword like *lessons* or *truths*. A longer-than-usual introduction could tell the story, and the body of the sermon could major on application.

When the purpose of the miracle seems to be evidential, it may be possible to use the Syllogistic method. The raising of Lazarus in John 11 suggests the following premises and conclusion:

I. The giving of life is a divine right or prerogative.
II. Jesus openly restored Lazarus to life.
III. Therefore, Jesus demonstrated a divine prerogative.

Keeping in mind the narrative nature of passages that present the miraculous, the preacher may design the sermon homiletically by using one of the narrative approaches discussed in chapter 11 of this book. A first-person account of a beneficiary of a miracle (such as the man at the pool of Bethesda in John 5:1-15 or the paralytic in Mark 2:1-12) could be a powerful way to communicate the personal significance of an encounter with the power of God. Similarly, the experience of Jairus in the raising of his daughter (Mark 5:21-43) has great possibility for being developed as either a first-person or third-person story sermon.

When preaching on miracles, the preacher will need to exercise caution in the following areas:

1. All of the time available for preaching should not be spent telling the story, unless, perhaps, the Narrative approach is being used.
2. If an apologetic element about miracles in general (or a particular one, for that matter) is a part of the sermon, the preacher must not get sidetracked to the detriment of the text at hand. The purpose of the immediate sermon must be kept clearly in view.
3. The preacher must not allegorize or spiritualize unless the text itself does so. This may be the case occasionally (for example, John 9), but this indeed is rare. To do otherwise is to make the preacher's imagination the only limitation in the matter of interpretation. Leprosy, the sea, wine, and other elements in the miracle stories are all tempting subjects for the allegorizer, but this temptation must be avoided.
4. Finally, the preacher should exercise care in his use of the term *miracle*. While the term can and should be freely applied to those events described in Scripture where God has acted in a truly supernatural and unusual way, it should not be used carelessly of events that are the natural result of the created order, or of occurrences that are highly unusual but not necessarily miracu-

lous. The birth of a baby, while a wonderful thing to behold, is not a miracle according to most definitions of the word. The earthquake that resulted in the release of Paul and Silas from jail (Acts 16) is not spoken of as a miracle in the text itself, though it may have been one. Caution is encouraged, for if "everything" is a miracle, then nothing is.

Notes

1. This brief discussion is based on the article by Gordon H. Clark, "Miracles," vol. 4 in *Zondervan Pictorial Encyclopedia of the Bible* (Grand Rapids, Mich.: Zondervan Publishing House, 1976), 241-250. Also recommended is C. S. Lewis, *Miracles: A Preliminary Study* (New York: Macmillan, 1963), as well as Colin Brown, *Miracles and the Critical Mind* (Grand Rapids, Mich.: Wm. B. Eerdmans Publishing Co., 1984); and T. R. McNeal, "Miracles, Signs, Wonders" in *Holman Bible Dictionary* (Nashville: Holman Bible Publishers, 1991), 973-974.

2. An example of this is what was done by William Barclay, *The Gospel of John*, vol. 2 in *The Daily Study Bible Series* (Philadelphia: Westminster Press, 1975), 103. Barclay apparently had a difficult time accepting the raising of Lazarus as a literal, physical event and concluded by saying that it "does not really matter whether or not Jesus literally raised a corpse to life in A.D. 30, but it matters intensely that Jesus is the Resurrection and the Life for every man who is dead in sin and dead to God today. There may be problems in this story; we may never know what exactly happened at Bethany so many years ago; but we do know for certain that Jesus is still the Resurrection and the Life. That is what the story tells us—and that is what really matters." This writer's opinion is that this represents exegetical irresponsibility at its worst. If there is historical doubt about whether Jesus raised the corpse of Lazarus to life again, there must also be historical doubt about whether Jesus actually uttered the words attributed to him in that same setting!

Likewise, the cavalier attitude of Eric Rust leaves much to be desired. See Rust's "Preaching from the Miracle Stories of the Gospels," *Biblical Preaching: An Expositor's Treasury*, ed. James W. Cox (Philadelphia: Westminster Press, 1983), 231 ff. He suggests, for example, that the cursing of the fig tree (Mark 11:12-25) may have "originated in a parable" and that the turning of water into wine (John 2:1-11) "may have been a saying like that of new wine in old wineskins transformed into a miracle, although here the details would *seem* to point to *some kind* of incident" (italics mine). If Rust's hermeneutical and critical methodologies were applied to all of Scripture, we would be left with very little of which we could be certain. There is no objective or compelling reason to handle miracle stories in this way.

On the other hand, a classic on the subject of the miracles of Jesus is Richard C. Trench's *Notes on the Miracles of Our Lord* (Grand Rapids, Mich.: Baker Book House, 1949; reprint).

Finally, Sidney Greidanus has a helpful discussion on the subject of miracles in *The Modern Preacher and the Ancient Text: Interpreting and Preaching Biblical Literature* (Grand Rapids, Mich.: Wm. B. Eerdmans Publishing Co., 1988), 38-41.

3. Merrill C. Tenney, *John: the Gospel of Belief* (Grand Rapids, Mich.: Wm. B. Eerdmans Publishing Co., 1976), 152-161. Tenney's treatment of the other sign-miracles in John's Gospel varies from this one, but all are helpful. The whole book is highly suggestive along homiletical lines as well as an excellent overview of the fourth Gospel.

21

PREACHING
ON PARABLES

Introduction to Parabolic Literature

Parables are found in various parts of the Bible, although the vast majority are found in the New Testament. In the Old Testament, passages such as 2 Samuel 12:1-7 and Isaiah 5:1-7 are in parable form, but these are few in number. By contrast, a total of 41 parables are found in the sayings of Jesus in the Synoptic Gospels alone.[1] Some are found in only one of the Gospels; some are found in two; and seven of them are found in all three Synoptics. There is a difference of opinion among scholars concerning the presence of parabolic material in John's Gospel. Donald Guthrie says there are "many sayings in John which are parabolic in style although not in form."[2] C. H. Dodd, likewise, mentions texts in John which are somewhat parabolic in form.[3]

What Is a Parable?

A parable is a type of literature (or "oral literature") in the general category of "figures of comparison."[4] It consists of a story that has elements of reality the hearer or reader may easily understand. Sometimes the story is quite simple and true to life.[5] At other times, parables may include "a most surprising point in them; something takes place that is certainly not impossible, but is at least amazing."[6] Still, a parable is always understandable as far as its story is concerned. The elements in the story are easily recognizable, as is the plot.[7]

The actual meaning of a parable, however, may be a different matter. While many parables are rather clear in their meaning and give the interpreter little difficulty, some are not as clear as they seem at first. As Thomas Long points out, parables can be a bit tricky for the interpreter, so they need to be handled carefully.

> But the more we get to know the parables, the less confident we become of our understanding of them. As soon as we reach out to grasp a parable's seemingly obvious truth, a trapdoor opens and we fall through to a deeper and unexpected level of understanding. Just as we are ready to play our interpretive hand, the parable deals us a new and surprising card, often making us unsure that we even know what game we are playing.[8]

In our quest to better understand how to deal with parables, contrasting them with other seemingly similar literary forms may be helpful. R. C. Trench, in his older but classic work, points out the following in this regard:[9]

1. Parables are different from fables, such as Aesop's. Trench identifies two fables in the Old Testament: Judges 9:8-15 and 2 Kings 14:9. He states that the fable reaches only the level of morality that the world understands and that it fails to reach the higher spiritual level. Fables, for the most part, are seldom true to life, for they often express their truths through the personification of animals or plants.

2. Parables are different from myths. Trench notes that the myth "presents itself not merely as the vehicle of the truth, but as being itself the truth; while in the parable we see the perfect distinctness between form and essence, shell and kernel."

3. Parables are different from proverbs, though there is but one Hebrew word for both (mashal), and the words are sometimes used interchangeably in the New Testament. For example, in Matthew 15:14-15 a proverb is given but is called a parable. Both proverbs and parables are comparative statements, and in many instances, the brief proverb could be expanded into a parable. In general, however, proverbs are shorter and more direct, while parables often take the form of a developed story, including the presence of an identifiable plot.

4. Parables are different from allegories, but the difference is more in form than in essence. The allegory has many points of comparison, whereas the parable ordinarily has only one such point. Further, an allegory may be somewhat fanciful, with people being represented by nonhuman things. Trench also points out that the allegory interprets itself, while the parable requires interpretation from without. (Leland Ryken does place the parable in the general category of allegory but explains that allegory should be thought of as a continuum, ranging from the very explicit to the barely understandable. He implies that the parable tends toward the very explicit. Ryken does not suggest that parables need to be interpreted on every point.)[10]

Parables are powerful communicators. They involve the hearer or reader in the process of making value judgments, sometimes about doctrinal concerns and at other times about behavioral matters. Ryken says in this regard:

> In one sense the parables are a very sophisticated literary form—they work by indication instead of direct statement. They force people to make a judgment on some commonplace situation and then to transfer that judgment to a spiritual plane.[11]

There is no "rule" about the length of a parable. Some of Jesus' parables are relatively long. The parable of the prodigal son is 22 verses in length, for example. Many others are from 6 to 10 verses. Yet, some are only a verse or two, as we see in Luke 13:19,21.

The purpose of the parables Jesus told seems to be twofold. Usually He sought to make spiritual truths clearer. Analogy (employed in parables) is an excellent means of teaching concepts. The parable of the good Samaritan (Luke 10:30-36) and the three parables of something lost and found (Luke 15) are good examples of parables Jesus used to make truth more understandable.

At other times, parables are evidently told to leave the hearers with a certain amount of confusion. This is seen in Luke 8:9-10 as a fulfillment of Isaiah 6:9. If this concept seems troublesome, Jesus' prayer in Luke 10:21-22 can also be noted.

Interpreting Parables

Before discussing the methodology of preaching on parables, we must first look at how they should be interpreted. Trench stated:

> Each one of the parables is like a casket, itself of exquisite workmanship, but in which jewels richer than itself are laid up; like fruit, which, however lovely to look upon, is yet more delectable in its inner sweetness.... In the interpretation of the parable, the question [is], how much is significant?[12]

Trench believed that some of the major details in a parable are important for the interpreter to understand and interpret in order to arrive at the meaning of the entire parable. More recent scholarship, however, tends to assert that only one major detail is really important because a parable has only one central meaning.

Both J. Robertson McQuilkin and A. Berkeley Mickelsen, in their respective books on hermeneutics, list the steps the interpreter should take to get a grasp on the meaning of a parable.[13] These steps might be summarized as follows:

1. When possible, determine the precise setting which led to the telling of the parable. Why was this parable told?
2. Identify the central meaning of the parable:
   a. Does the precise setting make the meaning clear?
   b. Does the teller explain the parable's meaning? Is there a stated application?
   c. Is there a surprising element in the parable? How does this affect its meaning?
   d. Can this central meaning stand on its own when the secondary details of the parable are removed?
3. Note the parts of the story that are important to stress the central meaning. Nonessential parts of the story do not contribute to the central meaning. They can be eliminated or skipped over. The essential parts can "fill out" the thrust of the parable without being regarded as allegory.

4. Compare the parable passage with parallel texts, if any.
5. Fit the central meaning of the parable into the other teachings of Scripture, beginning with the speaker's teachings.
6. Do not use parables to formulate doctrine but to clarify the doctrine of more literal passages.

In reference to Jesus' parables, Mickelsen states that "the parables serve to illustrate and unfold various aspects of the reign of God." He discusses a number of parables and gives the following as the various aspects illustrated:[14]

1. The presence of the reign of God (Matt. 13:24-30, the parable of the tares; and Matt. 13:33, the parable of the leaven).
2. The role of grace in the response to the reign of God (Matt. 21:28-32, the parable of the two sons; and Luke 15:1-7, the parable of the lost sheep)
3. The loyal adherents to the reign of God (Luke 14:25-33, the parables of the tower and the king going to battle).
4. Crisis in the reign of God (Matt. 21:33-46, the parable of the unfaithful husbandmen; and Matt. 25:1-13, the parable of the ten virgins).

Preaching on the Parables

A potential problem common to all preaching is especially dangerous when one prepares to preach on a parable. This is the danger of making the parable say more than was intended by the original teacher. This, of course, is the problem of eisegesis. If the preacher attempts to preach in any way similar to a verse-by-verse approach, he runs a great risk of doing just that.

Above all, the preacher must remember to preach on the central idea of the parable. This must, of course, be reflected in the stated theme (and subject, if any) of the sermon. The sermon method chosen must then effectively communicate this central idea.

One approach to preaching on a parable is similar to the Analytical method. Technically, it would not be a true analysis because the parable itself is not taken apart and scrutinized part by part. Instead, the whole parable is studied from various outside perspectives. This might be called a "faceting" approach, as if someone were holding a diamond and revolving it slowly to scrutinize it through its various facets.

When this approach is used, the theme would be "a study of the parable of the _____ [sower]." The proposition would be stated in the same way as that of a true Analytical sermon:

PROPOSITION: A study of the parable of the sower in Mark 4 will teach us how the gospel is received by various hearers.

The main points will then discuss the parable from various perspectives:

I. The story of the parable of the sower...
II. The meaning of the parable of the sower...
III. The relevance of the parable of the sower...

This approach uses a basic three-step hermeneutical approach: (1) What does the text say? (2) What does the text mean? (3) How does the text apply? This is an exegetically sound way to preach on a parable, but it is rather predictable and does little to gain or hold the audience's attention.

A second method for preaching on parables is similar to the Textual method of implication. The difference is that instead of using a verse or part of a verse as the proposition, the proposition is the central idea of the parable expressed in the preacher's own words. Each main point then is a truth implied by the parable's central idea.

The preacher should note that if a Textual approach is used, the sermon will tend to be somewhat topical in nature. This will be especially true if the parable is short. If it is several verses or longer, it may be possible to base some of the implied main points on details in the text related to the central idea. Caution must be exercised in doing this, however, so that a faulty hermeneutic is not employed. Remember that a parable is not a full allegory.

A third approach homiletically is the Comparative method. This will be especially useful with parables that are quite short, such as Matthew 13:33 (the parable of the leaven) or Matthew 13:44 (the parable of the hidden treasure). In shorter parables, the central point of comparison is usually quite clear. In effect, one is dealing with a figure of speech like a simile or metaphor. To use this method with a longer parable, it will be necessary to carefully discern the exact figure used in the central idea. Otherwise, exegetical allegorizing will result.

Finally, a parable can be preached using a Narrative pattern. As mentioned at the first of this chapter, parables sometime include an unexpected surprise. The parable of the good Samaritan (Luke 10:25-37) is an example of this sort of plot twist. Jesus' Jewish audience would have been shocked to hear him tell of a priest and a Levite passing the wounded man by, while a despised Samaritan stops and helps! Another example is that of the dishonest, but shrewd manager in Luke 16:1-9. Here we find Jesus commending this person, even though he had acted dishonestly. Either of these texts, and many other parable texts, could be preached by discovering this kind of twist in the plot. Then the story can be retold in an interesting way that highlights the unexpected and clarifies the theological or ethical principle that is the point of the parable.

A parable might be preached narratively by telling the story from the point of view of a chief person in the parable. With a little imagination, for instance, a great story could be told about the prodigal son from the perspective of the father, or even from the perspective of the older brother. A first-person approach could even possibly be used. Similarly, the parable of the good Samaritan could be told from the viewpoint of the Jewish traveler on his way to Jericho. The story might unfold according to the following movements:

1. The Jewish traveler knew the highway was dangerous but may have figured, *It can't happen to me.*
2. But then it happened. His person and possessions were violated, and he was left in critical condition.
3. Barely conscious, he saw help coming as a priest approached.
4. Probably fearing a trap or not wanting to get involved, the priest steers clear of the wounded man. Hope fades.
5. Ah, but again help approaches in the form of a Levite. Surely, he will help.
6. But again, help does not come. Hope continues to dwindle.
7. Finally, the traveler feels himself being given first aid and helped onto the back of a fellow traveler's donkey, and soon they arrive at an inn, where he receives further care.
8. The next day, after the stranger has paid the bill and given an advance to the innkeeper for any further expenses, the recovering victim comes to realize that his new "friend indeed" is a member of a hated minority.
9. What does that discovery do to his understanding of being a true "neighbor"?

It is also possible to retell this parable in a narrative form, using contemporary persons and details rather than things like the road to Jericho, Levites, Samaritans, or donkeys. The story/sermon would conclude by emphasizing the truth Jesus taught concerning loving one's neighbor as oneself, which is the single great truth of this text.

Notes

1. See the chart in *Disciple's Study Bible,* New International Version (Nashville: Holman Bible Publishers, 1988), facing p. 1187.

2. Donald Guthrie, "Jesus Christ," vol. 3 in *Zondervan Pictorial Encyclopedia of the Bible* (Grand Rapids, Mich.: Zondervan Publishing House, 1976), 563.

3. C. H. Dodd, *Historical Tradition in the Fourth Gospel* (New York: Cambridge University Press, 1975; reprint), 366 ff.

4. J. Robertson McQuilkin, *Understanding and Applying the Bible* (Chicago: Moody Press, 1983), 153.

5. McQuilkin, 153-154. McQuilkin states that "Although a parable by definition is not the record of a historical event, to be a parable it must be *true to life*" (italics mine).

6. Eduard Schweizer, "Preaching on the Parables," *Biblical Preaching: An Expositor's Treasury,* ed. James Cox (Philadelphia: Westminster, 1983), 248.

This writer points out some examples of surprising twists in several of Jesus' parables. He states that parables "tell of an amazing event that surprises everybody and is of a unique quality, without surpassing the limits of real life."

7. See Peter Rhea Jones, *The Teaching of the Parables* (Nashville: Broadman Press, 1982) and "Parables" in *Holman Bible Dictionary* (Holman Bible Publishers, 1991), 1071-1073.

8. Thomas G. Long, *Preaching and the Literary Forms of the Bible* (Philadelphia: Fortress Press, 1989), 87.

9. Richard C. Trench, *Notes on the Parables of Our Lord* (Grand Rapids, Mich.: Baker Book House, 1967; reprint), 3-5. It should be remembered that Trench's work was first published in 1861, prior to more recent scholarship on the subject.

10. Leland Ryken, *The Literature of the Bible* (Grand Rapids, Mich.: Zondervan Publishing House, 1974), 301-302.

11. Ryken, 303.

12. Trench, 15.

13. McQuilkin, 154-164; A. Berkeley Mickelsen, *Interpreting the Bible* (Grand Rapids, Mich.: Wm. B. Eerdmans Publishing Co., 1963), 229.

14. Mickelsen, 224.

22

PREACHING FROM THE EPISTLES

Of the 27 books in the New Testament, 21 are Epistles. There are also 8 additional letters found in the New Testament that possess apostolic authority. Seven of them are found in Revelation 2—3. The other one is located in Acts 15:23-29. No books in the Old Testament are in the epistolary form, but letters appear in some of the historical books.

An Overview of the Epistles

The Epistolary Form[1]
This form was quite common in the centuries immediately before and after New Testament times. Cicero (106-43 B.C.) saw the ancient letter as being one of three kinds: (1) the letter of information, (2) the friendly personal letter, and (3) the formal, argumentative presentation. Some overlap occurs in these categories, but they are still helpful.[2] (Incidentally, 835 of Cicero's own letters survive, while many others have been lost.)

Another well-known letter writer was the philosopher Seneca (d. A.D. 65), who was tutor and advisor to Nero. He practically governed the Roman Empire himself for some eight years (A.D. 54-62). The apostle Paul encountered Seneca's brother Gallio in Corinth (see Acts 18:12-17) in A.D. 52. Along with some 40 books, Seneca left behind many letters dealing with moralistic themes. In addition to non-Christian writers, many of the early church fathers made extensive use of the epistle to make known their views. These include Polycarp, Clement of Rome, Origen, and Ignatius.

The epistle is the earliest form of Christian literature in existence. Several New Testament epistles were written before the first Gospel (presumed by most scholars to be Mark). These include James, 1 and 2 Thessalonians, 1 and 2 Corinthians, Romans, and probably Galatians. Thus, these epistles were the earliest statements of the young church's interpretation and application of the teachings of Jesus. The richness of these and the later epistles in regard to ethics and theology cannot be overstated. Thomas Long remarked: "If it is true that the identity of the church's Lord was disclosed most clearly in the Gospels, it is also the case that the character of the church's life was shaped most tangibly by the letter."[3]

The Epistles are also rich in literary value. Some texts such as 1 Corinthians 13; Ephesians 1:15-23; Romans 8:28-39; and Philippians 2:5-11 are literary masterpieces. The Books of Hebrews and 1 Peter are written in a very fine classical Greek style.

The New Testament letters are also quite important historically. They, along, with Acts, unfold many of the events that took place in the early church, as well as give insight into the personalities of some of the key players in that drama. These letters, especially those of Paul, should always be studied along with Acts, as this book is often helpful for understanding the setting in which they were written and to which they were sent.

Although the epistle was a common literary form in New Testament times, those found in Scripture are unique:

> In general, the New Testament epistles do not conform closely to any existing models. For one thing, they show an unusual mixture of the personal letter and the more formalized literary epistle. They contain the personal notes, salutations, and news that informal letters contain, and they are addressed, for the most part, to specific readers (in contrast to literary epistles intended for publication, which assume a generalized audience and lack specific addresses to a reader). But along with this informality, there is much that is obviously formalized in the Epistles.[4]

William Larkin isolates two factors unique to the early church context that resulted in the transformation of the ancient epistle form into the form encountered in Scripture. "First, there was a spiritual dimension of life which was uppermost in the minds and hearts of Christians." He adds: "The second factor was apostolic authority."[5] These factors made the New Testament genre of epistle different from other ancient epistles.

Because of these factors, Larkin suggests, the actual form of the New Testament letters varies from their pagan counterparts. He mentions several differences, including the use of spiritual names for the sender and the addressee(s), the use of a benediction in place of the usual simple greeting, and the replacement of the "pagan prayer/ wish" with thanksgiving to God for spiritual health. The closings of the New Testament letters include prayers, benedictions, or other spiritually oriented materials. All of this is done with overtones of apostolic leadership and authority.[6]

Sidney Greidanus suggested that the New Testament epistles be thought of as "long-distance sermons."[7] These letters were stand-ins for the writers who, though unable to be present with the recipients, communicated the same truth to them in much the same way that it would have been done if they were able to be present. Richard LongenHecker, in fact, argues for identifying certain epistles as summaries or collections of the preaching done in synagogues by Paul or in churches by James, Peter, and John.[8]

The Epistles of Paul[9]

Of the 21 letters in the New Testament, Paul penned 13. He was an individual especially suited for that. Ladd states: "The greatest mind in the New Testament to interpret the meaning of the person and work of Jesus is the converted Pharisee, Paul."[10] Paul was a highly complex individual. Culturally, he was both Greek and Jewish. Religiously, he was trained as a rabbi and was an expert in matters of the Jewish faith. Then, the radical transformation brought about by his encounter with Jesus Christ gave him a perspective on the meaning of the gospel that was fathomed by few others. Paul's intellectual capabilities enabled him to argue convincingly and forcefully for truth, yet his letters also portray an individual who cared deeply about people. Furthermore, he was not only an intellectual force with which to reckon, he was also a practitioner. The truths he taught, the ethics he espoused, and the kind of life he motivated others to live were not just things to write or preach about, but things to do! He gave himself without reservation for the cause of Christ and His church.

Theologically, the Letters of Paul are quite diverse. This is certainly true when the whole collection of his letters is considered, but it is even true of some individual letters. In Ephesians, for example, Paul discussed topics such as the doctrine of God, Christology, pneumatology (study of the Holy Spirit), anthropology, harmartiology (study of sin), soteriology (theological doctrine related to salvation), angelology, and sanctification. He does this within the primary theme of ecclesiology (theological doctrine related to the church). As far as broad categories are concerned, it seems that only eschatology is untouched in Ephesians. As a whole, Paul's writings cover the entire spectrum of theological issues.

In matters related to the ethics of Christian living, the apostle was equally diverse. In Ephesians, again, he wrote about racial division and unity, assorted matters of personal morality, issues concerning interpersonal relationships among believers, proper relationships with unbelievers, and family and household matters. Elsewhere, he discussed the nature of love, proper behavior in church meetings, the conflict between law and gospel, the believer's personal responsibility to civil authorities, marriage and sexuality, and the responsibilities of church leaders. Either directly or in principle, Paul addressed most issues which have faced the church through the centuries.

Each of Paul's letters was situational. That is, each was written to address a particular need or problem. The preacher must first understand this situation, as other things in the book are often related to it. Without understanding this "purpose of the book," the preacher runs the risk of using texts in ways that run contrary to Paul's intention.

In 1 Corinthians, for example, Paul wrote to a church that was in deep trouble. After his opening remarks, the apostle immediately addressed the matter of divisions within the church that had been reported to him by some members of Chloe's household (1:11). Matters of sexual immorality (5:1) and lawsuits (6:1) may also have come from this source. Certain questions had also been directed to Paul's attention by means of a letter. He dealt with these questions beginning in 7:1. These questions concern marriage (7:1), food sacrificed to idols (8:1), the Lord's Supper (11:17), spiritual gifts (12:1), the doctrine of the resurrection (15:12), and a special offering for the needy church in Jerusalem (16:1). Thus, a number of explosive issues needed Paul's attention.

In Galatians, on the other hand, the situation can be reduced to one basic problem: the Galatians were turning from the message he preached to a different "gospel," which in reality was not good news at all (1:6-9). Paul also spoke briefly to the matter of church discipline (6:1). The letter, then, is a systematic apologetic of the message originally presented to the Galatians.

As with these examples, each of Paul's letters can be studied to determine the situation that led to its composition. Ephesians, perhaps, is the only one that is a bit troublesome in this regard. Yet, although a specific situation is not mentioned in this book, the theme is certainly clear. Paul wrote about the church, beginning with its origin and continuing on to discuss issues related to its nature, its role in the ultimate plan of God, its growth, its basic method of operation, its behavior, and its resources for spiritual battle. Judging from the theme and the way it is presented, the letter seems to be an epistle to the church at large, a sort of "ecclesiological manifesto." Once the preacher understands the basic thrust of a book as a whole, he can then proceed to isolate subthemes in order to arrive at suitable preaching texts.

The General Epistles

Eight New Testament letters are General Epistles, written by authors other than Paul and not addressed to specific churches or individuals. The apostle John wrote three of them; Peter, two; and James and Jude, one each. Hebrews is anonymous. Its authorship has been the source of much speculation through the centuries.

The longest of the General Epistles is Hebrews. It is also the one written in the most carefully outlined style. It lacks some of the form associated with true epistles, particularly in its openings, but the conclusion does conform to the epistolary style. The book traditionally has been considered an epistle, although Leon Morris calls our attention to its homiletical or oratorical style.[11] Epistle and sermon should not be thought of as mutually exclusive, however, for the more formal epistles of ancient times were often speeches cast in written form.[12]

Hebrews could be called the longest argument in the Bible. Its purpose is to set forth the superiority of Christ and the new covenant. The author argued that Christ is superior to all other spokespersons for God who had gone before. Further, His sacrificial work is not only superior to the Old Testament sacrificial system, but it is also God's only way to salvation. The writer argues that if the readers revert to Judaism, leaving behind the work of Christ, they abandon God's only means to save them.

The preacher should be aware that no other epistle in Scripture is as Christological in its orientation as Hebrews. The first 10 chapters are especially packed with texts which draw our attention to the Savior. This homiletical treasure is indeed rich!

Among the other General Epistles, three stand at the forefront in terms of pulpit usage. James Earl Massey identifies them and states reasons this is so:

> Across the long history of the Christian preaching tradition, the epistles of James, 1 Peter, and 1 John have been the most used of the seven. The reasons are rather obvious: The need to know and understand personal faith in its social dimensions [James] is perennial in church life; the need to encourage believers to be steadfast under stress and strain [1 Peter] is expected in proper pulpit work; and the colorful affirmations provided in 1 John about God, Jesus Christ, and the meaning of the Christian life lend themselves readily to fertile concern of the preacher who reads them with both mind and heart.[13]

Each of these three books is entirely different from the others, both in style and theme. James is hard-hitting and extremely practical. (A former teacher of this writer jokingly suggested that the preacher should prepare and preach his series on James only when he was planning to change places of ministry!) James deals with topics such as faith, temptation, wealth, wisdom, the tongue, patience, and prayer—all of which need to be addressed from the pulpit.

The Letter known as 1 Peter was written in a style of Greek considered more classical than koine. (Some critics have denied Peter's authorship because of this.) The letter was written to encourage Christians who were undergoing, or would soon be undergoing, trials of various kinds, perhaps even persecution (1:6). While much of the letter is intended to encourage these believers, the book also deals with assorted practical matters of Christian living such as human authority (2:13-25), the marriage relationship (3:1-7), and church leadership (5:1-4).

The Book of 1 John is, in a sense, the simplest of the three, yet it presents some difficulties for the preacher. Its main themes are clear and easy to understand, but the structure is sometimes awkward and circuitous, as themes are repeated in different parts of the book. The purpose of the writing is presented in 5:13: "I write these things to you who believe in the name of the Son of God so that you may know

that you have eternal life" (NIV). The author made this statement
after naming a number of characteristics of the true believer (see
2:15,23,29; 3:6). Thus, the structure of the book seems to emphasize
these "marks of the true believer." Even with this in mind, however,
the flow of the book is sometimes unclear.[13]

The Book of 2 Peter is best known for its emphasis on the sure
promises of God leading to the second coming of Christ. The letter
also contains a strong warning against false teachers. It says that false
teachers will eventually receive judgment and destruction.

The Letter of Jude is a short treatise about contending "for the
faith." It, too, warns of false teachers, their empty promises, and their
coming punishment. Jude 4-16 closely parallels 2 Peter 2:1-18. These
sections are not only similar thematically but verbally as well. Scholars have long debated the literary dependency one of these letters has
had on the other.

Finally, 2 and 3 John are very short letters which have had little
impact on the church as far as preaching is concerned. The Book of
2 John is addressed to "the elect lady and her children." This may be a
veiled reference to a specific church and its members. The Letter
known as 3 John is addressed to a man named Gaius. Both letters
repeat truths found in 1 John. The third letter also contains some
personal remarks about certain individuals known to the author and
his reader(s).

Preaching on the Epistles

Because the Epistles deal extensively with theological and ethical
concerns, as well as give us insights into the personal lives of their
writers and receivers, this part of the Scripture is virtually an inex-
haustible treasure mine for the preacher and the church. Sermons
preached on texts from the Epistles can easily range from those that
explore the deepest theological truths in Scripture to those which deal
with practical, everyday matters of behavior.

Relevance does not need to be a problem, even though many of the
issues discussed in the Epistles may seem foreign to the contemporary world (such as meat offered to idols, or Judaizing teachers). The
preacher who studies carefully will find that the issues faced by the
first-century authors are quite often similar to situations facing today's church and today's Christian. The words of Stendahl are in-
structive: "Thus preachers should not *make* the text relevant. They
should get deeply enough into the text and its original situation and
intentions to *find* its relevance."[14]

Homiletically, every conceivable sermon method can be used with
various texts from the Epistles. The following examples show how
some of these methods might be applied to specific passages.

The Keyword method is widely useful because the writers of these letters often wrote in a structured fashion, making use of parallelism in their presentation:

Romans 1:13-17 (Keyword: *affirmation*)
I. "I am obligated" (v. 14).
II. "I am so eager" (v. 15).
III. "I am not ashamed" (v. 16).

Philippians 4:4-19 (Keyword: *encouragement*)
I. Remember the presence of the Lord (v. 5).
II. Remember the peace of the Lord (vv. 6-7).
III. Remember the power of the Lord (v. 13).
IV. Remember the promise of the Lord (v. 19).

The Analytical method is also useful with many texts because of the kinds of materials in the Epistles. Both doctrines and ethical concepts can be developed sermonically using this method:

Ephesians 4:7-16 (*the doctrine of gifted church leadership*)
I. The source of gifted leadership (vv. 7-10).
II. The description of gifted leadership (v. 11).
III. The role of gifted leadership (v. 12).
IV. The results of gifted leadership (vv. 13-16).

Philippians 2:1-11 (*the concept of humility*)
I. The plea for humility (vv.1-4).
II. The example of humility (vv. 5-8).
III. The result of humility (vv. 9-11).

Various Textual patterns can be used with certain key verses scattered throughout the Epistles:

Hebrews 13:8 (*Implicational method*)
I. He is the same in the dignity of His person.
II. He is the same in the extent of His power.
III. He is the same in the tenderness of His compassion.
IV. He is the same in His faithfulness to His promises.
V. He is the same in the effectiveness of His sacrificial death.

Philippians 4:13 (*Telescopic approach*)
I. "I can do everything . . ."
II. "I can do everything through Him . . ."
III. "I can do everything through Him who gives me strength" (NIV).

1 Peter 5:7 (*Illustrational method*): "Cast all your anxiety on Him because He cares for you" (NIV).
I. This is illustrated in the life of Hannah in 1 Samuel 1.
II. This is illustrated in the experience of the three young men in Daniel 3.
III. This is illustrated in the life of Peter in Acts 12.

The Problem-solving pattern can be used with many of the practical issues encountered in the Epistles:

Romans 8:28-39 (*the problem of handling disappointments*)
I. We have a need to deal with this problem.
II. Many nonbiblical solutions have been suggested.
III. The Bible has four *truths* to help us:
    A. The operation of divine providence is for our ultimate good (v. 28).
    B. We are held steadfastly by God's love (vv. 35-37).
    C. God is on our side (v. 31).
    D. We are more than conquerors (v. 37).

The Comparative method can be used with some figures of speech in the Epistles:

Hebrews 12:1-3 (*"running the race of the Christian life"*)
I. Let us run without encumbrances.
II. Let us run with endurance.
III. Let us run with our eyes on the goal.

The Syllogistic pattern is useful with epistolary material because much of this material is argumentative, setting forth "bottom-line" conclusions:

2 Peter 3:3-13 (*categorical syllogism*)
I. God always keeps His promises (vv. 5-6,9).
II. God has promised that the "day of judgment" is coming (v. 7).
III. Therefore, the "day of the Lord" is surely coming (v. 10).
CONCLUSION: We ought to live holy and godly lives (v. 11).

Inductive methods can also be used from time to time when a series of examples or proofs lead to a conclusion:

Colossians 1:15-20 (*Why should people devote themselves to Jesus Christ?*)
I. Jesus Christ is the image of God (v. 15).
II. Jesus Christ is the means of creation (v. 16).
III. Jesus Christ is the force of coherence (v. 17).
IV. Jesus Christ is the head of the church (v. 18).
V. Jesus Christ is alive forevermore (v. 18).
PROPOSITION: Jesus Christ has the supremacy over all things!

Galatians 3:1-5 (*How does a person keep right with God?*)
I. Did we get right by law or by faith? (v. 2).
II. Was the Spirit's help only temporary in order to take us to the law? (v. 3).
III. Does God continue to work among us because we obey the law? (v. 5).

PROPOSITION: We are not kept by the law, but by grace through faith.

Narrative patterns can be used with texts which speak about an event or a person in the Epistles. The visit of Epaphroditus to Paul, as recorded in Philippians, is one example. Another would be a sermon based on the character of Philemon or his runaway slave, Onesimus. This can be done in a traditional third-person way, or it might also be done using a first-person approach. A sermon from the perspective of either Philemon or Onesimus, for example, could be a quite effective way to communicate biblical truths about relationships in the household of faith.

The writer of a given New Testament epistle could also become a narrator, presenting a representative text through a first-person style of sermon. Possible texts for this type of message might include:

1. Galatians 1 and 2: "Paul" could tell the story of his earlier mission to the churches of Galatia, their acceptance of the gospel, and his great disappointment of their turning to "another gospel."
2. First Peter 1:3-12: "Peter" could blend his own testimony of failure and redemption with these words of encouragement.
3. First John 1:1-4: "John" could tell about his experiences with Jesus during the Lord's earthly ministry in which he heard, watched, and touched the Messiah.

Notes

1. For a brief introduction to ancient letters, see Chris Church, "Letter Form and Function" in *Holman Bible Dictionary* (Nashville: Holman Bible Publishers, 1991), 874.

2. Some scholars, such as Leland Ryken, prefer to differentiate between ancient letters and literary epistles, with the latter being more formal and artistic in style. See his *The Literature of the Bible* (Grand Rapids, Mich.: Zondervan Publishing House, 1974), 317.

Krister Stendahl states: "An epistle is a recognized literary form in antiquity. Its intention is to be literature written for public consumption—in the form of a letter. A letter is a real letter to a person or the leaders of a group or a group at large. With this useful distinction in mind, we see that Paul's writings are letters rather than epistles, but with a certain spectrum in which Philemon is most clearly a letter and Romans tends most toward the epistle." It should be pointed out that Stendahl does not accept as authentic all 13 letters traditionally attributed to Paul. Of the books disputed by Stendahl, Ephesians is the one most clearly written in the style of the literary epistle. See Krister Stendahl, "Preaching from the Pauline Epistles," *Biblical Preaching*, ed. James W. Cox (Philadelphia: Westminster Press, 1983), 313.

3. Thomas G. Long, *Preaching and the Literary Forms of the Bible* (Philadelphia, Fortress Press, 1989), 107.

4. Ryken, 317.

5. William J. Larkin, *Manual of Greek Exegesis for Preachers* (Columbia, S.C.: Columbia Bible College and Seminary, 1987), 132.

6. Larken, 124-125.

7. Sidney Greidanus, *The Modern Preacher and the Ancient Text: Interpreting and Preaching Biblical Literature* (Grand Rapids, Mich.: Wm. B. Eerdmans Publishing Co., 1988), 314.

8. Richard N. Longenecker, "On the Form, Function, and Authority of New Testament Letters," in *Scripture and Truth*, eds. D. A. Carson and John D. Woodbridge (Grand Rapids, Mich.: Zondervan Publishing House, 1983), 104-105.

9. Oscar S. Brooks, "Paul" in *Holman Bible Dictionary* (Nashville: Holman Bible Publishers, 1991), 1079-1085, presents a brief overview of Paul's message and life.

10. George Eldon Ladd, *A Theology of the New Testament* (Grand Rapids, Mich.: Wm. B. Eerdmans Publishing Co., 1974), 360.

11. Leon Morris, "Hebrews," vol. 12 in *The Expositor's Bible Commentary,* gen. ed. Frank E. Gaebelein (Grand Rapids, Mich.: Zondervan Publishing House, 1981), 3.

12. C. W. Carter quotes O. J. F. Seitz as saying that some epistles "might more accurately be classified as public orations, philosophical treatises, political tracts, or moral exhortations . . . [and] have all the marks of having been written for general publications." See "Epistle," vol. 2 in *Zondervan Pictorial Encyclopedia of the Bible* (Grand Rapids, Mich.: Zondervan Publishing House, 1976), 337.

13. James Earl Massey, "Preaching from Hebrews and the General Epistles," *Biblical Preaching: An Expositor's Treasury,* ed. James W. Cox (Philadelphia: Westminster Press, 1983), 332.

14. The *Disciple's Study Bible* (Nashville: Holman Bible Publishers, 1988) gives clear preaching and teaching outlines for each Bible book.

15. Stendahl, 307.

BIBLIOGRAPHY

The Preacher and Preaching

Achtemeier, Elizabeth. *Creative Preaching: Finding the Words*. Nashville: Abingdon Press, 1980.

_____. *Preaching as Theology and Art*. Nashville: Abingdon Press, 1984.

Adams, Jay E. *Preaching with Purpose*. Grand Rapids, Mich.: Baker Book House, 1982.

Aycock, Don M., ed. *Heralds to a New Age: Preaching for the Twenty-First Century*. Elgin, Ill.: Brethren Press, 1985.

Bailey, Raymond. *Jesus the Preacher*. Nashville: Broadman Press, 1990.

_____. *Paul the Preacher*. Nashville: Broadman Press, 1991.

Bailey, Raymond and James L. Blevins. *Dramatic Monologues: Making the Bible Live*. Nashville: Broadman Press, 1990.

Bartow, Charles L. *The Preaching Moment: A Guide to Sermon Delivery*. Nashville: Abingdon Press, 1980.

Baumann, J. Daniel. *An Introduction to Contemporary Preaching*. Grand Rapids, Mich.: Baker Book House, 1972, 1988.

Black, James. *The Mystery of Preaching*. Reprint. Grand Rapids, Mich.: Zondervan Publishing House, 1978.

Blackwood, Andrew W. *Biographical Preaching for Today*. New York: Abingdon Press, 1954.

_____. *Doctrinal Preaching for Today*. New York: Abingdon Press, 1956.

_____. *Expository Preaching for Today*. New York: Abingdon Press, 1943.

_____. *Preaching from the Bible*. New York: Abingdon Press, 1941.

_____. *The Preparation of Sermons*. New York: Abingdon-Cokesbury Press, 1942.

Bodey, Richard Allen. *Inside the Sermon: Thirteen Preachers Discuss Their Methods of Preparing Messages*. Grand Rapids, Mich.: Baker Book House, 1990.

Bowie, Walter R. *Preaching*. New York: Abingdon Press, 1954.

Braga, James. *How to Prepare Bible Messages*. Portland, Oreg.: Multnomah Press, 1981.

Broadus, John A. *On the Preparation and Delivery of Sermons*. 4th ed. Completely revised by Vernon L. Stanfield. San Francisco: Harper and Row Publishers, Inc., 1986.

Brooks, Phillips. *The Joy of Preaching*. Reprint. Grand Rapids, Mich.: Kregel Publications, 1989.

———. *Lectures on Preaching*. Reprint of Yale lectures. Grand Rapids, Mich.: Baker Book House, 1978.

Brown, David M. *Dramatic Narrative in Preaching*. Valley Forge, Pa.: Judson Press, 1981.

Brown, Henry C. Et al. *Steps to the Sermon*. Nashville: Broadman Press, 1963.

Brueggemann, Walter. *Finally Comes the Poet: Daring Speech for Proclamation*. Minneapolis: Fortress Press, 1989.

Bugg, Charles. *Preaching from the Inside Out*. Nashville: Broadman Press, 1992.

Buttrick, David G. *Homiletic: Moves and Structures*. Philadelphia: Fortress Press, 1987.

Buttrick, George A. *Jesus Came Preaching*. Yale lectures. New York: Scribner and Sons, 1931.

Chatfield, Donald F. *Dinner with Jesus and Other Left-handed Story-Sermons*. Grand Rapids, Mich.: Zondervan Publishing House, 1988.

Claypool, John R. *The Preaching Event*. Yale lectures. Waco, Tex.: Word Books, 1980.

Cox, James W. *A Guide to Biblical Preaching*. Nashville: Abingdon Press, 1976.

———. *Preaching: A Comprehensive Approach to the Design and Delivery of Sermons*. San Francisco: Harper and Row Publishers, Inc., 1985.

Craddock, Fred B. *As One Without Authority*. Nashville: Abingdon Press, 1979.

———. *Overhearing the Gospel*. Nashville: Abingdon Press, 1978.

———. *Preaching*. Nashville: Abingdon Press, 1985.

Crum, Milton, Jr. *Manual on Preaching*. Wilton, Conn.: Morehouse-Barlow Co., 1988.

Daane, James. *Preaching with Confidence*. Grand Rapids, Mich.: Wm. B. Eerdmans Publishing Co., 1980.

Davis, H. Grady. *Design for Preaching*. Philadelphia: Fortress Press, 1958.

Diduit, Michael, ed. *Handbook of Contemporary Preaching*. Nashville: Broadman Press, 1992.

Demaray, Donald E. *Introduction to Homiletics*. 2nd ed. Grand Rapids, Mich.: Baker Book House, 1990.

Drakeford, John W. *Humor in Preaching*. Grand Rapids, Mich.: Zondervan Publishing House, 1986.

Eslinger, Richard L. *A New Hearing: Living Options in Homiletic Method*. Nashville: Abingdon Press, 1987.

Fant, Clyde E. *Preaching for Today*. 2nd ed. New York: Harper and Row Publishers, Inc., 1987.

Fasol, Al. *Essentials for Biblical Preaching*. Grand Rapids, Mich.: Baker Book House, 1989.

Faw, Chalmer E. *A Guide to Biblical Preaching*. Nashville: Broadman Press, 1962.

Flynn, Leslie B. *Come Alive with Illustrations*. Grand Rapids, Mich.: Baker Book House, 1988.

Ford, D. W. Cleverly. *The Ministry of the Word*. Grand Rapids, Mich.: Wm. B. Eerdmans Publishing Co., 1979.

_____. *Preaching Today*. London: Epworth Press, 1969.

Freeman, Harold. *Variety in Biblical Preaching: Innovative Techniques and Fresh Forms*. Waco, Tex: Word Books, 1986.

Hall, Thor. *The Future Shape of Preaching*. Philadelphia: Fortress Press, 1971.

Hicks, H. Beecher, Jr. *Preaching Through a Storm*. Grand Rapids, Mich.: Zondervan Publishing House, 1987.

Hobbs, Herschel H. *My Favorite Illustrations*. Nashville, Broadman Press, 1990.

Hostetler, Michael J. *Illustrating the Sermon*. Grand Rapids, Mich.: Zondervan Publishing House, 1989.

_____. *Introducing the Sermon: The Art of Compelling Beginnings*. Grand Rapids, Mich.: Zondervan Publishing House, 1986.

Howard, J. Grant. *Creativity in Preaching*. Grand Rapids, Mich.: Zondervan Publishing House, 1987.

Howe, Reuel L. *Partners in Preaching*. New York: Seabury Press, 1967.

Hybels, Bill. Et al. *Mastering Contemporary Preaching*. Portland: Multnomah Press, 1989.

Jackson, Edgar N. *How to Preach to People's Needs*. Grand Rapids, Mich.: Baker Book House, 1956.

Jensen, Richard A. *Telling the Story: Variety and Imagination in Preaching*. Minneapolis: Augsburg Publishing House, 1979.

Jones, Ilion T. *Principles and Practice of Preaching*. New York: Abingdon Press, 1956.

Jowett, John Henry. *The Preacher: His Life and Work*. Yale lectures. New York: Doran & Company, 1912, 1928.

Kemp, Charles F. *The Preaching Pastor*. St. Louis: Bethany Press, 1966.

Kennedy, Gerald. *His Word Through Preaching*. New York: Harper and Row Publishers, Inc., 1947.

_____. *God's Good News*. Yale lectures. New York: Harper and Row Publishers, Inc., 1955.

Killinger, John. *Experimental Preaching*. Nashville: Abingdon Press, 1973.

_____. *Fundamentals of Preaching*. Philadelphia: Fortress Press, 1985.

Koller, Charles W. *Expository Preaching Without Notes Plus Sermons Preached Without Notes*. Grand Rapids, Mich.: Baker Book House, 1962.

Kooienga, William H. *Elements of Style for Preaching*. Grand Rapids, Mich.: Zondervan Publishing House, 1989.

Kroll, Woodrow M. *Prescription for Preaching*. Grand Rapids, Mich.: Baker Book House, 1980.

Larson, David L. *The Anatomy of Preaching: Identifying the Issues in Preaching Today*. Grand Rapids, Mich.: Baker Book House, 1989.

Lenski, R. C. H. *The Sermon: Its Homiletical Construction*. Reprint. Grand Rapids, Mich.: Baker Book House, 1968.

Lewis, Ralph L. and Gregg Lewis. *Inductive Preaching: Helping People Listen*. Westchester, Ill.: Crossway Books, 1983.

_____. *Learning to Preach Like Jesus*. Wheaton, Ill.: Crossway Books, 1989.

Lischer, Richard. *Theories of Preaching: Selected Readings in the Homiletical Tradition*. Durham, N.C.: Labyrinth Press, 1987.

Lloyd-Jones, D. Martyn. *Preaching and Preachers*. Grand Rapids, Mich.: Zondervan Publishing House, 1971.

Logan, Samuel T. Jr., ed. *The Preacher and Preaching: Reviving the Art in the Twentieth Century*. Phillipsburg: N.J.: Presbyterian and Reformed Publishing Co., 1986.

Long, Thomas G. *The Senses of Preaching*. Atlanta: John Knox Press, 1988.

Lowry, Eugene L. *Doing Time in the Pulpit: The Relationship Between Narrative and Preaching*. Nashville: Abingdon Press, 1985.

_____. *The Homiletical Plot: The Sermon as Narrative Art Form*. Atlanta: John Knox Press, 1980.

_____. *How to Preach a Parable: Designs for Narrative Sermons*. Nashville: Abingdon Press, 1989.

Luccock, Halford E. *Communicating the Gospel*. Yale lectures. New York: Harper and Row Publishers, Inc., 1954.

_____. *In the Minister's Workshop*. Nashville: Abingdon-Cokesbury Press, 1944.

Lueking, F. Dean. *Preaching: The Art of Connecting God and People*. Waco, Tex.: Word Books, 1985.

Macartney, Clarence E. *Preaching without Notes*. New York: Abingdon Press, 1946.

McCracken, Robert J. *The Making of the Sermon*. New York: Harper and Row Publishers, Inc., 1956.

MacPherson, Ian. *The Art of Illustrating Sermons*. New York: Abingdon Press, 1964.

Malcomson, William L. *The Preaching Event*. Philadelphia: Westminster Press, 1968.

Markquart, Edward F. *Quest for Better Preaching: Resources for Renewal in the Pulpit*. Minneapolis: Augsburg Publishing House, 1985.

Massey, James Earl. *Designing the Sermon: Order and Movement in Preaching*. Nashville: Abingdon Press, 1980.

McClure, John S. *The Four Codes of Preaching: Rhetorical Strategies*. Minneapolis: Augsburg Fortress Press, 1991.

Meyer, F. B. *Expository Preaching: Plans and Methods*. New York: Doran Co., 1912.

Miller, Calvin. *Spirit, Word, and Story: A Philosophy of Preaching*. Dallas: Word Books, 1989.

Miller, Donald G. *The Way to Biblical Preaching*. New York: Abingdon Press, 1957.

Mitchell, Henry H. *Black Preaching: An Analysis of the Black Homiletic Tradition*. San Francisco: Harper and Row Publishers, Inc., 1979.

Nichols, J. Randall. *The Restoring Word: Preaching as Pastoral Communication*. San Francisco: Harper and Row Publishers, Inc., 1987.

Niles, Daniel T. *The Preacher's Task and the Stone of Stumbling*. Yale lectures. New York: Harper and Row Publishers, Inc., 1958.

Pattison, Thomas H. *The Making of the Sermon*. Philadelphia: Judson Press, 1941.

Pearce, J. Winston. *Planning Your Preaching*. Nashville: Broadman Press, 1979.

Perry, Lloyd M. *Biblical Preaching for Today's World*. Chicago: Moody Press, 1973.

_____. *Biblical Sermon Guide*. Grand Rapids, Mich.: Baker Book House, 1979.

_____. *A Manual for Biblical Preaching*. Grand Rapids, Mich.: Baker Book House, 1981.

Pitt-Watson, Ian. *A Primer for Preachers*. Grand Rapids, Mich.: Baker Book House, 1986.

Proctor, Samuel D. *Preaching About Crises in the Community*. Philadelphia: Westminster Press, 1988.

Read, David H. C. *Preaching About the Needs of Real People*. Philadelphia: Westminster Press, 1988.

_____. *Sent from God: The Enduring Power and Mystery of Preaching*. Yale lectures. Nashville: Abingdon Press, 1974.

Reu, Johann M. *Homiletics*. Grand Rapids, Mich.: Baker Book House, 1967.

Robinson, Haddon W. *Biblical Preaching*. Grand Rapids, Mich.: Baker Book House, 1980.

_____. *Biblical Sermons: How Twelve Preachers Apply the Principles of Biblical Preaching*. Grand Rapids, Mich.: Baker Book House, 1989.

Sangster, William E. *The Craft of Sermon Construction*. Philadelphia: Westminster Press, 1951.

Scherer, Paul. *For We Have This Treasure*. Yale lectures. New York: Harper and Row Publishers, Inc., 1944.

Shoemaker, H. Stephen. *Retelling the Biblical Story: The Theology and Practice of Narrative Preaching*. Nashville: Broadman Press, 1985.

Sider, Ronald J. and King, Michael A. *Preaching About Life in a Threatening World*. Philadelphia: Westminster Press, 1987.

Skinner, Craig. *The Teaching Ministry of the Pulpit*. Reprint. Lanham, Md.: University Press of America, 1988.

Sleeth, Ronald E. *God's Word and Our Words: Basic Homiletics*. Atlanta: John Knox Press, 1986.

_____. *Proclaiming the Word*. Nashville: Abingdon Press, 1964.

Spurgeon, Charles H. *Spurgeon's Lectures to His Students*. Reprint. Grand Rapids, Mich.: Zondervan Publishing House, 1955.

Stalker, James. *The Preacher and His Models*. Yale lectures. New York: A.C. Armstrong and Son, 1891.

Steimle, Edmund A. Et al. *Preaching the Story*. Philadelphia: Fortress Press, 1980.

Stevenson, Dwight E. and Charles F. Diehl. *Reaching People from the Pulpit: A Guide to Effective Sermon Delivery*. Grand Rapids, Mich.: Baker Book House, 1958.

Stewart, James. *A Faith to Proclaim*. Reprint of Yale lectures. Grand Rapids, Mich.: Baker Book House, 1972.

_____. *Heralds of God*. London: Hodder and Stoughton, 1946.

Stibbs, Alan M. *Expounding God's Word: Some Principles and Methods*. Grand Rapids, Mich.: Wm. B. Eerdmans Publishing Co., 1961.

Stott, John R. W. *Between Two Worlds: the Art of Preaching in the Twentieth Century*. Grand Rapids, Mich.: Wm. B. Eerdmans Publishing Co., 1982.

_____. *The Preacher's Portrait*. Grand Rapids, Mich.: Wm. B. Eerdmans Publishing Co., 1964.

Stratman, Gary D. *Pastoral Preaching: Timeless Truth for Changing Needs*. Nashville: Abingdon Press, 1983.

Sweazey, George E. *Preaching the Good News*. Englewood Cliffs, N.J.: Prentice-Hall, Inc., 1976.

Thielen, Martin. *Getting Ready for Sunday's Sermon: A Practical Guide for Sermon Preparation*. Nashville: Broadman Press, 1990.

Thompson, William D. and Gordon C. Bennett. *Dialogue Preaching: The Shared Sermon*. Valley Forge, Pa.: Judson Press, 1969.

Troeger, Thomas H. *Imagining a Sermon*. Nashville: Abingdon Press, 1990.

Vines, Jerry. *A Guide to Effective Sermon Delivery*. Chicago: Moody Press, 1986.

_____. *A Practical Guide to Sermon Preparation*. Chicago: Moody Press, 1985.

Walker, Alan. *Evangelistic Preaching*. Grand Rapids, Mich.: Zondervan Publishing House, 1988.

Whitesell, Faris D. *The Art of Biblical Preaching*. Grand Rapids, Mich.: Zondervan Publishing House, 1950.

Whitesell, Faris D. and Lloyd M. Perry. *Variety in Your Preaching*. Old Tappan, N.J.: Fleming H. Revell Co., 1954.

Willimon, William H. *Integrative Preaching: The Pulpit at the Center*. Nashville: Abingdon Press, 1981.

_____. *Peculiar Speech: Preaching to the Baptized*. Grand Rapids, Mich.: Wm. B. Eerdmans Publishing Co., 1992.

_____. *Preaching About Conflict in the Local Church*. Philadelphia: Westminster Press, 1987.

Wood, John. *The Preacher's Workshop: Preparation for Expository Preaching*. Chicago: Inter-Varsity Press, 1965.

Theological and Exegetical Perspectives

Achtemeier, Elizabeth. *The Old Testament and the Proclamation of the Gospel*. Philadelphia: Westminster Press, 1973.

Clowney, Edmund P. *Preaching and Biblical Theology*. Phillipsburg, N.J.: Presbyterian and Reformed Publishing Co., 1979.

Cox, James W., ed. *Biblical Preaching: An Expositor's Treasury*. Philadelphia: Westminster Press, 1983.

Dodd, Charles H. *The Apostolic Preaching and Its Developments*. New York: Harper and Row Publishers, Inc., 1936.

Duke, Robert W. *The Sermon as God's Word: Theologies for Preaching*. Nashville: Abingdon Press, 1980.

Forbes, James. *The Holy Spirit and Preaching*. Yale lectures. Nashville: Abingdon Press, 1989.

Gowan, Donald E. *Reclaiming the Old Testament for the Christian Pulpit*. Atlanta: John Knox Press, 1980.

Greidanus, Sidney. *The Modern Preacher and the Ancient Text: Interpreting and Preaching Biblical Literature*. Grand Rapids, Mich.: Wm. B. Eerdmans Publishing Co., 1988.

Horne, Chevis F. *Preaching the Great Themes of the Bible: Stimulating Resources for Doctrinal Preaching*. Nashville: Broadman Press, 1986.

Kaiser, Walter C., Jr. *The Old Testament in Contemporary Preaching*. Grand Rapids, Mich.: Baker Book House, 1973.

_____. *Toward an Exegetical Theology*. Grand Rapids, Mich.: Baker Book House, 1981.

Kinlaw, Dennis F. *Preaching in the Spirit*. Grand Rapids, Mich.: Francis Asbury/Zondervan Publishing House, 1985.

Klein, George, ed. *Reclaiming the Prophetic Mantle*. Nashville: Broadman Press, 1992.

Liefeld, Walter L. *New Testament Exposition: From Text to Sermon*. Grand Rapids, Mich.: Zondervan Publishing House, 1984.

Lischer, Richard. *A Theology of Preaching: The Dynamics of the Gospel*. Durham, N.C.: Labyrinth Press, 1991.

Long, Thomas G. *Preaching and the Literary Forms of the Bible*. Philadelphia: Fortress Press, 1989.

_____. *The Witness of Preaching*. Louisville, Ky.: Westminster/John Knox Press, 1989.

Macleod, Donald. *The Problem of Preaching*. Philadelphia: Fortress Press, 1987.

Mounce, Robert H. *The Essential Nature of New Testament Preaching*. Grand Rapids, Mich.: Wm. B. Eerdmans Publishing Co., 1960.

Piper, John. *The Supremacy of God in Preaching*. Grand Rapids, Mich.: Baker Book House, 1990.

Rust, Eric Charles. *The Word and Words: Towards a Theology of Preaching*. Macon, Ga.: Mercer University Press, 1982.

Thompson, William D. *Preaching Biblically: Exegesis and Interpretation.* Nashville: Abingdon Press, 1981.

Toombs, Lawrence E. *The Old Testament in Christian Preaching.* Philadelphia: Westminster Press, 1961.

Worley, Robert C. *Preaching and Teaching in the Earliest Church.* Philadelphia: Westminster Press, 1967.

Communication Theory

Abbey, Merrill R. *Communication in Pulpit and Parish.* Philadelphia: Westminster Press, 1973.

Adams, Jay E. *Communicating with 20th Century Man.* Phillipsburg, N.J.: Presbyterian and Reformed Publishing Co., 1979.

Chartier, Myron R. *Preaching as Communication: An Interpersonal Perspective.* Nashville: Abingdon Press, 1981.

Engel, James F. *Contemporary Christian Communications: Its Theory and Practice.* Nashville: Thomas Nelson Publishers, 1979.

Garrison, Webb B. *The Preacher and His Audience.* Old Tappan, N.J.: Fleming H. Revell Co., 1954.

Griffin, Em. *The Mind Changers: The Art of Christian Persuasion.* Wheaton, Ill.: Tyndale House Publishers, 1976.

Hughes, Robert Don. *Talking to the World in the Days to Come.* Nashville: Broadman Press, 1991.

Kraft, Charles H. *Communication Theory for Christian Witness.* Nashville: Abingdon Press, 1983.

Lewis, Ralph. *Speech for Persuasive Preaching.* Berne, Ind.: Economy Press, 1968.

McLaughlin, Raymond W. *Communication for the Church.* Grand Rapids, Mich.: Zondervan Publishing House, 1968.

————. *The Ethics of Persuasive Preaching.* Grand Rapids, Mich.: Baker Book House, 1979.

Nichols, J. Randall. *Building the Word: The Dynamics of Communication and Preaching.* San Francisco: Harper and Row Publishers, Inc., 1980.

Reid, Clyde. *The Empty Pulpit.* New York: Harper and Row Publishers, Inc., 1967.

Tizard, Leslie J. *Preaching: The Art of Communication.* London: Allen and Unwin Publishers, 1958.

Webber, Robert E. *God Still Speaks: A Biblical View of Christian Communication.* Nashville: Thomas Nelson Publishers, 1980.

The History of Preaching

Brilioth, Yngve. *A Brief History of Preaching.* Philadelphia: Fortress Press, 1965.

Dargan, Edwin C. *A History of Preaching.* 2 Vols. Reprint. Grand

Rapids, Mich.: Baker Book House, 1968. Turnbull, Ralph G. *A History of Preaching*. Vol. III of Dargan. Grand Rapids, Mich.: Baker Book House, 1974.

Fant, Clyde E. and Pinson, William M. *20 Centuries of Great Preaching*. 13 Vols. Waco, Tex.: Word Books, 1971.

Holland, DeWitte T. *The Preaching Tradition: A Brief History*. Nashville: Abingdon Press, 1980.

Jones, Edgar D. *The Royalty of the Pulpit*. Yale lectures. New York: Harper and Row Publishers, Inc., 1951.

Webber, F. R. *A History of Preaching in Britain and America*. 3 vols. Milwaukee: Northwestern Publishing House, 1952.

Wiersbe, Warren W. *Listening to the Giants*. Grand Rapids, Mich.: Baker Book House, 1979.

_____. *Walking with the Giants*. Grand Rapids, Mich.: Baker Book House, 1976.

Wiersbe, Warren W. and Lloyd M. Perry. *The Wycliffe Handbook of Preaching and Preachers*. Chicago: Moody Press, 1984.